Major Campaign Speeches of

ADLAI E. STEVENSON

1952

Major
Campaign Speeches
of
ADLAI E.
STEVENSON

1952

WITH AN INTRODUCTION
BY THE AUTHOR

RANDOM HOUSE
NEW YORK

STEPHENS COLLEGE
COLUMBIA, MO.

To those friends and associates whose loyalty, love and labor were mine from that day in January, 1948, when I became a candidate for Governor of Illinois to that day in January, 1953, when I became a private citizen again. They know who they are and what they did for me. My gratitude is boundless.

A. E. S.

Contents

Introduction

"*Reason is one of the very feeblest of Nature's forces, if you take it at any one spot and moment. It is only in the very long run that its effects become perceptible. Reason assumes to settle things by weighing them against one another without prejudice, partiality, or excitement; but what affairs in the concrete are settled by is and always will be just prejudices, partialities, cupidities, and excitements. Appealing to reason as we do, we are in a sort of forlorn hope situation, like a small sandbank in the midst of a hungry sea ready to wash it out of existence. But sandbanks grow when the conditions favor; and weak as reason is, it has the unique advantage over its antagonists that its activity never lets up and that it presses always in one direction, while men's prejudices vary, their passions ebb and flow, and their excitements are intermittent. Our sandbank, I absolutely believe, is bound to grow—bit by bit it will get dyked and break-watered.*"

WILLIAM JAMES

October 7, 1904

Introduction

Why this book? It is because several publishers, shortly after the election, proposed a volume of my speeches during the campaign of 1952. I put the proposal aside and busied myself with my work in Illinois and with the flood of messages that has engulfed me since the election. Many of these letters are remarkable. They range from the labored scrawls of the unlearned to the felicitous phrases of famous writers and scholars; they range from Maine to India, from a single kind word to fine essays on politics, philosophy and religion. They have moved me deeply, particularly the admonitions not to be downhearted and not to lose faith in the ultimate triumph of reason. Well, I am not downhearted or even disappointed, and I believe more than ever that "our sandbank" of reason in major political campaigns is bound to grow.

So many of these messages requested copies of speeches that the copies soon gave out and my meager staff gave up. I thought better of the book proposal and agreed to do it after my term as Governor of Illinois, when I might find a little time to scratch among the dry bones of the campaign and put something together.

That I have now done, for better or for worse. What follows is a collection of fifty speeches covering much of what I talked about during the campaign. In all I find in my files whole or partial texts of some 250 speeches, to as many groups, large and small, in almost as many places. How many more times I spoke I shudder now to think, and that no record remains disturbs me not at all.

What *does* disturb me is what remains! Reading them over hurriedly recalls uncomfortably some words of Froude in his life of

Bunyan: "The excitement of perpetual speechmaking is fatal to the exercise of the highest powers." To "excitement" I would add "exhaustion," for sheer physical exhaustion was for me a continuous and disquieting menace to equilibrium, judgment and creative concentration. "Sleep is stealing me away" is a lovely West Indian phrase, and that wretched, blessed thief was ever at my weary elbow while I tried to think and read and write in interrupted intervals in planes and trains and hotel rooms for almost three interminable months.

But it was a glorious, heart-filling, head-filling odyssey for which I shall be forever grateful to my party, to my staff and to my fellow Americans. Their faces are a friendly, smiling sea of memory stretching from coast to coast. Bitter, ugly, false things were said and written during the campaign, I know, but not by those people. Millions of them believed in me and my party and voted for Senator Sparkman and me. Thousands even wrote gracious, flattering letters, after the election, explaining why they did *not* vote for me. They seemed to feel they owed me an explanation. I was touched and flattered, but I confess the thought occurred to me now and then that a little "X" in the right place on the ballot would have been so much easier than a long, thoughtful letter.

At least for an inexperienced candidate, I suppose we have contrived few more exacting ordeals than a Presidential campaign. You must emerge, bright and bubbling with wisdom and well-being, every morning at 8 o'clock, just in time for a charming and profound breakfast talk, shake hands with hundreds, often literally thousands, of people, make several inspiring, "newsworthy" speeches during the day, confer with political leaders along the way and with your staff all the time, write at every chance, think if possible, read mail and newspapers, talk on the telephone, talk to everybody, dictate, receive delegations, eat, with decorum—and discretion!—and ride through city after city on the back of an open car, smiling until your mouth is dehydrated by the wind, waving until the blood runs out of your arm, and then bounce gaily, confidently, masterfully into great howling halls, shaved and all made up for television with the right color shirt and tie—I always forgot —and a manuscript so defaced with chicken tracks and last-minute jottings that you couldn't follow it, even if the spotlights weren't blinding and even if the still photographers didn't shoot you in the eye every time you looked at them. (I've often wondered what happened to all those pictures!) Then all you have to do is make a great, imperishable speech, get out through the pressing crowds with a few score autographs, your clothes intact, your hands bruised, and back to the hotel—in time to see a few important people.

But the real work has just commenced—two or three, sometimes four hours of frenzied writing and editing of the next day's immortal mouthings so you can get something to the stenographers, so they can get something to the mimeograph machines, so they can get something to the reporters, so they can get something to their papers by deadline time. (And I quickly concluded that all deadlines were yesterday!) Finally sleep, sweet sleep, steals you away, unless you worry—which I do.

The next day is the same.

But I gained weight on it. And it's as tenacious as a campaign deficit! Somehow the people sustain you, the people and a constant, sobering reminder that you are asking them to entrust to you the most awesome responsibility on earth. And, too, there is mirth mingled with the misery all along the way. They shout, "Good old Ad-lie!" If you run for office and have a slightly unusual name, let me advise you either to change it before you start, or be prepared to take other people's word for it. And I shall not soon forget about the woman in the crowd in San Francisco who reached into the car to shake hands with me, and not long after discovered that she had lost her diamond ring. Nor will I forget the warm welcome I received on a whistle stop in Bethlehem and my thanks to "the people of Allentown." My only hope is that *they* forget it! Again, out West, I warmly endorsed the impressive chairman of a meeting as a candidate for Congress, only to discover that he was not running for Congress or anything else.

But recollections of these happy, weary weeks of travel and travail could go on and on to no one's advantage, including mine. And my assignment from the publishers is an "Introduction" to these speeches, uttered in halls, parks, public squares, railroad stations, in darkness and light, rain and shine.

I selected these particular speeches from the larger mass because they seem to cover much of what I wanted to say and said. There are others, of course, that I should like to have included, and some that have been included might advantageously be forgotten, and quickly, as "campaign oratory" generally is. But I have not "edited" my campaign, nor have I edited its record, these speeches, from the vantage point of hindsight and afterthought. Hence there is repetition, redundancy and restatement. But they are the words, unchanged, that were born and spoken in a great variety of circumstances and under incredible pressures. I have relied upon stenographic transcriptions in most cases. Where lacking, I have used my own typescript with my accompanying notes to reconstruct what I said as accurately as possible. The only deletions are purely local matter, meaningful only at the time and place, like comments about local candidates and local references or jokes which are difficult or impossible to reconstruct from the materials at hand, even if they had any value. Yet in an effort to furnish an example of a "whistle stop" I have left in the text of the Ypsilanti talk at least those improvisations which the stenographer was able to catch. I should add that in a few instances I have checked and corrected quotations for accuracy. The arrangement is chronological.

How did I organize the campaign and why? Why was I defeated? Do I regret the kind of campaign I tried to conduct? Why was I the Democratic candidate? What is my political philosophy? Why am I a Democrat? What is the future of the Democratic Party? What is my future? All these, and many other questions I've been asked to answer in this Introduction.

Of course, it's impossible, but I can say that I am a Democrat because I believe that the Democratic Party has been faithful to the people as a whole, and to the root concept of equal rights for all and special privileges for none. And I believe that over its long history, the Democratic Party has been much more alert and adaptable to our needs, be they defenses against economic misfortune, or the realities of the uneasy world about us. I believe that properly informed, continuously and accurately informed, the people will know best in the long run, better than any one of us or any group of us, better than Alexander Hamilton's "rich and well born" or Karl Marx's "proletariat."

The Democratic Party has survived the Federalists, the Whigs and all manner of less enduring parties because, by and large, it has clung to the broad concept of a people's party. I hope it will not become just a labor party, or a farmer's party, or a minorities party, or a small-business party, or reflect predominantly the views and economic interest of any group in our society. When it does, it will fail in its historic mission as a means to an end—as a mechanism for the expression of general opinion and for the development of public policy for the attainment of the basic objective of a truly democratic society—the always imperfect but ever-expanding well-being and freedom of *all* the people.

These are broad strokes of the philosophic brush and there is much more I could say about the Democratic Party, critical as well as approving, for I make no pretenses about the wisdom, virtue, or infallibility of Democrats. Indeed, I think self-examination and criticism are the great and not-so-secret weapons of democracy. And criticism and nonconformity seem to come naturally to us Democrats who represent such diversity and have no taste for the irons of rigid uniformity and discipline. As Marse Henry Watterson said, "Things have come to a pretty pass when a man can't cudgel his own jackass."

But this is not the place nor have you the patience for me to attempt to review all the successes and failures, the virtues and vices, of a political institution that has survived 150 years of our history, and made much of it. After all, what I think and why I am a Democrat, is set forth, ad infinitum I fear, in the speeches that follow.

Besides, I must add that I was born a Democrat! And I think there is a story somewhere in this volume which attempts to explain that.

My father's family moved to Kentucky from Virginia and North Carolina, and a generation or so later they moved on to Bloomington, Illinois, before the Civil War. They were Scotch-Irish Presbyterians and Democrats, and strong in the faith, both political and religious. Miraculously, Grandfather Stevenson flourished politically in Republican Illinois and was elected Vice-President with Grover Cleveland in 1892. He was nominated again with Bryan in 1900, and, as a feeble old man, was a reluctant but very strong candidate for Governor in 1908. My father's Democratic allegiance and activity ended only with his death in 1929.

But my mother's family were Pennsylvania Quakers who came early to Illinois. Her grandfather, Jesse Fell, was a "liberal" of those days, I suppose, an abolitionist, educator and a founder of the Unitarian Church in Bloomington. Discontented with the Whigs, he took the leading part in organizing a "Republican Party" in Central Illinois and worked tirelessly for the advancement of his long-time friend, Abraham Lincoln. His son-in-law, my grandfather, William Osborn Davis, was also a Pennsylvania Quaker who found the Unitarian Church in Bloomington much to his liking. For forty years he was a leading Republican editor and publisher of Illinois.

So it is hardly surprising that when the son of the Democratic Vice-President married the daughter of the Republican editor of the same town, the newspapers of the country headlined the event as a "triumph of love over politics."

Small wonder, then, that as I grew up in Bloomington, I found myself in Mother's beloved Unitarian Church and Father's beloved Democratic Party. I guess I was a compromise to begin with, which may have predestined a political career for which I had no conscious stomach, and, I might add, no positive encouragement from my father at any time.

There was little of black and white in our home as I look back on it. Visiting the two grandfathers on Sundays and vacations, I was often in Presbyterian churches and saw and listened to as many articulate Republicans as Democrats, perhaps more, because the local Democrats were few—but hardy!—in Bloomington in those days.

Thinking of political influences brings back one unhappy incident of those days. It was a Sunday dinner at Grandfather Stevenson's with William Jennings Bryan. From prior visits, I recalled with awe how much fried chicken he could eat and I resolved to match him, piece for piece. I did, and when we reached the great Chautauqua tent for his speech, I promptly fell sound asleep at his feet, to the great discomfiture of my parents. But I still love fried chicken—and Democrats.

My father's principal interest was agriculture as I grew up. In the twenties he was active in the fight for the McNary-Haugen Bills, and a better break for farmers. It was natural then that I accepted an invitation to join the staff of George N. Peek of Illinois, a Republican leader in the farmers' long struggle, and the first Administrator of the Agricultural Adjustment Act. I dropped my law practice in Chicago and moved to Washington in the summer of 1933. While I did not contribute much to the relief of the unhappy plight of the Illinois farmer, I did have an intensive course in agricultural economics and a most enlightening introduction to the perishable "special crops" on the West Coast—everything from the dates of the desert of Southern California to the apples of Washington.

With the repeal of the prohibition amendment, in December,

1933, I was "loaned" to an agency called the Federal Alcohol Control Administration, hastily improvised to regulate all the alcoholic beverage industries until more permanent legislative controls could be devised. The FACA, as it was called, was also headed by a Republican, Joseph H. Choate, Jr., of New York. For most of a year I labored prodigiously with the infinite problems of those industries, emancipated after fifteen years, and so heavily freighted with social interest.

Then, after almost a year and a half of the intensity of the early days of the Roosevelt Administration in Washington, I returned to my law firm in Chicago in the autumn of 1934. And there I stayed, occupied with the law and my first interest, foreign affairs, until I moved again to Washington in June, 1941. This time it was to join my beloved friend, Colonel Frank Knox, the Secretary of the Navy, also a Republican, as his Special Assistant and Counsel. In large part, Colonel Knox's request to join him and the confidence he reposed in me during those three relentless years of the war, until his death in April, 1944, sprang from an earlier common conviction that involvement in the war seemed inevitable. I am sure that is why he disregarded the counsels of Republican regularity and the cautious advice of lesser men, and, like Henry Stimson, accepted the call of his President to head the Navy in an hour of peril and imperative preparedness.

From the fall of France in June of 1940, I had spent much of my time in Chicago agitating and exhorting about the sinister threat of Hitler and fascism and for aid to the Allies. Colonel Knox's newspaper, the Chicago *Daily News*, rode gallantly to battle with the Chicago *Tribune* every day in the citadel of isolation and "America First." Finally, with the clouds gathering ever darker and the pressure gauges rising rapidly in Washington, Colonel Knox asked me to drop the public-opinion battle in Chicago and join him in the Navy Department. I did, in July of 1941, and from that day until this repose or relaxation have never been my lot.

My duties with Secretary Knox in the rapidly expanding Navy Department were many and varied. And there was much travel, including a memorable and early journey to the South Pacific with Secretary Knox and Admiral Nimitz, a journey I can never forget because of what I saw of the enormity and the cost in heroism and treasure of our undertaking to bridge and conquer the Pacific.

In the fall of 1943, Secretary Knox "loaned" me to head an

economic mission to see what should and could be done about devastated, hungry, confused Italy behind the allied armies, then painfully fighting their way up the peninsula.

I think it was in Naples on a wet, cold night in that ugly winter that I naively asked Ernie Pyle if the G.I.'s up at the front were much interested in the soldier-vote legislation I had just been working on in Washingon. He looked at me incredulously. "No," he said, "I don't think so, but I can tell you what they *are* thinking about. They're thinking about a dry spot where they can place their bottoms and wring out their socks." Later I went up there in the mud and blood of the Liri Valley and saw for myself. He was right.

Somewhere, there in Italy, I think, I read about a public-opinion poll which reported that some seven out of ten American parents disapproved their sons going into politics or public service, or something like that. From what I had already seen of the war at home, in the Pacific, in the Mediterranean and from what I was still to see in Europe, I've often thought of that little morsel of news: fight, suffer, die, squander our substance, yes; but work in peacetime for the things we die for in war, no! There seemed to me something curiously inconsistent about the glorious, eager, uncomplaining sacrifices of war for the security of our homeland and its cherished institutions, and the active distaste of so many respectable people for peacetime participation in the politics and service of that homeland and its institutions. Die for them—yes; work for them—no. Small wonder, I thought, that our "politics" is no better, and great wonder that it is as good as it is. It seems to me sad that "politics" and "politician" are so often epithets and words of disrespect and contempt, and not without justification, in the land of Jefferson and in a government by the governed.

But it is an old story. Dickens and everyone else has had something to say about it, and there's a speech about it somewhere in this volume. Of one thing I am sure, however; the regeneration of our politics and public life at our maturity and zenith is moving apace and in the right direction. But there is a long way to go.

A year later, in the autumn of 1944, I was in England and along the Western Front in France and Belgium on an Air Force job. Like so much of "my war" there was little time to think, to meditate on it all. I was always in a hurry. I guess I've always been in a hurry, which probably does not distinguish me much from most of my fellow Americans! Yet standing one day—wet and cold—in

Eschweiler, a battered little town on the German frontier, I thought of Italy, just a year before, wet, cold and bloody too, of the South Pacific the year before that, hot, steaming and bloody, of North Africa, West Africa, the Caribbean, and all the places I had been, all the things I had seen, like the soldiers there in Eschweiler, moving up to the lines, and the ambulances moving back. I thought of the ghastly burns I had seen long before on those "Pearl Harbor boys" in the rows of white beds in California. I thought, too, of how the desperately wounded little Japanese prisoners had struggled to sit up and bow in a stinking, suffocating hospital hut in a coconut grove on the other side of the war-wrenched globe.

Was this the everlasting destiny of man, indicted for his stupidity and sin, convicted, sentenced forever to kill or be killed? No, it would end soon. "The weather is too bad for tactical flying," the officer was saying, "but the Eighth Air Force will be over tonight to flatten some more of Berlin, I suppose." And beyond, I thought, was the Russian juggernaut pounding, grinding toward us; the noose was tightening—yes, it would be over soon; and then we must start on something better; pick up where Wilson left off, with a broken heart and a broken body, and push on to end this ugly business before it ends us all; what was it Wilson said in his sorrow with the prescience of revelation: "For I can tell you, my fellow citizens, I can predict with absolute certainty that within another generation there will be another world war if the nations of the world do not concert the method by which to prevent it."

It wasn't a long reverie, just a moment, there near the command post, in December, 1944, before the big push across the Rhine. The next day we started back across Belgium by automobile on the way to London. That night the Battle of the Bulge commenced, and the last Nazi convulsion was smothered in the forest of Ardennes which had been so still and beautiful in the soft fresh snow.

Back home, when my friends, Edward Stettinius, then Secretary of State, and Archibald MacLeish, Assistant Secretary, asked me to come into the State Department to help out "for a few months" with the United Nations planning, I accepted.

They used to say that if you worked in wartime Washington, you would get one of three things: galloping frustration, ulcers or a sense of humor. I guess I got them all and I also got a great education in war, the world, our Government and my fellow man under every sort of trial and tension, from Congressional investigations to that shattering evening in the Secretary of the Navy's office while the news from Pearl Harbor was coming in. But I think my most intensive postgraduate education commenced that day I entered the State Department as Assistant to the Secretary, late in February, 1945.

Instead of a few months I stayed a year. Instead of going back to Chicago after the San Francisco Conference, as I had planned, I went to London as deputy to Stettinius on the Preparatory Commission of the U.N. When he shortly fell ill and had to return to the United States, I succeeded him as chief of our delegation and lived in London for almost six months. It was the most exacting, interesting and in many ways the most important interval of my life. After almost four years of preoccupation with war, the satisfaction of having a part in the organized search for the conditions and mechanics of peace completed my circle.

After our work in London was done, Secretary of State Byrnes asked me to go to Argentina or Brazil as our Ambassador, but I went back to Chicago, my family and law firm, in March, 1946. President Truman asked me to serve on our delegation to the United Nations that fall and I spent three more sleepless months at the General Assembly in New York. He appointed me again in 1947, and for another three months I worked with our delegation in New York, an interval which confirmed with finality misgivings I had sorrowfully expressed early in 1946 about Russian intentions and our hopes for future tranquility.

When I returned to Chicago in December, 1947, some of the Democratic leaders asked me to run for Governor. This was a new departure indeed. I had never run for any office, had never wanted any, had never been active in city or state politics and knew almost none of the party leaders in Chicago or downstate. Moreover, 1948 didn't look like a very good year for Democrats anywhere, let alone in Illinois where only three had been elected Governor in ninety years. But I accepted. Why? I don't know exactly; perhaps it was because of Father and Grandfather Stevenson and Great-Grandfather Fell who had all served Illinois; perhaps it was restlessness about settling down again after eight feverish years of war and peace; perhaps it was the encouragement of some determined friends . . . and perhaps the public-opinion poll I saw in Italy had something to do with it.

Anyway, I did it. I worked at it day and night, from January to November, and was elected by the largest majority in the State's history. There followed four years of toil in Springfield, more rewarding and satisfying than I dreamed possible. The governorship of a great state is an intensive education in politics, people and public administration that has few counterparts in American public life. There I discovered that in a political job there are usually two ways to do things: the politically expedient way or the right way. Sometimes they do not coincide but in the long run the right way is the best politics. But the story of what was done in Illinois has been told before. I would like to tell it again some time, myself, but not here.

How did I happen to be nominated for President when I didn't seek the nomination and didn't want it? In late December, 1951, I decided after long reflection on the trials and hazards, the changes and chances of political life, to run for Governor again. There was much, much more to do in Illinois; there would be no primary contest, my chances of re-election looked very bright regardless of what happened nationally, my principal associates had agreed to stay with me for another term, the government was well organized at last, the party political tribulations of the early years had subsided, and the Governorship of Illinois was a dramatic opportunity to demonstrate to all and sundry, in and out of politics, that reason will prevail—"our sandbank is bound to grow"—and that, simply stated, the best government is in fact the best politics and will pay off in public confidence and votes manyfold what it loses in patronage, profit and political organization.

So I announced for Governor again. Very shortly articles began to appear about me as a Democratic Presidential possibility, seldom taking any note of the fact that even if I wanted the nomination I was already committed to run for Governor and it was too late under Illinois law for anyone else to file.

All winter and spring people were coming to Springfield and telephoning from all over the country—newspapermen, columnists, commentators, political leaders, friends, leaders of organizations, etc., etc. The mail became a real burden. First it was exhortation to announce my candidacy and enter primaries—"fight for the nomination." To all, my explanation was the same: I was a candidate for Governor of Illinois; I was committed to run for that office and one could not run for two offices at the same time in good conscience, or treat the highest office within the gift of the people of Illinois as a consolation prize. Moreover, as the executive head of a huge business, the State of Illinois, I had little time to go around the country campaigning for an unwanted nomination for an unwanted office—an office, moreover, of such appalling difficulty and responsibility in the year of grace, 1952, that I felt no sense of adequacy.

Later the pressure changed. It was no longer, "Will you be a candidate for the nomination?", but "Will you accept the nomination?" This was more difficult. If I said, "Yes," publicly or covertly, it would start the draft movement in earnest. If I said, "No," how would it reconcile with all my preaching about public service and politics? How could I foretell then, long before the convention, what manner of deadlock and bitterness might develop to the lasting damage of my party? And, finally, could anyone in good health and already in public life refuse the greatest honor and greatest responsibility in our political system? So I concluded to keep still and say nothing more to anyone, contenting myself with confidence that no one could in fact be drafted by a modern convention against his often-expressed wish. As the convention approached, that is what I told everyone, while I busied myself with the formation of committees, preparing my program and campaigning for Governor.

All this time, from January to July, I read stories speculating that I wanted to run if Senator Taft was nominated by the Republicans, but not against General Eisenhower; that I was being coy and playing hard to get; that I had promised President Truman to run if he didn't, etc., etc. And only occasionally did I see anything suggesting that I meant what I said and that another term as Governor of Illinois really was the full measure of my ambition.

I was a district delegate to the convention, and the day before it convened I asked a caucus of the Illinois delegation not to nominate me and not to vote for me, if nominated. At the opening of the convention, I made a welcoming speech as Governor of the host state, along with Martin Kennelly, the Democratic Mayor of Chicago. Something of a demonstration followed; so, after one more appearance in the hall, I stayed away on the other side of the city. Hearing that Archibald Alexander, candidate for Senator in New Jersey, or Governor Shricker of Indiana might nominate me, I called them both by phone and asked them not to. Alexander agreed, but my esteemed friend, Governor Shricker, rebelled—and a very good nominating speech he made, too!

Contrary to the impression of some, I had no understanding whatever with President Truman at any time that I was available. To set at rest still another rumor, I think my friend, Colonel Arvey, the National Committeeman from Illinois, would testify that during those six months I repeatedly urged him to do nothing in my behalf and repeatedly he assured me he neither had nor would, always adding that he was bedeviled with incessant pressures and inquiries.

In the circumstances that I have here attempted hastily to sketch I was nominated and accepted the nomination at about three o'clock on the morning of July 26th. And I was delighted with the selection the following day of a very uncommon American, Senator John Sparkman of Alabama, as my running mate.

The delegates went home, most of them, I suspect, a little bewildered about the unknown, reluctant dragon they had just selected. I went to Springfield, there to contemplate the wreckage of my hopes to run for Governor and the problems of a highly inexperienced candidate for the Presidency. I had limited political acquaintance, no manager, no staff, little money in the till, little press support. And I was running against General Eisenhower, a national hero for ten years, and also the inevitable accumulation of irritations and anxieties of twenty years of government in a time of profound changes—irritations and anxieties which had been vigorously, if not objectively, cultivated for a long time by Republican orators and most of the press. The best confidential polls indicated that we had no more than 35 per cent of the popular vote.

But the Republican Party was badly split and the election was three months off. Like Dr. Johnson, I saw no point in expressing a consternation I didn't feel for a calamity that had not occurred. And, besides the great Democratic Party and the social revolution it had wrought, I had some other assets, too; among them the prompt, warm and sincere encouragement and loyalty of all the disappointed contenders for the nomination—Senator Kefauver, Averell Harriman, Senator Kerr, Senator Russell, and my great kinsman, Alben Barkley. There was still another asset, little noted in the newspapers, which meant a great deal to me—I had literally no obligations to anyone.

I suppose, like the unsought and unwanted nomination itself, this was something new in our political history. Nor, let me add, did anyone ever ask anything of me in exchange for support or money, which, I daresay, is also something unique in Presidential campaigns.

I concluded to organize and run my part of the campaign my own way. As I was still Governor I established my headquarters in Springfield instead of New York, as in the past. I enlisted an old Chicago friend, Stephen Mitchell, as Chairman of the National Committee in Washington and induced Wilson Wyatt of Louisville to come to Springfield to organize and manage my headquarters. And I finally persuaded Dwight R. G. Palmer of New York along with Beardsley Ruml to undertake the thankless and indispensable job of raising the money to finance the campaign. For myself, I set about the business of what I was going to say and left to the others the decisions as to where and when I would say it.

Platforms are supposed to be solemn, sincere public declarations of party principles and intentions. In fact, they are more often, in our times, disingenuous appeals to as many interests as possible to catch as many votes as possible. The people know this, by and large, and the result has been, it seems to me, that platforms per se not only attract fewer and fewer votes, but have come to mean less and less to more and more, candidates included.

I had nothing whatever to do with writing it, but the Democratic platform of 1952, while if not the perfection of political probity, was, I thought, a very good one indeed. I decided to adhere to it as closely as I could and, thereby, perhaps further a little the classical purpose of a periodical restatement of principles and program for the public's enlightenment.

For years I have listened to the nauseous nonsense, the pie-in-the-sky appeals to cupidity and greed, the cynical trifling with passion and prejudice and fear; the slander, fraudulent promises, and the all-things-to-all-men demagoguery that are too much a part of our political campaigns. Sometimes in the deafening clamor of political salesmanship, I've thought that the people might be better served if a party purchased a half hour of radio and TV silence during which the audience would be asked to think quietly for themselves.

Politicians all applaud and support public education as democracy's great monument and cornerstone, but does the politician, the agent and spokesman of democracy, have no responsibility for public education? Government by the consent of the governed is the most difficult system of all because it depends for its success and viability on the good judgments and wise decisions of so many of us. But judgment and decision depend on information and understanding. In matters of public policy, candidates then have the greatest responsibility of all to inform truthfully, so that the people will understand and will have the tools of good judgment and wise decision.

One can argue, indeed, that candidates claiming the people's confidence have even a higher mission; honestly to help man to know, as St. Thomas Aquinas said, what he ought to believe; to know what he ought to desire; to know what he ought to do.

It is an old, old story. Call it the duty of aspirants for public office to inform, to educate, to reason with the people they seek to lead, if you please. Believing utterly in democracy and the collective reason of properly informed people, I have always thought that political campaigns for offices of great responsibility are both an opportunity and an obligation to talk sensibly and truthfully about public questions and their full implications.

I felt that the danger, not only to the Democratic Party politically, but to the country, in this national campaign was that it would follow the preconvention line and turn largely on Korea, corruption, communists in government, etc., which were really not controversial issues between the two candidates at all. No one was running on a pro corruption ticket or in favor of treachery. Everyone wanted to arrest inflation, reduce the cost of living and end the stalemate in Korea as quickly as possible. These were all questions of men and methods for dealing with them, not of objectives or good intentions. But of basic and fundamental importance in the campaign was that we Americans who were destined to lead, whether we liked it or not, must face stern decisions at home and the brutal facts of a world half slave, half free, a world besieged from the east for the first time since the Turks were turned back at the gates of Vienna, a world in which two-thirds of the people were hungry and half could neither read nor write—a world, in short, in which tolerance, understanding and peace were not to be had easily, quickly or cheaply. Unless people faced these realities at home and abroad, unless they knew that sedatives are not solutions and peace and prosperity goals, not gifts, we would dissipate a great opportunity to "dyke and break-water," as William James put it, our sandbank of reason.

For these reasons, I said in accepting the nomination that I viewed the campaign not as a crusade to exterminate the opposition, "but as a great opportunity to educate and elevate a people whose destiny is leadership, not alone of a rich, prosperous, contented country, but of a world in ferment." And because you cannot banish the evils of society by banishing reason or waving wands, I also said in that speech: "Let's talk sense to the American people. Let's tell them the truth. . . . Better we lose the election than mislead the people."

I tried to do that during the campaign, with, I fear, indifferent success. First, with my hastily recruited staff and the ever-wise counsel of a long-time friend and assistant in Springfield, Carl McGowan, we prepared a list of some twelve or thirteen major topics or issues which I wanted to discuss, like agriculture, foreign policy, labor, natural resources, inflation, corruption, etc. Feeling that the "time for a change" sentiment was the greatest hazard of all, I concluded also to devote an early speech to the vaporous anxiety of people to vote themselves out of trouble.

Next, I decided that I would discuss these major questions one by one in separate speeches during September, thereby setting forth my whole program and identifying myself and my views as quickly as possible. One must bear in mind that I had not campaigned in the primaries and that my views as well as myself were little known about the country. So it seemed to me wise to take the initiative at once and set forth my position as clearly, comprehensively and unequivocally as possible, reserving October, the second half of the campaign, for the exigencies and opportunities that were bound to develop as the campaign progressed, and for amplification and rebuttal in the debate that I thought would develop on some of the domestic issues at least. It did not develop and as the battle of words progressed, I felt more and more that people cared little about the issues and party records, or about precise definition of positions. They were weary of conflict, impatient and eager for repose. While discouraging, it was not surprising. Having said my piece with some precision on the problems of our country, I tried to stir deeper waters and talked more and more philosophically about faith and fear, and about the mighty and wondrous powers for good of free and independent-thinking Americans.

If my early assumption that some reasoned and precise debate would develop was a mistake, I made some other miscalculations too. I had not anticipated that responsible Republican spokesmen, not including General Eisenhower, would trumpet plain falsehoods about my administration in Illinois. Nor had I assumed that many Republican leaders, but never General Eisenhower, would impugn my loyalty and good "judgment" because I told the simple truth— that the reputation of Alger Hiss was good when I knew him. Truth is *not* a matter of judgment in such a situation. "Thou shalt not bear false witness" is still the law of God and man, I hope. And thou shalt not be afraid to bear true witness is, I think, a good rule for all of us, including timid politicians. I withheld any comment about the relations of Mr. Dulles, now Secretary of State, and General Eisenhower himself with Hiss as long as I felt I could, until October 23rd, and I wish I had not felt obliged to mention such irrelevancies at all.

While foreign affairs was bound to enter the campaign significantly and properly, I had assumed that it and our unhappy situation in Korea particularly would not be a politically fruitful tree to shake in view of my adversary's past utterances. In early August I decided, if elected, to make a quick journey to Japan, Korea and India "to see for myself," meet the people with whom I would have to deal, and to give the best possible evidence of our profound concern for the Orient. We kept the plan secret, fearful that it might be construed as a political gesture. This may have been a mistake, and while I cannot approve the General's speech about going to Korea and the implication of early settlement or the misleading use that was made of it, I think he did the right thing to go out there and that we will all benefit from his first-hand information. I only wish that time and circumstances had permitted him to travel farther.

Did I talk over the people's heads? No—and that's about the only aspect of the campaign I am sure of! As I have said above, I think candidates for important offices, let alone for the Presidency of the United States in this age and day, should not treat us as fourteen-year-olds but as adults, challenging us, in the ancient tradition of all civilized people, with the assumption that we should and can and will respond to the appeal of reason and imagination.

What's more, I doubt if I could have talked over people's heads even if I had foolishly wanted to. As Franklin P. Adams said, "The average man is a great deal above the average." To be sure, many of us may be taken in now and then by professionalized emotionalism, showmanship and huckstering. And I concede that radio, television and press create the means of mass manipulation and the "sale" of political ideas and personalities. But I am not much troubled by that danger. There are too many evidences of growing political maturity and discernment in America. While the campaign of 1952 is not a good illustration because so many imponderable factors were involved, like "time for a change," Korea and my opponent's great popularity, it is safe to say that many people voted for the Democratic candidates not because we held out any comforting hope of early tax reduction, an end to the war, peace on earth and easy solutions for all our frustrations, but for exactly the opposite reason—because we did not. There were many like the woman who flattered me with her thanks for "a shot in the intellect," and the one who wrote, "I am easily swayed by emotion until I think, which I occasionally do."

Of course those who lose are not easily persuaded that the winners evidenced any maturity, and likewise the winners are always convinced that the losers were benighted. Each of us thinks the other mature if he votes the same way for the same reasons. And, because intellectual pride is here to stay, each of us is likely to feel that he understands things a little better than the next man, just as so many were sure they understood what I was saying, but doubted if the other fellow did. Jan Struther illustrated it by these engaging verses which I immodestly repeat:

STEVENSON'S SPEECH

John Doe, he heard a speech.
It didn't plead, it didn't preach,
It wasn't loud, it wasn't wild,
It didn't treat him like a child.
It even carried one or two
Words he hadn't known he knew.
John Doe scratched his head:
John Doe smiled, and said:
"Richard wouldn't understand—
But as for me, I think it's grand."

Richard Roe, he heard it too;
Listened hard the whole way through.

It made him feel he wasn't dense—
Addressed him like a man of sense.
It made him feel, "I'm not a fool—
I still remember stuff from school."
Richard Roe, he rubbed his eyes
With a kind of proud surprise.
"'Tisn't quite in Johnny's line—
But as for me, I liked it fine."

Doe and Roe met face to face
Just outside the polling-place.
"Well, what's new?" said Doe to Roe.
"Nothing much," said Roe to Doe.
"Whaddya know?" said Roe to Doe.
"Not a thing," said Doe to Roe.
In they went, and out they came,
Looking just about the same.
He, and he alone (thought each)
Had *really* understood that speech . . .

This Introduction was written by the blue Caribbean in a happy state of half-wakefulness on my first real vacation in many years. What I believed and much of what I said in the memorable campaign of 1952 is in the pages that follow.

Because I have profound respect for my fellow countrymen I gave them the best I had. It can never be good enough, and my apology is that in the fever and haste of the campaign I could not better express what was in my heart and head.

We live in a time for greatness and greatness cannot be measured alone by the conventional yardsticks of resources, know-how and production. There are moral dimensions, too. It is the urgent duty of a political leader to lead, to touch if he can the potentials of reason, decency and humanism in man, and not only the strivings that are easier to mobilize.

The challenge of our faith and time "is the insensate worship of matter" organized in a vast international conspiracy. But the goal of life is more than material advance; it is now, and through all eternity, the triumph of spirit over matter, of love and liberty over force and violence.

In a world where masses of people at all levels of degradation and elevation are going to decide their own destiny, more and more, in a world where words like "freedom" and "justice" are meaningless to many, we are struggling to *meet* grievous assault by better satisfying the basic material needs of man. But we shall *master* the assault only by better satisfying the basic spiritual needs of man. These are hungers, too, and we alone, those of us around the globe who are free to follow the great teachers, free to believe and free to speak, are the only ones who can. For communism knows no God, and cannot satisfy the hungry heart.

To find the true balance between security and freedom, between initiative and anarchy, between tolerance and conformity, to organize vast patience and understanding for the peaceful resolution of our conflicts, to communicate the material and spiritual goals of life by the example of a superior system of self-management and self-discipline, these are the tasks of democratic statesmanship in our tense times. And these are tasks for adults, not children, for reason, not emotion, for faith, not fear.

We lost the election; we were soundly defeated. But if I talked sense, if I succeeded in expressing my ideas as I set out to do, if I educated and elevated any of us, then I am richly rewarded.

I have no regrets about losing the election, except for the disappointment of so many dedicated supporters who share my hope of revitalizing a basic assumption of democracy: honest political leadership that despises the easy road to popularity and insists on focusing attention on reality and truth, however distasteful. Unless the great political parties and their spokesmen assume responsibility for educating and guiding the people with constant candor, how can we be sure that majority rule will meet the test of these searching times?

I am an optimist, as these speeches will disclose. Anyone who has seen the might and majesty of America and Americans as I have must be an optimist—the America that "asks nothing for herself except what she has a right to ask for humanity itself."

In a letter to John Tyler almost 150 years ago, Thomas Jefferson wrote: "No experiment can be more interesting than that we are now trying, and which we trust will end in establishing the fact, that man may be governed by reason and truth. . . .

"I hold it, therefore, certain, that to open the doors of truth, and to fortify the habit of testing everything by reason, are the most effectual manacles we can rivet on the hands of our successors to prevent their manacling the people with their own consent. The panic into which they were artfully thrown in 1798, the frenzy which was excited in them by their enemies against their friends, and their apparent readiness to abandon all the principles established for their own protection, seemed for a while to countenance the opinions of those who say they cannot be trusted with their own government. But I never doubted their rallying; and they did rally much sooner than I expected. On the whole, that experiment on their credulity has confirmed my confidence in their ultimate good sense and virtue."

To that I say "Amen."

ADLAI E. STEVENSON

Barbados, B.W.I.
February 7, 1953

Major Campaign Speeches of

A D L A I   E.   S T E V E N S O N

1952

Welcoming Address

Democratic National Convention

CHICAGO, ILLINOIS

July 21, 1952

As Governor of the host state to the 1952 Democratic Convention, I have the honor of welcoming you to Illinois. And, in the name of our nine millions of people, I extend to you the heartiest of greetings. Chicago and Illinois are proud that once again the party conventions by which we restate our principles and choose our candidates for the greatest temporal office on earth, are held here in Chicago—at the crossroads of the continent.

Here, on the prairies of Illinois and the Middle West, we can see a long way in all directions. We look to east, to west, to north and south. Our commerce, our ideas, come and go in all directions. Here there are no barriers, no defenses, to ideas and aspirations. We want none; we want no shackles on the mind or the spirit, no rigid patterns of thought, no iron conformity. We want only the faith and conviction that triumph in free and fair contest.

As a Democrat perhaps you will permit me to remind you that until four years ago the people of Illinois had chosen but three Democratic governors in a hundred years. One was John Peter Altgeld, a German immigrant, whom the great Illinois poet, Vachel Lindsay, called the Eagle Forgotten; one was Edward F. Dunne, whose parents came here from Ireland; and the last was Henry Horner, but one generation removed from Germany. Altgeld was a Protestant, Dunne was a Catholic, and Horner was a Jew.

That, my friends, is the American story, written by the Democratic Party, here on the prairies of Illinois, in the heartland of the nation.

You are very welcome here. Indeed, we think you were very wise to come here for your deliberations in this fateful year of grace. For it was in Chicago that the modern Democratic story

3

began. It was here, just twenty years ago, in the depths of shattering national misery at the end of a dizzy decade of Republican rule that you commenced the greatest era of economic and social progress in our history—with the nomination of Franklin Roosevelt; twenty years during which we fought total depression to victory and have never been more prosperous; twenty years during which we fought total war to victory, both East and West, and launched the United Nations, history's most ambitious experiment in international security; twenty years that close this very month in grim contest with the communist conspiracy on every continent.

But, our Republican friends say it was all a miserable failure. For almost a week pompous phrases marched over this landscape in search of an idea, and the only idea they found was that the two great decades of progress in peace, victory in war, and bold leadership in this anxious hour were the misbegotten spawn of socialism, bungling, corruption, mismanagement, waste and worse. They captured, tied and dragged that ragged idea in here and furiously beat it to death.

After listening to this everlasting procession of epithets about our misdeeds I was even surprised the next morning when the mail was delivered on time! I guess our Republican friends were out of patience, out of sorts and, need I add, out of office.

But we Democrats were not the only victims here. First they slaughtered each other, and then they went after us. And the same vocabulary was good for both exercises, which was a great convenience. Perhaps the proximity of the stockyards accounts for the carnage.

The constructive spirit of the great Democratic decades must not die here on its twentieth anniversary in destructive indignity and disorder. And I hope and pray, as you all do, that we can conduct our deliberations with a businesslike precision and a dignity befitting our responsibility, and the solemnity of the hour of history in which we meet.

For it is a very solemn hour indeed, freighted with the hopes and fears of millions of mankind who see in us, the Democratic Party, sober understanding of the breadth and depth of the revolutionary currents in the world. Here and abroad they see in us awareness that there is no turning back, that, as Justice Holmes said, "We must sail sometimes with the wind, sometimes against it; but we must sail and not drift or lie at anchor." They see in us, the Democratic Party that has steered this country through a storm of spears for twenty years, an understanding of a world in the torment of transition from an age that has died to an age struggling to be born. They see in us relentless determination to stand fast against the barbarian at the gate, to cultivate allies with a decent respect for the opinion of others, to patiently explore every misty path to peace and security which is the only certainty of lower taxes and a better life.

This is not the time for superficial solutions and endless elocution, for frantic boast and foolish word. For words are not deeds and there are no cheap and painless solutions to war, hunger, ignorance, fear and to the new imperialism of Soviet Russia. Intemperate criticism is not a policy for the nation; denunciation is not a program for our salvation. Words calculated to catch everyone may catch no one. And I hope we can profit from Republican mistakes not just for our partisan benefit, but for the benefit of all of us, Republicans and Democrats alike.

Where we have erred, let there be no denial; where we have wronged the public trust, let there be no excuses. Self-criticism is the secret weapon of democracy, and candor and confession are good for the political soul. But we will never appease, nor will we apologize for our leadership in the great events of this critical century from Woodrow Wilson to Harry Truman!

Rather will we glory in these imperishable pages of our country's chronicle. But a great record of past achievement is not enough. There can be no complacency, perhaps for years to come. We dare not just look back to great yesterdays. We must look forward to great tomorrows.

What counts now is not just what we are *against*, but what we are *for*. *Who* leads us is less important than *what* leads us—what convictions, what courage, what faith—win or lose. A man doesn't save a century, or a civilization, but a militant party wedded to a principle can.

So I hope our preoccupation here is not just with personalities but with objectives. And I hope the spirit of this Convention is confident reaffirmation that the United States is strong, resolved, resourceful and rich; that we know the duty and the destiny of this heaven-rescued land; that we can and we will pursue a strong, consistent and honorable policy abroad, and meanwhile preserve the free institutions of life and of commerce at home.

What America needs and the world wants is not bombast, abuse and double talk, but a sober message of firm faith and confidence. St. Francis said: "Where there is patience and humility there is neither anger nor worry." That might well be our text.

And let us remember that we are not meeting here alone. All the world is watching and listening to what we say, what we do and how we behave. So let us give them a demonstration of democracy in action at its best—our manners good, our proceedings orderly and dignified. And—above all—let us make our decisions openly, fairly, not by the processes of synthetic excitement or mass hysteria, but, as these solemn times demand, by earnest thought and prayerful deliberation.

Thus can the people's party reassure the people and vindicate and strengthen the forces of democracy throughout the world.

Speech of Acceptance

I accept your nomination—and your program.

I should have preferred to hear those words uttered by a stronger, a wiser, a better man than myself. But, after listening to the President's speech, I feel better about myself!

None of you, my friends, can wholly appreciate what is in my heart. I can only hope that you may understand my words. They will be few.

I have not sought the honor you have done me. I *could* not seek it because I aspired to another office, which was the full measure of my ambition. One does not treat the highest office within the gift of the people of Illinois as an alternative or as a consolation prize.

I *would* not seek your nomination for the Presidency because the burdens of that office stagger the imagination. Its potential for good or evil now and in the years of our lives smothers exultation and converts vanity to prayer.

I have asked the Merciful Father—the Father of us all—to let this cup pass from me. But from such dread responsibility one does not shrink in fear, in self-interest, or in false humility.

So, "If this cup may not pass from me, except I drink it, Thy will be done."

That my heart has been troubled, that I have not sought this nomination, that I could not seek it in good conscience, that I would not seek it in honest self-appraisal, is not to say that I value it the less. Rather it is that I revere the office of the Presidency of the United States.

And now, my friends, that you have made your decision, I will fight to win that office with all my heart and soul. And, with your help, I have no doubt that we will win.

You have summoned me to the highest mission within the gift of any people. I could not be more proud. Better men than I were at hand for this mighty task, and I owe to you and to them every resource of mind and of strength that I possess to make your deed today a good one for our country and for our party. I am confident too, that your selection of a candidate for Vice President will strengthen me and our party immeasurably in the hard, the implacable work that lies ahead for all of us.

I know you join me in gratitude and respect for the great Democrats and the leaders of our generation whose names you have considered here in this Convention, whose vigor, whose character, whose devotion to the Republic we love so well have won the respect of countless Americans and have enriched our party. I shall need them, we shall need them, because I have not changed in any respect since yesterday. Your nomination, awesome as I find it, has not enlarged my capacities. So I am profoundly grateful and emboldened by their comradeship and their fealty, and I have been deeply moved by their expressions of good will and support. And I cannot, my friends, resist the urge to take the one opportunity that has been afforded me to pay my humble respects to a very great and good American, whom I am proud to call my kinsman, Alben Barkley of Kentucky.

Let me say, too, that I have been heartened by the conduct of this Convention. You have argued and disagreed, because as Democrats you care and you care deeply. But you have disagreed and argued without calling each other liars and thieves, without despoiling our best traditions in any naked struggles for power.

And you have written a platform that neither equivocates, contradicts nor evades. You have restated our party's record, its principles and its purposes, in language that none can mistake, and with a firm confidence in justice, freedom and peace on earth that will raise the hearts and the hopes of mankind for that distant day when no one rattles a saber and no one drags a chain.

For all these things I am grateful to you. But I feel no exultation, no sense of triumph. Our troubles are all ahead of us. Some will call us appeasers; others will say we are the war party. Some will say we are reactionary. Others will say that we stand for socialism. There will be the inevitable cries of "throw the rascals out"; "it's time for a change"; and so on and so on.

We'll hear all those things and many more besides. But we will hear nothing that we have not heard before. I am not too much concerned with partisan denunciation, with epithets and abuse, because the workingman, the farmer, the thoughtful businessmen, all know that they are better off than ever before and they all know that the greatest danger to free enterprise in this country died with the great depression under the hammer blows of the Democratic Party.

Nor am I afraid that the precious two-party system is in danger. Certainly the Republican Party looked brutally alive a couple of weeks ago, and I mean both Republican parties! Nor am I afraid that the Democratic Party is old and fat and indolent. After 150 years it has been old for a long time; and it will never be indolent as long as it looks forward and not back, as long as it commands the allegiance of the young and the hopeful who dream the dreams and see the visions of a better America and a better world.

You will hear many sincere and thoughtful people express concern about the continuation of one party in power for twenty years. I don't belittle this attitude. But change for the sake of change has no absolute merit in itself. If our greatest hazard is preservation of the values of Western civilization, in our self-interest alone, if you please, is it the part of wisdom to change for the sake of change to a party with a split personality; to a leader, whom we all respect, but who has been called upon to minister to a hopeless case of political schizophrenia?

If the fear is corruption in official position, do you believe with Charles Evans Hughes that guilt is personal and knows no party? Do you doubt the power of any political leader, if he has the will to do so, to set his own house in order without his neighbors having to burn it down?

What does concern me, in common with thinking partisans of both parties, is not just winning the election, but how it is won, how well we can take advantage of this great quadrennial opportunity to debate issues sensibly and soberly. I hope and pray that we Democrats, win or lose, can campaign not as a crusade to exterminate the opposing party, as our opponents seem to prefer, but as a great opportunity to educate and elevate a people whose destiny is leadership, not alone of a rich and prosperous, contented country as in the past, but of a world in ferment.

And, my friends, more important than winning the election is governing the nation. That is the test of a political party—the acid, final test. When the tumult and the shouting die, when the bands are gone and the lights are dimmed, there is the stark reality of responsibility in an hour of history haunted with those gaunt, grim specters of strife, dissension and materialism at home, and ruthless, inscrutable and hostile power abroad.

The ordeal of the twentieth century—the bloodiest, most turbulent era of the Christian age—is far from over. Sacrifice, patience, understanding and implacable purpose may be our lot for years to come. Let's face it. Let's talk sense to the American people. Let's tell them the truth, that there are no gains without pains, that we are now on the eve of great decisions, not easy decisions, like resistance when you're attacked, but a long, patient, costly struggle which alone can assure triumph over the great enemies of man—war, poverty and tyranny—and the assaults upon human dignity which are the most grievous consequences of each.

Let's tell them that the victory to be won in the twentieth century, this portal to the Golden Age, mocks the pretensions of individual acumen and ingenuity. For it is a citadel guarded by thick walls of ignorance and of mistrust which do not fall before the trumpets' blast or the politicians' imprecations or even a general's baton. They are, my friends, walls that must be directly stormed by the hosts of courage, of morality and of vision, standing shoulder to shoulder, unafraid of ugly truth, contemptuous of lies, half truths, circuses and demagoguery.

The people are wise—wiser than the Republicans think. And the Democratic Party is the people's party, not the labor party, not the farmers' party, not the employers' party—it is the party of no one because it is the party of everyone.

That I think, is our ancient mission. Where we have deserted it we have failed. With your help there will be no desertion now. Better we lose the election than mislead the people; and better we lose than misgovern the people. Help me to do the job in this autumn of conflict and of campaign; help me to do the job in these years of darkness, doubt and of crisis which stretch beyond the horizon of tonight's happy vision, and we will justify our glorious past and the loyalty of silent millions who look to us for compassion, for understanding and for honest purpose. Thus we will serve our great tradition greatly.

I ask of you all you have; I will give to you all I have, even as he who came here tonight and honored me, as he has honored you—the Democratic Party—by a lifetime of service and bravery that will find him an imperishable page in the history of the Republic and of the Democratic Party—President Harry S. Truman.

And finally, my friends, in the staggering task you have assigned me, I shall always try "to do justly and to love mercy and to walk humbly with my God."

The Beginning
of the Campaign

Governor's Day
Illinois State Fair

SPRINGFIELD, ILLINOIS

August 14, 1952

I notice from the program that today is still entitled Governor's Day. But I thought we had rechristened this as Barkley Day some two or three years ago.

So I welcome you all to Barkley Day at the greatest show on earth—the centennial of the Illinois State Fair. And we welcome for the fifth time running the noblest Kentuckian of them all, our beloved friend, Alben Barkley. What's more, Mr. Vice President, you have expiated the sins of omission of last year and we give you a double welcome this year because you have brought Mrs. Barkley with you. We Democrats think one Barkley is wonderful, but two are terrific.

You've heard so much *about* me today I think you should be spared hearing *from* me. Besides, this is the fifth year that you have listened to me too. I use "me too" in the grammatical, not the political sense. Which reminds me that there was a big meeting out here yesterday—a sort of bi-partisan gathering with representatives from both branches of the Republican Party. I don't know how the peace conference got along but they had a good time criticizing us for everything, as usual. They even accused me of the crime of visiting President Truman the other day —a crime that hasn't been committed since Rutherford B. Hayes, because the party in power has not nominated a candidate who was neither a member of Congress nor the Cabinet in seventy-five years. I thought I detected an explanation of their difficulty in finding something to say, however, when the orator of the day [Senator Nixon] revealed that out at the camp in Colorado [Gen-

11

eral Eisenhower's vacation headquarters] they ate fried mush most of the time.

I said this was the fifth year you had listened to me—an affliction that you have borne with admirable patience and fortitude. The Democratic days at the Fair have been among the proudest moments of my life. And now I must go away in quest of an even greater office, and leave behind not only you, my friends, but also my work here in Springfield. It is not easy to say farewell to you or to that work which has been my total life. For all the sweat and tears I have been richly rewarded.

What we set out to do when I first talked to you from this platform as a candidate for Governor in August, 1948, we have done in three and a half short years. We have eliminated the useless payrollers, put state purchasing on a businesslike basis, enacted a great road reconstruction program, raised the sights of the Illinois school system, put the state police on a professional non-political basis, taken the Commerce Commission out of politics, put Illinois out in front in the care and treatment of our mental patients, amended the Constitution, extended aid to tuberculosis hospitals, reorganized many aspects of state government, knocked out commercial gambling, enforced the truck weight laws to protect our highways, instilled a new sense of public responsibility among the state's employees—and I could go on and on. And in contrast to most all the other states, we have not raised taxes for the general purposes of the state.

You will forgive me for hurriedly mentioning these things. I mention them because they and many others have meant much to me, and, I think, to our party. It has been said that perhaps no state in our time has done so much so quickly. I don't know whether you call it a "New Deal" for Illinois, or a "Fair Deal," or a "Square Deal," but I know that it has been a no deal state government. We have just been trying to give the people the right change, which seems to be a novel and appealing idea.

But the importance of this work is not measured by my personal interest or satisfaction or by yours. It is important because the states are important. We talk about and deplore incessantly the increasing centralization of power over our lives in Washington. But that tidal drift toward the capital will go on and on unless those necessary functions of government which don't have to be performed in Washington are performed, and properly performed, at the state or local level. The people will demand the services, and if they don't get them at home they will turn to Uncle Sam. And every dollar you send to Washington to pay for them will shrink before it gets back home. Because our enemies are big, because business and labor and agriculture are big, because everything is big and organized nowadays, our Federal Government has inevitably become bigger too. But it should be unencumbered in the discharge of its monstrous major duties by a lot of other jobs it need not do. And the states are the dikes which we can build more strongly against the flood waters sweeping toward the District of Columbia.

While I want you to sweep me down there, don't sweep any more government jurisdiction down there! Sometimes one must overcome a feeling of reluctance about changing jobs. But the reluctance I feel about bigger and bigger jobs for the Federal Government is a reluctance I won't get over!

Because what we have been doing here in Illinois is important to our citizens, because it is important to our federal system, because public confidence is important to our party, and because much remains to be done, I had wanted to stay here and have a hand in putting this business of good government on a more permanent basis in Illinois. But I have been assigned another task, an assignment, which, I gather, has been greeted with enthusiasm in some sections of Illinois. One of our United States Senators, indeed, has said that I have been the worst Governor Illinois has had since the turn of the century. But I'm not the only Governor on whom he has poured his rich and reckless invective. I can well understand why he should look back with sentimental regret to the more bounteous days of my predecessor here in Springfield.

But because the citizens of the state will take a more charitable view of our efforts to give them the right change here in Springfield, and because you have a new leader exceptionally equipped by character and experience to carry on the work we have commenced, I am just as confident as I am standing here that Sherwood Dixon, Herbert Paschen, Eddie Barrett, Ben Cooper, Ivan Elliott and Fred Cain will all be elected next November. And I intend to be standing right here with them next summer—as President of the United States.

I am about to leave you on a long journey, and the route, by the way, won't be a military or political secret. I intend to cover as much ground as time and strength and our resources permit. And I won't call it a "crusade" to exterminate Republicans. I like a lot of Republicans, even some very new converts to that faith, whatever it is. Indeed there are some Republicans I would trust with anything—anything, that is, except public office. No, my journey won't be a crusade; we'll just call it Operation Victory.

And before I leave I want to say to you, shamelessly and sentimentally, that my heart will always be here in Illinois. Here five generations of my family have lived and prospered. My roots are deep in our prairies and I owe Illinois a great debt. I have tried my best to discharge that debt honorably and well. But in the process I have only increased my obligations.

Four years ago, when you entrusted me with the reins of state government, I found myself committed to tasks and responsibilities which were new to me and staggering in complexity and magnitude. I have learned more than I can say in these short years. It is easy enough to have bright ideas about the art of civil government in the abstract; but you never really can understand government until you are confronted with the concrete pressures and the day-to-day operating responsibilities. The essence of republican government is not command. It is consent. The experience and training of four years in Springfield have given me a unique opportunity to explore and, I hope, to master in some measure the means by which competing parties, competing branches of government, competing groups in the community can be brought to common action for the common good.

I want to thank you all for the opportunity you have afforded me. The experience has vastly enhanced my self-confidence for the new and appalling assignment I face in the future. My greatest ambition is to discharge that responsibility in a manner that will preserve the confidence and respect of my friends in Illinois who have given me the courage to face a future limitless with danger and opportunity.

I have learned other things in the past four years too. And most recently I have been hearing a great deal about the need for a change. I had always thought that Americans liked change for the better and disliked change for the worse. But a new doctrine is abroad in the land—the doctrine of change for the sake of change. Whether that change is to be for the better or for the worse is apparently something we are to find out after the election. It is like buying a surprise package at a novelty store. Maybe the cigar is a good one, or maybe it will explode in your face.

This whole problem of the need for a change is very interesting to me in a family way. From 1860 to 1912—a period of fifty-two long years—this nation had only one Democratic President. I can say this with feeling, because, as some of you may remember, Grover Cleveland's Vice President during his second term was my grandfather. I've read a good deal about that period and I don't recall the Republicans during those fifty-two long years saying very much about the sacred principle of change. Evidently "change" is a sound principle only when the Republicans are out and the Democrats in.

I've learned some other things of late. At the Republican Convention, an eminent party leader, a former President of this country, aged 77 years, made one of the main addresses. His speech was deeply melancholy in tone. This would probably be his last Republican Convention, he kept saying—a note of pessimism which we all sincerely hope will turn out to be wholly unjustified. He described the state of the nation in equally funereal language. The whole effect was one of black, unrelieved gloom.

In marked contrast to this venerable and melancholy figure of 77 at the Republican Convention was the stripling of 74 who stole the show at the Democratic Convention—and whom you are patiently waiting to hear today. Where the Republican despaired of the Republic, the Democrat exulted in the prospects of democracy, speaking with robust and youthful confidence about the exciting years ahead. Where the first wondered mournfully about whether he—or the nation—would last much longer, the second described how he spent last Christmas eating with the troops in Korea and looked forward to new travels and adventures. If the Vice President had suggested that he might not be back in four years, the convention hall would have exploded with incredulous laughter.

There are many fine people in the Republican Party. I am frank to say that I hope many of them will vote for me in November, as many of them voted for me here in Illinois four years ago. But it seems to me the leadership hardly does justice to the rank and file, let alone to the truth. They describe me as a "captive" candidate. They say I am a "captive" of the city bosses, and then of the CIO, and then of the Dixiecrats, and then of President Truman, and then of Wall Street, and then of an organization called A.D.A. Next week that will probably be a girl named Ada, but I haven't met her yet. Anyway I had no idea I was so popular, and I hope I can bear this multiple courtship and captivity with becoming modesty.

The fact that my captors generously assault one another reminds me of a story I heard about a scout who was captured by a group of Indian tribes, who soon began to argue among themselves about which tribe he belonged to. Tempers rose and so did the tomahawks. The rival tribesmen laid each other on the ground and Davy Crockett, or whoever he was, made his escape. Maybe there's hope for me! Meanwhile, it's not too uncomfortable to be captured by most everybody—except the Republican Old Guard!

But I have kept you much too long. Let me just add that I have often wondered how best to describe the essential difference between our two major parties. But when I think about the contrast between the speaker at the Fair yesterday and the speaker at the Fair today, the meat of the difference becomes obvious. The Republican Party is the party which makes even its young men seem old. The Democratic Party is the party which makes even its old men seem young. It is my pride and pleasure to present to you the youngest of them all, our beloved Vice President, Mr. Democrat himself—Alben Barkley.

The Nature of Patriotism

American Legion Convention

Madison Square Garden

NEW YORK CITY

August 27, 1952

I have attended altogether too many conventions not to know how you are all beginning to feel here on the afternoon of your third day. You work hard at Legion business, and then devote the balance of your time to the museums, art galleries, concerts and other cultural monuments of New York. And, of course, you have to listen to speeches too! I console myself with the thought that this punishment, while cruel, is not unusual.

I have no claim, as many of you do, to the honored title of old soldier. Nor have I risen to high rank in the armed services. The fact that a great General and I are competing candidates for the Presidency will not diminish my warm respect for his military achievements. Nor will that respect keep me from using every honest effort to defeat him in November!

My own military career was brief. It was also lowly. An Apprentice Seaman in a naval training unit was not, as some of you may also recall, exactly a powerful command position in World War One. My experience thus provided me with a very special view—what could be called a worm's-eye view—of the service. In 1918 I doubt if there was anything more wormlike than an Apprentice Seaman. I must add, though, that from a very topside job in the Navy Department during the frenzy of the last war I sometimes had nostalgic recollections of apprentice seamanship when someone else had to make all the decisions.

After the first war, many Americans lost sight of the fact that only the strong can be free. Many mistook an ominous lull for permanent peace. In those days the American Legion knew, however, that he who is not prepared today is less so tomorrow, and

17

that only a society which could fight for survival would survive.

The Legion's fight to awaken America to the need for military preparedness is now largely won. We have made great advances in understanding the problem of national security in the modern world. We no longer think in terms of American resources alone. For the most part we now understand the need for a great international system of security, and we have taken the lead in building it.

We have joined our strength with that of others—and we have done so in self-protection. We seek no dominion over any other nation—and the whole free world knows it! If there are those behind the Iron Curtain who don't know it, it is because their masters don't want them to know it.

I am not sure that, historically, there has been another powerful nation that has been trusted as the United States is trusted today. It is something new under the sun when the proudest nations on earth have not only accepted American leadership in the common defense effort, but have also welcomed our troops and bases on their territory. Ports the world around are open to American warships by day or night. Our airmen are stationed in the most distant lands.

Yet all is not perfect. There are still vital interests which we and our allies are not militarily prepared to defend.

Some of us are reluctant to admit that security cannot be won cheaply by some clever diplomatic maneuver or by propaganda.

We have not yet really faced up to the problem of defending our cities against the rapidly growing threat of Soviet air power. There is, for example, a great shortage of volunteers for our civil defense ground observation corps.

And many only partly understand or are loath to acknowledge that the costs of waging the cold war are but a fraction of the costs of hot war.

So there remain important tasks for us. I believe in a strong national defense, and I believe that we must press forward to improve our position and not waver or hesitate in this interval when the scales are so precariously balanced. While I think it is true that today the fight for preparedness is going well, there are other and even more difficult tasks that we dare not neglect.

The United States has very large power in the world today. And the partner of power—the corollary—is responsibility. It is our high task to use our power with a sure hand and a steady touch —with the self-restraint that goes with confident strength. The purpose of our power must never be lost in the fact of our power —and the purpose, I take it, is the promotion of freedom, justice and peace in the world.

We talk a great deal about patriotism. What do we mean by patriotism in the context of our times? I venture to suggest that what we mean is a sense of national responsibility which will enable America to remain master of her power—to walk with it in serenity and wisdom, with self-respect and the respect of all mankind; a patriotism that puts country ahead of self; a patriotism which is not short, frenzied outbursts of emotion, but the tranquil and steady dedication of a lifetime. The dedication of a lifetime— these are words that are easy to utter, but this is a mighty assignment. For it is often easier to fight for principles than to live up to them.

Patriotism, I have said, means putting country before self. This is no abstract phrase, and unhappily, we find some things in American life today of which we cannot be proud.

Consider the groups who seek to identify their special interests with the general welfare. I find it sobering to think that their pressures might one day be focused on me. I have resisted them before and I hope the Almighty will give me the strength to do so again and again. And I should tell you—my fellow Legionnaires—as I would tell all other organized groups, that I intend to resist pressures from veterans, too, if I think their demands are excessive or in conflict with the public interest, which must always be the paramount interest.

Let me suggest, incidentally, that we are rapidly becoming a nation of veterans. If we were all to claim a special reward for our service, beyond that to which specific disability or sacrifice has created a just claim, who would be left to pay the bill? After all, we are Americans first and veterans second, and the best maxim for any administration is still Jefferson's: "Equal rights for all, special privileges for none."

True patriotism, it seems to me, is based on tolerance and a large measure of humility.

There are men among us who use "patriotism" as a club for attacking other Americans. What can we say for the self-styled patriot who thinks that a Negro, a Jew, a Catholic, or a Japanese-

American is less an American than he? That betrays the deepest article of our faith, the belief in individual liberty and equality which has always been the heart and soul of the American idea.

What can we say for the man who proclaims himself a patriot —and then for political or personal reasons attacks the patriotism of faithful public servants? I give you, as a shocking example, the attacks which have been made on the loyalty and the motives of our great wartime Chief of Staff, General Marshall. To me this is the type of "patriotism" which is, in Dr. Johnson's phrase, "the last refuge of scoundrels."

The anatomy of patriotism is complex. But surely intolerance and public irresponsibility cannot be cloaked in the shining armor of rectitude and righteousness. Nor can the denial of the right to hold ideas that are different—the freedom of man to think as he pleases. To strike freedom of the mind with the fist of patriotism is an old and ugly subtlety.

And the freedom of the mind, my friends, has served America well. The vigor of our political life, our capacity for change, our cultural, scientific and industrial achievements, all derive from free inquiry, from the free mind—from the imagination, resourcefulness and daring of men who are not afraid of new ideas. Most all of us favor free enterprise for business. Let us also favor free enterprise for the mind. For, in the last analysis, we would fight to the death to protect it. Why is it, then, that we are sometimes slow to detect, or are indifferent to, the dangers that beset it?

Many of the threats to our cherished freedoms in these anxious, troubled times arise, it seems to me, from a healthy apprehension about the communist menace within our country. Communism is abhorrent. It is strangulation of the individual; it is death for the soul. Americans who have surrendered to this misbegotten idol have surrendered their right to our trust. And there can be no secure place for them in our public life.

Yet, as I have said before, we must take care not to burn down the barn to kill the rats. All of us, and especially patriotic organizations of enormous influence like the American Legion, must be vigilant in protecting our birthright from its too zealous friends while protecting it from its evil enemies.

The tragedy of our day is the climate of fear in which we live, and fear breeds repression. Too often sinister threats to the Bill of Rights, to freedom of the mind, are concealed under the patriotic cloak of anti-communism.

I could add, from my own experience, that it is never necessary to call a man a communist to make political capital. Those of us who have undertaken to practice the ancient but imperfect art of government will always make enough mistakes to keep our critics well supplied with standard ammunition. There is no need for poison gas.

Another feature of our current scene that I think invites a similar restraint is the recurrent attacks in some communities upon our public schools.

There is no justification for indiscriminate attacks on our schools, and the sincere, devoted, and by no means overpaid teachers who labor in them. If there are any communist teachers, of course they should be excluded, but the task is not one for self-appointed thought police or ill-informed censors. As a practical matter, we do not stop communist activity in this way. What we do is give the communists material with which to defame us. And we also stifle the initiative of teachers and depreciate the prestige of the teaching profession which should be as honorable and esteemed as any among us.

Let me now, in my concluding words, inquire with you how we may affirm our patriotism in the troubled yet hopeful years that are ahead.

The central concern of the American Legion—the ideal which holds it together—the vitality which animates it—is patriotism. And those voices which we have heard most clearly and which are best remembered in our public life have always had the accent of patriotism.

It was always accounted a virtue in a man to love his country. With us it is now something more than a virtue. It is a necessity, a condition of survival. When an American says that he loves his country, he means not only that he loves the New England hills, the prairies glistening in the sun, the wide and rising plains, the great mountains, and the sea. He means that he loves an inner air, an inner light in which freedom lives and in which a man can draw the breath of self-respect.

Men who have offered their lives for their country know that patriotism is not the *fear* of something; it is the *love* of something. Patriotism with us is not the hatred of Russia; it is the love of this

Republic and of the ideal of liberty of man and mind in which it was born, and to which this Republic is dedicated.

With this patriotism—patriotism in its large and wholesome meaning—America can master its power and turn it to the noble cause of peace. We can maintain military power without militarism; political power without oppression; and moral power without compulsion or complacency.

The road we travel is long, but at the end lies the grail of peace. And in the valley of peace we see the faint outlines of a new world, fertile and strong. It is odd that one of the keys to abundance should have been handed to civilization on a platter of destruction. But the power of the atom to work evil gives only the merest hint of its power for good.

I believe that man stands on the eve of his greatest day. I know, too, that that day is not a gift but a prize; that we shall not reach it until we have won it.

Legionnaires are united by memories of war. Therefore, no group is more devoted to peace. I say to you now that there is work to be done, that the difficulties and dangers that beset our path at home and abroad are incalculable. There is sweat and sacrifice; there is much of patience and quiet persistence in our horoscope. Perhaps the goal is not even for us to see in our lifetime.

But we are embarked on a great adventure. Let us proclaim our faith in the future of man. Of good heart and good cheer, faithful to ourselves and our traditions, we can lift the cause of freedom, the cause of free men, so high no power on earth can tear it down. We can pluck this flower, safety, from this nettle, danger. Living, speaking, like men—like Americans—we can lead the way to our rendezvous in a happy, peaceful world.

Thank you—and forgive me for imposing on you for so long.

Equal Rights

Lest you think I entertain any ill feeling, let me say at the outset that I have forgiven my friend Averell Harriman and the New York delegates to the National Convention for what they did to me there!

It is with great pride that I come among you this evening as the nominee of the Democratic Party. I must add that I also come here with some trepidation, because even in Chicago we have to admit that New York is important—at least on election day!

I am a Democrat by inheritance—but I am also a Democrat by conviction. I believe in the progressive policies of the Democratic Party. I believe that they are the best policies for our country to follow, and I believe the people think so, too, and that the Democratic Party will win again in November. And I expect to win running like a singed cat. The singeing hasn't been very painful so far.

There is one face I miss here this evening—your great Senator and my honored friend, Herbert Lehman. But I don't begrudge him one minute of his well-earned holiday in Europe. And I doubt if he begrudges me one minute of my campaign in the United States! For many years Senator Lehman has been one of the best and purest influences in our public life. And today he exerts in the Senate a moral authority and leadership comparable to that provided twenty years ago by George Norris.

We have a good time ahead of us this autumn. We have a good platform. A group of honest men got together in Chicago and made an honest attempt to grapple with the great problems of our day. They came out with good answers. I stand on that platform.

And I don't feel the need—so understandably felt by my distinguished opponent—of having my campaign manager say that I will write my own platform.

We have a great Vice Presidential candidate. I hope you in New York will soon get to know him better. To me he is somehow the physical embodiment of the social and economic progress of the past two great decades of Democratic leadership.

John Sparkman was the son of a tenant farmer. He worked his way up from rural poverty to win an education, a law degree, and an outstanding position as a legislator. But John Sparkman has never forgotten his beginnings. It has been his ambition in life to make more freely available to other poor boys and girls the opportunities which only stubborn determination could win for himself.

He is a leading representative of the new liberalism which is changing the face and the folkways of the South. He has been the devoted champion of legislation promoting farm ownership, better housing, social security, the T.V.A., rural electrification, soil conservation, and crop insurance. None know the problems of the small businessman better than he, and his intimate knowledge of the revolutionary convulsions that torment our world has been accentuated by service on the United States Delegation to the United Nations Assembly. He has enlisted for life in the struggle to improve the economic lot and the security of all our people. I am very proud to have John Sparkman as my running mate. And I hope I can keep up with him.

We have, in addition, a Presidential candidate. Perhaps the less said about him the better. You know what we have done and tried to do in Illinois. I propose to outline in the next few weeks what I should like to do in the nation. Let me say now that I shall do my best to conserve our gains and to carry forward the great Democratic tradition of government in the service of all the people, the tradition of Franklin Roosevelt and Harry Truman.

The Republicans have been talking of late as if I was ashamed of the accomplishments in war and peace of the past twenty years which they, by some miraculous agility, both embrace and condemn at the same time. I have been tempted to say that I was proud to stand on that record, if only the General would move over and make room for me!

But it is not enough, it seems to me, just to stand on the successes of the past. The people know what *has* been done, and now they want to know what *will* be done. A party cannot live on laurel leaves. We remember what happened to Lot's wife. And the people whom we seek to govern, though prosperous and well, are sorely taxed and troubled by war and threats of war.

The transcendent problem before us and the great unfinished business of our generation is peace in the world. There is only one way to work for peace. It is not an easy way. There is no substitute for the long, complex and patient processes of building strength and unity in the free world—political strength, economic strength, military strength, and moral strength—the strength of a common faith that nations can be free and people can stand erect and unafraid.

I am disturbed by some of the Republican contributions to the foreign-policy debate. A Republican foreign-policy expert said the other day that the Democratic Party was interested only in Europe and regarded all other nations as "second-class expendables." This kind of statement is not simply absurd; it is also irresponsible and dangerous. And I hope that such excessive partisanship does not do irreparable damage to our country. Of course, we are interested in Europe. But if this country, and I mean Democrats and Republicans alike, stands for anything, it stands for freedom and against the expansion of communist dominion anywhere in the world. Does Mr. Dulles think that President Truman by his prompt and courageous decision of June 27, 1950, treated Korea like "a second-class expendable"? If he does not think so, he would serve his party and his country and our friends in Asia better by more candor and less claptrap.

I hope that the Republican leaders will permit us to discuss our somber foreign problems on the plane where they belong—not on the plane of demagoguery, but on the plane of serious, factual discussion, and in terms of alternatives that are real, rather than epithets that are false.

And we could well apply the same rule to the problems here at home. One of these I want to mention here tonight is civil rights.

The phrase civil rights means a number of concrete things. It means the right to be treated equally before the law. It means the right to equal opportunity for education, employment and decent living conditions. It means that none of these rights shall be denied because of race or color or creed. The history of freedom in our country has been the history of knocking down the barriers to equal rights. One after another they have fallen, and great names in our history record their collapse: the Virginia Statute of Religious Freedom, the Bill of Rights, the Emancipation Proclamation, the Woman's Suffrage Amendment, down to the 1947 Report of the President's Commission on Civil Rights.

The record of our progress is a proud one, but it is far from over. Brave and important tasks remain. We cannot rest until we honor in fact as well as word the plain language of the Declaration of Independence.

This is our goal. It requires far more than action by government. Laws are never as effective as habits. The fight for equal rights must go on every day in our own souls and consciences, in our schools and our churches and our homes, in our factories and our offices—as well as in our city councils, our state legislatures and our national Congress. In this discussion, of all discussions, let us not be self-righteous. Let us work for results, not just empty political advantage. We are dealing here with fundamental human rights, not just votes.

This is a job for the East, the North and the West, as well as for the South. I know. I have been a Governor of a great Northern state. I have had to stop outrages committed against peaceful and law-abiding minorities. I have twice proposed to my legislature a law setting up in our state an enforceable fair employment practices commission. I am proud to say that the Democrats in our legislature voted almost solidly for the bill. But I must report in simple truth that the bill was lost in Springfield, Illinois, because of virtually solid opposition from the party which claims descent from Abraham Lincoln. All the same, gratifying progress has been made in Illinois toward the elimination of job discrimination by the initiative of business itself. And I would be less than fair if I didn't acknowledge it gratefully.

In saying this is not a sectional problem, I do not mean to say that there is no particular problem in the South. Of course there is a problem in the South. In many respects, the problem is more serious there than elsewhere. But, just as it is chastening to realize our own failures and shortcomings in the North, so it is both just and hopeful to recognize and admit the great progress in the South. Things are taking place in the South today that would have seemed impossible only a few years ago. In the last two years alone ten state universities have admitted Negro students for the first time to their graduate and professional schools. And that is only one of many examples that could be cited of the wonders that are working in the South.

We can agree that the problem is nationwide; we can agree that good progress has been made; but I think we can also agree that unremitting effort is the cause of most of that progress, and that unremitting effort is the way to assure more progress in the future. Part of that effort must be legislative. The Democratic platform of 1952 states the goals of Federal legislation.

I have often affirmed my belief in strong state and local administration. I believe—with your own great Governors, Al Smith and Franklin Roosevelt and Herbert Lehman—that affirmative state government can rise to meet many pressing social problems, and can thereby arrest the trend toward overcentralized Federal power. In Illinois I have worked to make the state government responsive to the needs of the people so that it would not be necessary for them to turn to Washington for help. I like to think that people are becoming more and more conscious of the role of the states in the Federal system; more and more conscious that we will save more money by doing the jobs at home than by screaming about waste and extravagance in Washington.

In the case of equal opportunity for employment, I believe that it is not alone the duty but the enlightened interest of each state to develop its own positive employment practices program—a program adapted to local conditions, emphasizing education and conciliation, and providing for judicial enforcement. That is the kind of law I proposed in Illinois.

I think the time has come to talk sensibly about how we can make more rapid progress in this field rather than how we can make more votes. I think—indeed, I know—that there are leaders in the South who are just as anxious as we are to move ahead. But we must frankly recognize their local difficulties. We must recognize, too, that further government interference with free men, free markets, free ideas, is distasteful to many people of good will who dislike racial discrimination as much as we do.

This is not the time to discuss all these familiar obstacles. Let me only say that in a spirit of give and take, of tolerance and understanding, we can clean up this fire hazard in our basement faster and more effectively.

But our platform also favors Federal legislation—particularly, I assume, when states fail to act and inequalities of treatment persist. The problem, of course, is what kind of legislation.

Personally, I have been much impressed by a bill recently reported favorably by the Senate Labor Committee. Only three members opposed it, one of whom was Senator Richard Nixon. Both your New York Senators joined in sponsoring the bill.

It creates a Federal Commission and encourages it to stay out of any state with an effective commission; by the same token, however, it encourages the states to act because, if they do not, the national government has the power to do so. The bill requires the Federal Commission to undertake a nonpartisan and nationwide educational program, to proceed by persuasion as far as possible, and, in cases of complaints of violation, to proceed by very careful deliberation and full and fair hearings. Enforcement would be by order of a court, not an administrative body.

You know as well as I do that we have reached a sort of legislative stalemate in this field in the Congress. In so far as this is due to real, legitimate objections to the substance of the legislation, I think this Senate bill goes a very long way toward meeting such objections. It may be that it can be improved still further, especially in the direction of giving the states a reasonable time in which to act.

In so far as the present stalemate is due to misuse of the processes of deliberation and debate in Congress, the problem is somewhat different.

I believe firmly in the principle stated in our platform—the principle that majority rule shall prevail, after reasonable debate, in both houses of our Congress. And from my experience, with the practical workings of representative government, I would interpret "reasonable" very liberally, because majorities can be tyrannical too.

This principle of majority rule is important in a much broader area than that of civil rights—it is of vital importance, for example, in the field of foreign policy. One of the most famous of all filibusters occurred in 1917 in the debate over President Wilson's proposal to arm merchant ships for the protection of American lives and property against power-mad aggression. It is not inconceivable that a similar situation might occur today or tomorrow in the delicate state of our foreign relations. In these perilous times we cannot risk submerging our national purposes in a sea of interminable conversation.

The precise nature of the changes that should be made in the present rules of Congress, is, of course, a problem for the Congress itself, for each House, under our Constitution, makes its own rules for doing business. As President I could not make the decision, but I could and would use whatever influence I may have to encourage the Congress to shake off its shackles.

I would urge in these fields and in many others that affect national policy that all of us resolve to take a fresh look. There has been too much freezing of positions, too much emotion, too many dogmatic statements of irrevocable attitudes. We are dealing with human situations, with human emotions, with human intelligence; our purpose must be to reason together for the common betterment of us all; our interest must be, not in controversy, but in results.

This has been my attitude, and this will be my attitude. If there are those who disapprove, I will be sorry but not surprised. If there are those who approve, I bespeak their best efforts and pledge them mine, confident that in the long run results will be more eloquent than oratory.

I have been talking about methods. About goals there can, of course, be no disagreement. We believe in the equality of rights and the equality of opportunity for all Americans. In affirming this belief, the Democratic platform was but the mirror of our own conscience. We must continue this fight until it is won.

Faith in Liberalism

The State Committee of the Liberal Party

NEW YORK CITY

August 28, 1952

I appreciate very much this opportunity to meet with you men and women of the Liberal Party, and I'm deeply grateful for your confidence and for the honor that you have done me. That your nomination of me (for President) was unanimous only increases my respect for your judgment and discrimination!

After listening to what Mr. Dubinsky had to say a moment ago, I was tempted to think that when he concluded he was going to introduce not me but Benjamin Franklin. Evidently he couldn't get here.

Dr. Counts said here a moment ago that the Liberal Party has tried to serve us as sort of a political conscience. Now I have, of course, read about you in the published writings of certain columnists and I am fully aware that you are very dangerous characters. I'm informed that attacks on you from the right are equaled in violence only by denunciations in the communist press.

Well, I know how that is. In my very brief political career I've sometimes wondered if I had any friends left. And then they suddenly nominated me for President, and I wondered if I hadn't too many friends. But if I have, by any chance, too many friends I am sure time will take care of that!

You know how it is in an election year—they pick a President and then for four years they pick on him.

I hope that the alert members of the press here present will note that I arrived at your convention under my own power. I was not escorted or dragged to this platform. And what's more I think I'm standing on my own feet. And, to the best of my knowledge, I've neither been drugged nor hypnotized. Now I offer this testimony in advance since, as you know, I'm alleged by the Repub-

licans to be in a state of multiple captivity and you will, sooner
or later, undoubtedly be included on the distinguished list of my
jailers.

I've been much interested in the continued debate that's been
raging in the newspapers as to whether I was headed right, center
or left. I think it would have been rather more relevant had they
asked: Is the man moving forward, backward, or is he grounded?

Now I sometimes think we're far more tolerant of a quarter-
back than we are of our candidates. An advance on the football
field through left guard, or through right guard, or even straight
through center, is generally counted as yardage gained. I think that
is the sports writer's word for it. The only unforgivable thing is to
be trapped by the Old Guard behind your line. Whatever may
happen, I trust that it will at least be said of me that I know the
difference between the goal line and the sideline.

Now there's no mystery about my program, whatever label may
attach to it. I am running on the Democratic platform. I am for
it; and I'll fight for it and I expect to win on it.

No platform, of course, can resolve all of our dilemmas. As vital,
it seems to me, as the written word is the spirit and the resolution
of those who embrace the written word. The real question is
whether a platform represents the clicking of a ghost's typewriter, if
I may put it that way, or the beating of a human heart.

Our opponents also have a platform. In modern times they've
honored us Democrats by borrowing many phrases from past Democratic platforms. Now because of the timing of the conventions,
this inevitably leaves them four years behind. But I suppose
plagiarism must, nevertheless, be considered a form of progress.

And this is open season for that kind of progress. This is the
time when even the most obsolete Republican becomes momen-
tarily reconciled to the machine age. He listens—he's very apt to
listen with a stiff upper lip—while his candidate calls for those
greater social gains which a few minutes before they called wild-
eyed socialism. In this season Republican candidates are even forgiven for whispering that there could be a better law than the
Taft-Hartley Act.

The season when Republican hearts regularly throb with such
thoughts is, of course, the autumn of Presidential years. This is
indeed a truly remarkable interval, a sort of pause in the Republican occupation and I've often thought that it might well be called

the liberal hour. But it should never be confused with any period when Congress is in session.

Now it's a misfortune—deserved, I fear—of the Republican leadership not just to be taken too seriously during these moments of imitation. Their forward look sometimes seems to me like a costume taken out of the closet every four years for the big masquerade ball. It often looks nice after a dry cleaning, but the stuffed shirt still shows.

I think it's ironic—but nonetheless revealing—that my distinguished opponent, my very distinguished opponent, feels compelled to prove that he was innocent of any association with Franklin Roosevelt and Harry Truman. After all, there were four occasions on which the people of the United States indicated their desire to continue such an association. Nevertheless, my opponent's trepidation is perhaps understandable. Joe McCarthy may get him if he doesn't watch out.

I certainly, for one, don't envy the General having to listen to all the conflicting advice about how to treat the slanderers of his dear friend and senior officer, General Marshall. You can tell the size of a man by the size of the thing that makes him mad, and I hope that, regardless of my own political advantage, this matter is not finally resolved by the counsel of those who favor what has been described as the middle-of-the-gutter approach.

There is some low comedy in this minor Republican spectacle, but there is also, it seems to me, symbolic tragedy, too. For everything that our distinguished fellow citizen has accomplished in his great service to his country is imperiled by many men who propose to ride to Washington on his train.

They are not just the men who hunt communists in the Bureau of Wild Life and Fisheries while hesitating to aid the gallant men and women who are resisting the real thing in the front lines of Europe and Asia. They are also the men who would rather hold post-mortems over the loss of China than do something now to save India.

And they are, finally, the men who seemingly believe that we can confound the Kremlin by frightening ourselves to death. They would rather battle Democrats than communists any day. And, like the communists, their favorite sport is prophesying our imminent doom.

As I indicated at the start of this campaign, I don't intend to tell anyone that complicated things are simple and that all of the answers are in the back of a book which I will shortly produce. Only men who confuse themselves with God would dare to pretend in this anguished and bloody era that they know the exact road to the promised land.

You of the Liberal Party will perhaps understand me best when I vigorously disclaim infallibility. For it seems to me that an authentic humility, an awareness of the complexity of men's choices, a tolerance for diverse opinions, and a recognition for brave experimentation are the heart of any liberal faith.

But let no one make the mistake of believing that the liberal's tolerance for conflicting opinion makes him incapable of fighting hard for the things that he believes in.

For example, I yield to no man—if I may borrow that majestic parliamentary phrase—I yield to no man in my belief in the principle of free debate, inside or outside the halls of Congress. The sound of tireless voices is the price we pay for the right to hear the music of our own opinions. But there is also, it seems to me, a moment at which democracy must prove its capacity to act. Every man has a right to be heard; but no man has the right to strangle democracy with a single set of vocal cords.

There's another text that I should like to take from the Democratic platform. The near unanimity with which the civil rights plank was adopted at the Democratic Convention this year is in great part the result of things that have happened to us as a nation during the past decade. At the moment, as on so many occasions during World War Two, Negro Americans are fighting and working side by side with their white countrymen in many parts of the world. I venture to say that there are few men of either race who are not affected by that experience. And one could point to many other examples of the remarkable progress of the past decade, and I mean in the South as well as in the North.

The Federal Government has a direct responsibility to maintain this progress by helping to secure equal rights for all of our people.

I told the Democratic State Convention earlier this very evening that I have been impressed by the recent bill reported by Senator Humphrey on behalf of the Senate Labor Committee. Both your New York Senators joined in sponsoring the bill. We must continue to press forward along such lines as these—in our national Congress as well as in our states and our communities—

until we have eradicated the curse of discrimination in this nation.

To meet the crisis of our day, we must have affirmative values and clear-cut objectives. The challenge to all of us is to prove that a free society can remain free, humane and creative, even when it is under heavy and ruthless fire; that it can combat poverty, injustice and intolerance in its own midst, even while resisting a monstrous foreign despotism; and that it can give man a glimpse of serenity and of hope, even while calling on them for sacrifice.

We shall be accused of idealism or some such crime for projecting so optimistic a vision. To which the only truthful answer is that we plead guilty. This is not to say that we guarantee a happy ending; it is only to say that we retain our confidence in man's ability to achieve the triumph of decency and of compassion in our lifetime.

After all, there was a man named Hitler, and it looked for a while as if he were invincible. Yet we despised and "decadent" peoples are still talking—and he hasn't made a speech in seven years. The "thousand-year Reich" already belongs to the history books while the idea of freedom has endured, even in the dreariest dungeons behind the Iron Curtain. So I say, let the demagogues beware.

I believe we are living in the twilight of the totalitarian gods; beyond the fury and the turmoil of our times lies an horizon of new hope for embattled humanity. With liberal faith, with cool heads, with warm hearts, we shall make that hope real for our nation and for our century.

War and Peace

Broadcast to the Armed Forces Overseas

August 30, 1952

Men and women of our Armed Services overseas:

I am grateful to the Secretary of Defense and to the Armed Forces Radio Service for this chance to speak to you.

My campaign for the Presidency has this in common with yours: now that I have been drafted, I am fighting to win.

Two World Wars have dragged our two generations, yours and mine, through the bloodiest years of the Christian era. Many of you are now fighting in Korea and many more are standing guard in Europe to prevent a third world war. When Captain James Jabara of Wichita, an Air Force ace on leave from Korea, was asked why we are fighting there, his answer was: "So we won't have to fight in Wichita." I think the Captain hit the nail on the head. It is almost as simple and certainly as important as that.

None of us has the gift of prophecy. In these tense days none of us can be sure what to expect from one moment to the next. But I want to make one thing very definite: I don't expect a third world war, and I reject the notion that a third world war is inevitable. That is familiar communist talk. And I hope that regardless of the dire prophecies of our political adversaries, neither I nor any Democratic candidates will give such foolish confirmation to Soviet propaganda during this campaign in the United States.

What we know, and you who serve in Korea know better than the rest of us, is that the enemy is implacable, sullen, determined, and dangerous. Communism has already enveloped and enslaved many hapless millions through the world. It has drawn people to serve under false gods; and—as you in Korea well know—it has imbued them with the devil's own fury.

35

The grimmest knowledge of all is the certainty of the enemy's relentless ambition to rule our lives—as he already rules the lives of millions in Europe and Asia. But we know, too, that he is not superhuman. He can be stopped, punished and beaten back. You have already gone far to restrain his limitless ambitions. On your continued strength and success rest the aspirations of all people for a peaceful world. If we should now falter and fail, then all our hopes for decent lives would be drowned in another brutalizing war of God knows what extent and duration and at what dread cost to all that is most dear to us. But we need not falter and we shall not fail.

And if war is not inevitable, neither is peace inevitable.

I am an optimist because I believe Americans will make good use of the time your efforts in Korea and in Europe are winning for us. People often ask: Is time working for us or against us? It seems to me a silly question. Time works for the fellow who makes the best use of his time. And America can make better use of time than our adversaries. We must—or we will lose this struggle.

You have heard it said, as I have, that the Korean War is a "useless" war. Nothing seems to me more mischievous than this idea which has been so extensively used for political purposes in this country. Had we not resisted aggression in Korea, then we would not only have lost Korea but we would have invited the Soviet Union to pursue aggression elsewhere. The line had to be drawn somewhere and, the earlier it was drawn, the better the chance and the greater the hope of averting general war. The logic of not fighting in Korea, as Captain Jabara put it, is to fight in Wichita. No one knew this better than President Truman when he made his courageous decision in the summer of 1950 to stand up to the communists.

You have probably heard, too, that America has gained nothing in the last year of the Korean War—that we are right where we started when we sat down with the communist negotiators more than a year ago. I sometimes wonder how shortsighted some people can get, especially in campaign years. We have gained a year's time. And we have used that year to accomplish three significant and quite possibly decisive victories.

One. We have enormously expanded our defense production. T-47's are rolling off the lines in large numbers and the new and better T-48's are coming along fast. F-86's are being produced much faster, and newer models are going into production. Production of all the other essential and complicated gear of modern warfare is rising. Rapid progress is being made in perfecting guided missiles and other weapons that a year or two ago were only paper projects.

I will not say that we have yet won the battle for production, but we are well on our way to winning it. The victory is already affecting the Kremlin's calculations and strategy. Stalin respects and fears the strength of the free world, which is largely the productive power of America.

Two. In the past year the strength of our allies has grown mightily. Alongside you in Korea there are now ten fire-hardened and battle-tested ROK divisions. More divisions can and will be organized.

In Indo-China, where, until recently, our French allies were fighting almost alone, there are now well over a hundred thousand native Indo-Chinese fighting men. Many more units are to be formed. Their American military advisers say that the Indo-Chinese are good fighting men, skilled in the kind of jungle tactics used by the communist guerrillas.

Our Western European allies now have two and a half million men serving in their armed forces. In Southern Europe the Greeks and the Turks and the Yugoslavs are fierce and formidable allies. You have seen Greek and Turkish units in action in Korea. You know their worth in battle.

All these figures represent big improvements over a year ago. These forces need more and better equipment. They need more training. They need better organization. But these things are all do-able and they are being done. There are no more easy pickings in the Far East or in Europe, and the Kremlin likes to gamble only on sure things. And now that you have fought the enemy to a standstill in Korea, the only sure thing is that a new act of aggression anywhere would be very risky indeed.

This growing strength of our allies has great significance for you. What you all want to know is when you will climb on board the transport that will bring you home. The only honest answer to that is that when our allies become strong enough for their initial defense, most of you can come home. And the only way to speed that day is to speed the arming of our friends.

Three. We have won another important victory during the past year. We have done what many doubters of democracy thought a democracy could not do. We have yielded neither to the hot-heads who wanted to extend the war nor to the weak-kneed who wanted to quit when they found that the going was tough. The Republican leaders, impatient and torn by conflicting counsels, have wavered between recklessness and weakness.

I trust that the Democratic Party will not try to win votes by encouraging the cruel illusion that there is an easy solution to this struggle. There isn't any magic by which the hammer and sickle of world communism can be beaten into a ploughshare of peace. Most Americans know that nothing less than discipline, restraint and concentration by all of us on the objectives of survival and triumph is sufficient in this fateful hour of history. Nothing less can insure the safety of the America we know and want our children to know.

This third victory—the victory over timidity, on the one hand, and recklessness, on the other—has won for us the respect which men of sober strength always enjoy. And such respect is a powerful deterrent to aggression.

These are no mean accomplishments for a year's time. I think they fully justify my faith that world war is not inevitable. I think they justify the hope that by persevering in this difficult and some-times exasperating path we can win our way to a peaceful world. It is a goal worth the price, heavy as it is. At any rate, there are no safe alternatives. To plunge the world into greater war or to capitulate to hopelessness is no solution.

If I could make one rule for both parties in this campaign, it would be that no candidate for high office would weaken our perseverance in this struggle by indulging in promises that are easy to make and impossible to keep. We are living in a cruel and dangerous world—a world in which the wise man keeps his rifle clean, his guard up, and tries to think as straight as he can shoot. And, as much as we need straight-shooting, we need straight-thinking even more.

I shall not try to win your vote by an "all this and heaven too" campaign. Moreover, I could not, because you who are overseas know the score better than many here at home. The party that comes to power in November is going to have to ask the American people to put away childish things and do manful things. There are no shortcuts to national security. There are only shortcuts to defeat. The Democratic Party has had to deal with this world problem and deal with it responsibly for many years. Because we have faith in the people, we dare to tell them the facts and to ask them to work harder, and to make the sacrifices that are necessary to back you up, because that is the only way to get you back home. So long as you are asked to do the unusual, so long must we put aside politics as usual, profits as usual, strikes as usual and pleasure as usual.

This is the basic message which I hope to bring to the American people before the November election. Perhaps it isn't good politics. I don't know yet whether one can win an election with hard, distasteful truths, but this is the only way I want to win it. Seekers after high office owe it to their own sense of self-respect as Americans, they owe it to the American people, and they owe it to you who are serving overseas, to say in this 1952 campaign what they ask of the people, not just what they promise them. This, I believe, is the only kind of political honesty which fits the savage circumstances of our time.

There are a few things I am going to ask the American people.

First, I ask that everyone register and vote. More than a million of you who are serving overseas are eligible. There are politicians in this country who hope that many of you and many of your fellow citizens at home will not vote. And the reason is not hard to find. Every victory for reaction in our country and every setback to progress has been caused by the voters who wouldn't bother to vote.

Reaction at home threatens what we all want most: Peace and prosperity. Not peace or prosperity—but peace and prosperity. It has to be both or neither, because without enduring peace there can be no enduring prosperity. Conversely, there can be no enduring peace without a healthy, strong, productive United States on which the stability of the whole world depends. A change to a rampaging reactionary Republican domestic policy means therefore not only disaster at home but disaster abroad.

The Republican theme song in this campaign is that "it is time for a change." You are going to hear that tune over and over from now to November. Now I am not against change. It is always time for a change—for the better. The Democratic Party is not against change. The changes brought during this past twenty years of progress under Democratic administrations is the best proof of that. I hope the Democratic Party will always lead the way to constructive change.

I hope you will vote and participate in the great decisions of the America you serve so far away. The Department of Defense has issued a pamphlet which tells you how to register and vote. It may be a little complicated, but it is worth your trouble.

Almost every state has tried to make it easy for you. The pamphlet is called "Voting Information, 1952." And there is someone in each of your units who will be glad to give you any help you need.

The second thing I ask is that you measure all candidates for high office—not just the Presidential candidates, but the Vice-Presidential candidates and the candidates for the Senate and the House of Representatives—against the bitterly difficult issues of our time and decide whether they measure up. Ask yourselves which party has the best-balanced team and is most likely to give you the kind of government you think the country needs.

I hope you won't forget that the man in the White House cannot make laws. He can suggest, he can urge, he can even plead, but laws are made by the men in the House of Representatives and the Senate. Their greatness can make him great; their smallness can bring his best efforts to naught. It is something like baseball. The pitcher who doesn't get good support is not likely to win many ball games.

What kind of support do you think the Old Guard Republicans in the Congress will give, and what kind of a change do you think they want? Their batting average is one of almost total opposition to every forward step America has taken. The truth is that they are frightened men, frightened by progress and they want to march backwards into a comfortable and safely Republican past that no longer exists and cannot be disinterred.

I must say that it frightens me to think that such men might influence the fate of the nation. At home and abroad they are the champions of a "little America" huddled behind its ocean barriers and hoping to stem the riptides of history by damning the Democrats.

And so I also ask you to ask yourselves this very serious question: What kind of America do you want to find when you come back? Is it an America of boom-and-bust? An America where free men are intimidated by smear and slander? An America which has no faith in itself and its future? Or is it an America which has solved the problems of depression and provides abundant opportunities for useful, contented and peaceful lives? Is it an America that is making steady progress toward equal rights, equal justice and equal opportunity for education and employment? I am sure that that is the kind of America you want to find.

Perhaps we can afford the "little America" policy of the little, frightened men. Perhaps we don't need strong friends and good neighbors. Perhaps Stalin is not really up to any mischief. Perhaps if we had let him take Korea, that is all he would have wanted— just as Hitler had only one last territorial demand—only one, that is, before he was ready to launch the bloodiest war in history. Perhaps we can all relax and go to the ball game—all of us, that is, except you.

The Democratic Party doesn't think so. The Democratic Party thinks that that would be playing Russian roulette with all our futures. The Democratic Party is not afraid to ask the American people to do the hard jobs that have got to be done to back you up, for we have unlimited faith in the wisdom and the backbone of an informed people.

My time is up. I thank you for listening to a solemn speech. But these are solemn times. Whether I win or lose the election may not be important, but how best we can win peace and prosperity for America is all-important. You are doing your share and I am going to do mine as best I can.

Bi-Partisan Foreign Policy

Campau Square

GRAND RAPIDS, MICHIGAN

September 1, 1952

I am very glad to be able to be here in Grand Rapids on this Labor Day holiday. As a boy I spent my holidays up in Northern Michigan. But now I have made the unhappy discovery that in politics and public office there are no holidays—especially in campaign years.

I am privileged to count myself among the friends and admirers of one of your great citizens. I knew Arthur Vandenberg well, and served with him at four or five of the great international conferences following the war. He paid me the courtesy of some flattering correspondence and proposed me as his successor on one of the major committees of the United Nations in 1947. He was a great champion of our bi-partisan—or, as he preferred to call it, our un-partisan—foreign policy. Senator Vandenberg was never doctrinaire. He was a practical and realistic man whose primary concern was the protection and advancement of the welfare and safety of his country—a foreign policy that far-seeing men and women of both parties could support. And Arthur Vandenberg refused to play politics with foreign policy.

These are good rules to follow today. I, for one, intend to do my best to follow them because foreign policy is a deadly serious business these days. I think it should be discussed in this campaign soberly and with restraint. We could pay a sad price in misunderstanding or miscalculation abroad by what we say intemperately, unwisely and hypocritically to beguile the voters in this campaign. Our purpose should not be to exploit people's fears, not to make empty promises of magic solutions, but instead to discuss the real problems that confront our country in the world, and what we actually can and should do about them.

I want to say, clearly and unmistakably, that I believe the essential direction of our foreign policy is right—building the unity and collective strength of the free countries to prevent the expansion of Soviet dominion and control over one nation after another. I think we must join other nations in building military, economic and political strength which can gradually but surely lessen the relative power of the Soviet Union on world events. And I think we must continue to work steadily at the frustrating task of putting international affairs on a permanent basis of law and order.

These are the key purposes of our present policy as I understand it. They are the purposes that we are seeking to accomplish through the United Nations; through the Atlantic, Pacific and Western Hemisphere regional security treaties; through our programs of military and economic aid to other countries; through the Point Four program; and through our financial and commercial policies, including the reciprocal trade program. These things make sense. If we continue with steps like these, adjusting and changing and improving them as we can, war becomes an alternative of diminishing hope to the enemy, and communism an alternative of diminishing attraction among the vast uncommitted peoples of the world.

Now in all I have said here, I do not believe there is any fundamental issue between the Republican candidate for President and myself. As far as I know, he, like myself, approves the basic direction our foreign policy has been following.

Where there is an issue, however, is between the two Republican Parties that contested the nomination with such violence at Chicago, because the Republican Party is hopelessly divided over foreign policy. Senator Vandenberg, with all his great prestige and persuasiveness, was never able to win over the reactionary wing of his party to his own enlightened understanding of the twentieth century.

That wing of the party seems stronger if not wiser since we lost the benefit of Senator Vandenberg's leadership. And I say that with no partisan satisfaction, because the difficulties we confront as a nation in this revolutionary age transcend any considerations of political advantage. And I say to you in all sincerity that winning the peace is far dearer to me, as it is to you, Democrats and Republicans alike, than winning the election.

My distinguished opponent has already had occasion to disagree with conspicuous Republicans on foreign-policy issues. He has differed sharply with members of his party who have assailed the American action in Korea to stop and turn back communist aggression. He has gone further to set himself against the views of important members of his party who have called for enlarging the Korean War.

I think he has done us all a service by saying these things. He knows, as every realistic American knows, that if we had not chosen to fight in Korea, sooner or later we would have had to fight a bigger war somewhere else. The memory of Munich is still fresh. The quicker aggression is stopped the better. And, as it is, even with all the heartbreak and suffering and cost of Korea—even with the frustration of the long stalemate over the armistice—it is quite possible that our action in Korea may have headed off World War Three. We may never know the answer to that, but the tragic consequences of piecemeal aggression even in our lifetime are plain for all to see.

I don't envy the General's impossible dilemma as a result of the conflict within the party he now heads. Carrying out an effective, positive, forward-looking foreign policy in a democracy requires support not only in the executive, but also in the legislative branch of government. How is it possible when a large proportion of his party's members in the Senate, and more than half of them in the House, have consistently opposed what he approves? And if elected—he would probably carry back to Washington with him most of the same Republicans.

But the Republican leaders evidently have a solution for this dismal dilemma because their vice-presidential candidate the other day asserted his belief that Republicans in Congress who have opposed our bi-partisan foreign policy will change and reverse their attitude if their party is successful in this election. (Maybe this is what they mean by "it's time for a change"!) Now must we conclude from this that a lot of Republican leaders have been opposing our foreign policy just for political reasons? Should matters of this extreme gravity be entrusted to men who trade their convictions so lightly? I may be naive but I don't think a man should be in public office whose attitude on our most important business depends on whether a Democrat or a Republican is in the White House. Surely a vote on foreign policy in the Congress is more important than voting in a popularity or a beauty contest.

Happily the Democratic Party is united on foreign policy. We have our differences. If we didn't we would hardly be Democrats, but our differences are not over foreign policy. Democratic support of this policy is no new, sudden, confused or pretended attitude. We have worked for the building of that program from the beginning with the advice and help of some far-sighted Republicans like Arthur Vandenberg. We know much about its weak points and its strong points, and the ugly and the happy realities of our period in history. We believe passionately in the rightness of our directions. Our deepest convictions and highest hopes are involved, for this is the means of preserving our most cherished institutions, our freedoms, our future as a Christian nation.

The price is high, dangerously high, and we look hopefully to the time when it can be reduced, but meanwhile we must forge the great tools for man's noblest work—achieving freedom, justice and dignity for nations and individuals. For a century, from Waterloo to the Marne, the British fleet protected us, but now it is our turn. It is up to this mighty nation with our allies to advance the hopes through which man may eventually fulfill his destiny as a child of God.

Improving Our Labor Laws

Labor Day Rally—Cadillac Square

DETROIT, MICHIGAN

September 1, 1952

Let me say at the outset that I am very much flattered, indeed, by the presence here of His Honor the Mayor of Detroit. I am conscious of your recent serious illness, Mr. Cobo, and I trust that your participation in this tremendous holiday festivity and your association with so many Democrats won't cause any relapse.

I stand before you today as a fugitive from a sweatshop down in Springfield, Illinois. Down there the speed-up is in full force, but we aren't complaining a bit. In fact, we like it because we believe in our job and our job is to win in November.

This, my friends, is Labor Day of an election year, and I think candidates ought to get a day off too. But if they got off they might not get in. So I've welcomed the invitation to come to Detroit to talk to you about the relationship between the Democratic Party, which I represent, and the working people, which you represent.

Contrary to the impressions fostered by some of the press, you are not my captives, and I am not your captive. On the contrary, I might as well make it clear right now that I intend to do exactly what I think right and best for all of us—business, labor, agriculture—alike. And I have no doubt that you will do exactly what you think right and best at the election.

You are freeborn Americans—a proud and honorable station, carrying with it the right and the responsibility to make up your own minds—and so am I. So if either of us thinks in terms of captivity, let's agree right here and now on a mutual pact of liberation.

The interest and the obligation of the President must be the common interest. His concern for labor, as for industry, is only as a part of the common interest. I would intend to honor that office by complete freedom to serve not one man or a few, but the whole nation. And I think that is precisely what you would want me to do.

The relationship between the Democratic Party and the working people of America is a very simple one. We both believe in equal rights for all and in special privileges for none. We both believe that the objective of our country and of its Government is to achieve human decency, to meet human needs, and to fulfill human hopes.

We take honest open pride in what the tremendous progress of the last twenty years has meant, not for the Democratic Party, but for the whole nation. We pulled ourselves, as you know, out of the quicksand of depression. In fighting an awful war we did our part and we did it gloriously.

We have made America the best place to live and work in the world has ever known—a land where men are assured a decent wage and security when their work is done; a land where the mother can know that her children's opportunities are bright and limitless.

But these things, my friends, are not permanent. They have to be fought for, fought for by each succeeding generation. So it's my obligation, I think, to give you my ideas of our common interests, my thoughts about our common future.

I see three sets of common interests in the labor field. These are positive interests, constructive interests. We have talked, it seems to me, too much in terms of labor wars, too little in terms of labor peace, too much in terms of stopping things by law, too little in terms of establishing industrial democracy.

There is our first common interest in securing to all who work the minimums of human decency. This means, among other things, that the men and women in our working force, some 62,000,000 of us, shall receive a decent living wage, insurance against the risks of disability and unemployment, and the assurance of solid, not token, security when life's work is done.

It means, too, that we must struggle tirelessly to add to these assurances, equality of work opportunity for every one of us— regardless of race, of color or of creed. Human decency is the theme of our history and the spirit of our religion. We must never cease trying to write its guarantees not just into our laws, but into the hearts and the minds of men.

A second key to our common interest is that the men and women in our working force are consumers as well as producers.

Our welfare is not measured by what we get from the payroll clerk, but by what we get at the store and the school and the hospital, and by what we have left to put in the bank. Meeting such problems as inflation, as housing and the high cost of living, is not part of a labor policy, it's part of a national policy. It's not just part of a labor program because it's part of a national problem.

The working man cannot and must not think of his welfare as something separate and apart from the common good. The interests of the factory worker, the white-collar worker, the employer, the farmer, are all rooted in the soil of national well-being. If your employer's business fails, for example, you are out of a job. We are utterly dependent on one another, and what is best for the nation is best for all of us and is best for each of us.

Our third common interest is in the process of collective bargaining—the keystone of industrial democracy, of free enterprise.

Democracy is working when free men solve their own problems in their own way and in their own political and industrial communities. The 80,000 private collective bargaining agreements today in effect are alternatives to laws—and better than laws.

They are voluntary private solutions which make unnecessary involuntary government decisions. They prove that the most useful thing the Government can do is to assure a fair bargaining balance by guaranteeing to employes the right to act together.

The only legitimate purpose of a Federal labor relations law is to make private bargaining work better. And that purpose has not, in my judgment, been served by the Taft-Hartley Act.

Now, in 1947, we needed some revisions of the old Wagner Act. We needed some new rules for labor peace. Well, we got a new law all right—a tangled snarl of legal barbed wire, filled with ugly sneers at labor unions and built around the discredited labor injunction.

I don't say that everything in the Taft-Hartley Act is wrong. It isn't, and I don't think it's a slave labor law, either. But I do say that it was biased and politically inspired and has not improved labor relations in a single plant.

We must have a new law and my conclusion is that we can best remedy the defects in the old law by scrapping it and starting over again. What should be retained from the old law can best be written into the new law after the political symbolism of the Taft-Hartley Act is behind us.

Now, if I may, I—and I hope I don't impose upon you—I should like to suggest five general principles as the basis for a new labor relations law. I believe they represent the public interest in a fair, solid, durable pattern of free collective bargaining. And I think labor and management can agree on them too, if they'll only throw their guns on the table.

Point number one is that the law must accept labor unions, like employer corporations, as the responsible representatives of their members' interests.

The Taft-Hartley Act assumed that the unions could not be trusted to determine whether their members wanted a union shop. After the expenditure of millions of dollars to hold thousands of Government-conducted elections, in 95 per cent of which the employes voted for the union shop, the Congress last year finally repealed this gratuitous insult to the labor unions.

But the act still prohibits other forms of union security arrangements developed over many years by labor and management together in such cases as the maritime industry, the building trades and the printing trades.

The Congress arbitrarily said, "We know better than unions what is good for employes." The result could have been predicted. Today several thousand employers and several million employes are operating under bootleg agreements in flagrant violation of the statute.

Point number two is the other side of point number one. If labor unions are to be accepted as the full representatives and guardians of employe interests in the collective-bargaining process, then labor unions must conform to standards of fair conduct and equal protection in the exercise of their stewardship.

A few unions, my friends, made by law the exclusive representatives of certain groups of employes, abuse that trust by excluding from membership some who want to work, denying them a vote, denying their seniority rights because of the color of their skin or because of restrictive notions about employment security. That's not right.

And, my friends, that's not democracy. Unions which are given powers by Government, should be open to all on equal terms. I know it's the view and the practice of the vast majority of American unions and union members to reject any idea of second-class citizenship based on race or monopoly.

And speaking of industrial democracy, let me say that you, too, have a responsibility to participate in the affairs of your unions.

The union exists for your benefit. If there is anything wrong with it, if you don't approve of the officers, if you don't like the union's policies, if there are racketeers or communists, then it's up to you and your fellow members to do something about it. You have your own democratic cleansing process.

But you can't do it by sitting at home and complaining, any more than you can get better men in Government by staying away from the polls. Those who really work at self-government, moreover, will find deep satisfaction, and so will you.

Now number three of my suggestions is that a new Federal labor law must outlaw unfair bargaining practices by companies or unions.

The Taft-Hartley Act, like the Wagner Act, prohibits certain types of unfair labor practices by employers, such as discriminating against union members or forming company unions. The Taft-Hartley Act added a list of union unfair practices. The unions have protested vigorously against this addition.

Yet I think it is only common sense to acknowledge that we must forbid such practices as jurisdictional strikes, and strikes or boycotts attempting to force an employer to deal with one union when another has been certified as the representative of his employes.

It is equally clear, however, that the prohibitions in the Taft-Hartley Act are so broad and so jumbled as to outlaw proper, along with improper conduct—even, on occasion, to require union members to act as strikebreakers.

These provisions must be completely rewritten, with the intention, not of stripping unions of as much bargaining power as possible, but only to prohibit resort to those extremes which fair-minded judgment identifies as unreasonable.

Point number four is rejection of the labor injunction. We agreed to this once. In 1932, Congress overwhelmingly passed the Norris-La Guardia Act to prohibit the labor injunction. The vote was 326 to 14 in the House and 75 to 5 in the Senate.

Then, fifteen years later, in the Taft-Hartley Act, the labor injunction—the process of haphazard prejudgment—was disinterred. No showing of need was made for it, and that tyrannical power to have men and women ordered back to work in smothered silence has no place in today's labor law.

My fifth, and the last point that I presume to make to you, is that new methods must be found for settling national emergency disputes.

We are willing, as a nation, to put up with serious inconveniences when bargaining stalemates result in shutting down production. Collective bargaining is a form of free competition. And, in Justice Holmes' phrase, "free competition is worth more to society than it costs."

We cannot, however, tolerate shutdowns which threaten our national safety, even that of the whole free world. The right to bargain collectively does not include a right to stop the national economy.

The Taft-Hartley answer for this problem was the injunction. All that law boils down to is that in national emergency disputes employes shall be ordered to work for another eighty days on the employers' terms.

This remedy has been administered now nine times. Fair-minded critics have concluded that in only two of these cases did it do the slightest good. In the others it either had no effect at all or actually delayed private settlement.

I have no miracle-drug solution for this problem. I am clear, though, that where the Government must intervene in these private disputes, its purpose must be not just to stop the strike, but to see that the dispute gets settled.

I am clear, too, that the new law must recognize that these emergency cases are always different. It's a proven mistake for Congress to prescribe in advance the same old patent medicine for all of them.

What we need is a completely new law—one that will provide for investigation and reporting to the public on the issues involved, one that will provide for more effective mediation between the parties. Its purpose should be to keep these cases out of the White House, not to put them in.

But the Congress should give the President a choice of procedures, not present him with no alternative when voluntary agreement proves impossible: seizure provisions geared to the circumstances; or arbitration; or a detailed hearing and recommendation of settlement terms; or a return of the dispute to the parties.

Such a law would leave the obligation to settle these disputes where it belongs—and that's with the parties. But it would not straitjacket this settlement process.

It would express the firm voice of a nation which demands a fair and a quick settlement, and offers constructive help toward a solution.

Now these, my friends, are the outlines of a law consistent, it seems to me, with our democratic practices. They outline a minimum law, and a minimum law is what we need. And, I would hope, indeed, I expect that in the larger area of common agreement that exists today the representatives of labor and of management, meeting in a spirit of give and take and of sincere search for industrial peace in the national interest, could agree on such a law.

Finally, let none of us forget that labor problems are human problems. The ultimate answers do not lie in the legislator's inkpot or in the lawyer's brief.

The common denominator of all I have said today is confidence —confidence not in law or government, but in one another, in free men and free women; confidence in the private organizations they have set up, the private processes they have worked out to meet their common problems. For, if I can leave anything of certainty with you, it is that the greatest hope for industrial peace is not in laws, but in private agreements.

It's hard to remember that here in Detroit fifteen years ago a mighty industry was paralyzed, and fighting in the streets between bitter men was an imminent possibility. Today the automobile companies and the workers have a five-year contract, giving the nation an assurance of labor peace infinitely firmer than any Congress could ever supply.

My friends, when we have come so far we know we can go farther.

Is It Liberation?

HAMTRAMCK, MICHIGAN

September 1, 1952

I am glad that I can spend a few minutes here with you this afternoon in Hamtramck. You know one of tests you have to pass in the freshman class in American Politics is to pronounce that name.

This noon I spoke to a great crowd in Cadillac Square about labor and my hopes, indeed the hopes of all of us, management and labor alike, for industrial peace in the United States which is the arsenal of an embattled world. I made some suggestions about what is needed in my judgment to replace the Taft-Hartley Act. And I'm happy to say that they treated me very cordially. I hope they even agreed with me.

Here in Hamtramck I want to talk with you about an entirely different matter. It is a very serious matter. Last week the Republican candidate for President made a speech in New York. His speech aroused speculation here and abroad that if he were elected, some reckless action might ensue in an attempt to liberate the peoples of Eastern Europe from Soviet tyranny.

Many of you here in Hamtramck and in other cities across the country have friends and relatives who are suffering behind the Iron Curtain. Last Thursday I discussed their plight with Representative Machrowicz and others. We agreed that we would all deeply regret it if a false campaign issue were to be built on the hopes and fears of these suffering people and on the anxieties of all Americans for their liberation.

The freedom of the descendants of Pulaski, Kosciuszko and Masaryk and other heroes of the fight for liberty in Eastern Europe is an issue between all the free nations and the Soviet Union. It should never be an issue among Americans, for we are all united in our desire for their liberation from the oppressor and in confidence that freedom will again be theirs.

But I want to make one thing very plain: Even if votes could be won by it, I would not say one reckless word on this matter during this campaign. Some things are more precious than votes.

The cruel grip of Soviet tyranny upon your friends and relatives cannot be loosened by loose talk or idle threats. It cannot be loosened by awakening false hopes which might stimulate intemperate action that would only lead your brothers to the execution squads; we remember only too well how thousands went to their death in Warsaw but a few short years ago.

It cannot be loosened by starting a war which would lead to untold suffering for innocent people everywhere; such a course could liberate only broken, silent and empty lands.

We have a responsibility to these suffering peoples. We must continue our efforts to outlaw genocide. We must review our immigration policies. We must help provide better care for those who succeed in escaping from behind the Iron Curtain.

Above all, we must work with others to build strong and healthy societies in the free nations, for we know that the future freedom of Poland, Czechoslovakia, Hungary, Eastern Germany, and the other peoples who have fallen under Soviet rule depends on the outcome of the vast worldwide struggle in which we are engaged. Not in the ashes of another world war; only in the atmosphere of a peaceful world can the reaffirmation of the right of self-determination have any meaning, or can the enslaved nations be free and independent again.

I have hoped that this political campaign might reaffirm America's dedication to the ideal of freedom and independence for all nations as the only solid foundation for a just and durable peace.

Stalin pledged his word to us to grant these countries liberty after World War Two. He has violated that pledge. But we have not forgotten his pledge and we shall not forget his violation. We will continue to work for the day when all peoples will be free to choose their own government and to walk again erect and unafraid.

I tell you now that I will never fear to negotiate in good faith with the Soviet Union, for to close the door to the conference room is to open a door to war. Man's tragedy has all too often been that he has grown weary in the search for an honorable alternative to war, and, in desperate impatience, has turned to violence.

Action for action's sake is the last resort of mentally and morally

exhausted men. The free nations must never tire in their search
for peace. They must always be ready to sit down at the conference
table, insisting only that any agreement must conform to the spirit
of our great wartime pledges and the Charter of the United
Nations.

With our friends we will seek patiently and tirelessly for the
rule of law among nations. That law has been written. It is the
Charter of the United Nations. It remains for every nation to respect it. That is the goal.

I think that progress toward that goal depends more on deeds
than on angry words. I think the Soviet Union will be influenced
only by a steady, serious, undeviating determination to build up
the strength of the free world—not with a view toward war but
with a view toward preventing war and negotiating the conditions
of peace.

It is on this road to peace that I ask you to join me, if you see
fit to charge me with the honor and burden of the Presidency. I
honor that office too much to seek votes at the risk of the safety
and security of our nation. I humbly request that you consider
carefully what I have said. I deeply fear that great injury could be
done to our nation and to ordinary men and women everywhere
if this political campaign were to descend to the level of competi-
tive threats and veiled hints of imprudent action.

My opponent is an honorable man. He has given the most distinguished military service to his country. I believe that he wants
to serve the interests of peace and justice just as well and as much
as I do. I respect his integrity.

I hope that recent statements by him and his advisers have been
misunderstood. I cannot believe that they deliberately intend to
arouse doubts and apprehensions about the steadiness with which
America will pursue its peaceful purposes.

I think that their words can be interpreted, if we read them
carefully, as an endorsement of the European policies which this
Government has been following and with which they have been
closely identified. This is, I note, the conclusion of the New York
Times, a great and responsible newspaper which is supporting
his candidacy.

I deeply hope that this will prove to be the case, for we are
dealing here with something more than the awful abstractions of

power politics; we are dealing with the lives of millions of our fellow men and our kinsmen across the seas.

Defeat begins in the heart. The peoples of Eastern Europe will never lose heart. They have kept their faith alive before, through long periods of darkness. We too must keep faith. We must not allow the recklessness of despair to find any lodging in our hearts. With indomitable faith and courage, with unfaltering determination, we must continue to strive for a future in which all peoples will know the joys of liberty for which their fathers have bled and died so often in the eternal struggle between freedom and tyranny.

Time for a Change—?

Colorado Volunteers for Stevenson Dinner

DENVER, COLORADO

September 5, 1952

When this visit to Denver was arranged for me I had thought to find here a bustling and hostile campaign headquarters. But evidently all is quiet in Denver. The tents have been folded and the captains and the kings have departed.

I am informed, if not very reliably, that with both discordant elements of the Republican Party here in Denver suddenly someone realized that Denver is very close to the Great Divide. And I guess they thought it was time for a change before this unhappy symbolism became too apparent.

Whatever the reason, I am afraid my neighbors in Springfield, Illinois, are not going to get the same relief you in Denver have had. My headquarters will continue to be there on November 4th.

Now there is deep personal satisfaction for me in the fact that this, my first talk on my first extended campaign trip, is sponsored by the independents who are organizing around the country on my behalf.

I'm reminded of the lonely days of my first venture into political life in 1948. Few really believed then that I, a Democrat, could be elected Governor of an overwhelmingly Republican state. But there were a lot of independent-minded people in Illinois who believed in me enough to work hard for my election.

In Illinois the independents—and I include in that term all those who wear a party label over their hearts but not over their eyes—those people in Illinois shared with me, I think, certain ideals and objectives for government at all levels. We believed in these things:

Government—any government—is not an end in itself. It exists to serve certain human purposes. These purposes should be enlarged only with caution. Indeed, the effort should be always to

57

leave as wide a range of activity as possible in private hands and to keep public intervention as far down the scale and as close to the people governed as possible.

What ought to be done by Government for the public welfare should be done. There should be no wistful dragging of the feet or turning backward to a dead, irrelevant past.

Government should be competent. Its personnel must not be under the heavy hand of purely political selection or influence. It must not be afraid of raising and spending money for worthy purposes, but it must detest and fear waste and dishonesty as ever-present threats to the whole moral basis of government by the consent of the governed because people don't consent voluntarily to be cheated or abused.

We believe above all else that those who hold in their hands the power of government must themselves be independent—and this kind of independence means the wisdom, the experience, the courage to identify the special interests and the pressures that are always at work, to see the public interest steadily, to resist its subordination no matter what the political hazards.

Now this simple principle is not peculiar to Illinois, nor is it foreign to the majority of those who participate in political activity. It's my common ground with those who are devoting their time and their effort and their money to the Volunteers for Stevenson, under whose auspices I speak here in Denver tonight.

This election year can set the stage for great ideas and great events. This is a year which opens out on challenges, on opportunities and decisions as big as history itself. There are awesome things for any citizen to ponder. They are more awesome for a Presidential candidate.

Feeling this, I must assume that my opponent, whom I honor for the proud page he has written in American history, feels it too. And I can imagine nothing more false or hollow than to conceal these things from the American people in order to put on a show of politics as usual. If we do this, we will succeed only in making a show of ourselves. In a contest for the greatest office and in a time for greatness I think we owe it to the people to talk sense.

I don't think many people are beguiled by denunciations and generalizations (and I don't mean a pun). I may be wrong, my friends, but I must persist in that conviction—at least until November.

So I propose to go on saying just what I think about our public questions one by one, with little hope of pleasing everyone, but with confident certainty that honesty is the best policy and that for this office, in this anxious year, you don't want a political free-for-all, and you do want to know all you can about me and about my views. Frankly, until recently not many people cared about either. It's a little hard to get accustomed to this importance.

Now, having stated the ground rules as far as I'm concerned, I should like to talk a little about one of the biggest hazards of this campaign, as far as I'm concerned. As divided, as silent as both wings of the Republican Party are on major objectives, on policies to guide the nation, they have wholeheartedly united on one profound proposition: "It's time for a change."

You will hear this phrase many times—usually at the end of a long string of invectives in which each of the following words will appear at least once: crime, corruption and cronies; bossism, blundering and bungling; stupidity and socialism (either the creeping or galloping variety, depending on the inflammation of the speaker). Indeed, my friends, apparently you are going to hear little else. The question must come to your mind: "Change to what?" But don't pause for an answer because you may pause indefinitely.

Now, I've read the Republican platform, which is pretty good as a "Whodunit," but it doesn't tell us what kind of a domestic or foreign policy they are going to change to. I've listened to the speeches, too, and I don't yet know what legislation of the past twenty years is to be changed or changed to what. Nor have I heard yet to what new foreign policy we should be committed, unless it's the reckless suggestion of a war of liberation in Europe, which has frightened everyone except the Russians.

No, the guideposts and the road maps to the new Utopia which change will build are not yet visible. But meanwhile the Republican candidates seem to have clasped all of the social gains of the past twenty years to their bosoms with a "me-too" fervor that is touching to a Democrat, for imitation still remains the sincerest form of flattery.

I confess it's all a little perplexing. The Democrats are denounced for not wanting changes and then they are denounced for a subversive desire to change everything. I'm beginning to wonder if the Republican campaign rests on the proposition that Democrats are social revolutionaries who want to keep things exactly as they are.

But, and more seriously, "change" is about the most important word in the world today. In fact, I would be perfectly willing to have the outcome of this election decided on these questions:

Which party best understands the meaning of change in the modern world?

Which party has ignored it?

Which has anticipated the need for a change and done something about it?

Which party has resisted about every important change for the past twenty-five years?

And looking ahead now, which party is most likely to cope effectively with the vast changes already in the making?

You'll forgive me if I'm a little cynical when I hear shouting the loudest for change the politicians who have consistently opposed change at every turn as far back as most of us can remember.

Timing, timing with respect to change, is as important as change itself. It's when the problem is a live one that change becomes important. In fact, if my party had not met the challenge of change at the right time, there would be no program in America for the Republican leaders to endorse.

I have a hunch that the American people would like to see them get out in front with something besides criticism—for a change. And I have a hunch that there are a lot of us who would be more impressed by specific ideas about the making of a better world than by these hoarse denunciations and demands for a blank check made out to "change."

I believe there are a lot of changes still to be made. I'm for continuing the process of gradual and economic betterment which began at the depths of despair in 1932. The changes wrought in these twenty years have steadily raised the standards of life of our people, given new hope to the underprivileged and proven to the slave world the capacity of free men to provide security for themselves within the framework of freedom.

I'm glad that the General has apparently embraced these changes. But I don't detect any roars of approval from the Old Guard—you know what they are, they're the men who don't want anything done for the first time. My fellow townsman, Colonel McCormick, has even deserted—he's "gone over the hill" as the

G.I.'s say. And Senator Taft, it's reported, wants commitments and he wants them in writing.

Some commentators tell us that there are really two Republican Parties, which of course has been obvious to most of us for a long time. The comparatively modern men and the powerful Old Guard who are still fighting valiantly to keep us out of World War Two.

Now they tell us that if the Republicans lose this year, as usual, the Old Guard will come raging in and drive the so-called me-tooers into shameful exile. And, therefore, the thing for independ-ents and Democrats to do is to let the Republicans win, thereby assuring the triumph of moderation and enabling us all to live happily ever after.

I believe that this is the first time in history that it has been contended that now is the time for all good Democrats to come to the aid of the Republican Party.

Now, at the risk of seeming to lack compassion and humanity, that's too high a price to save enlightened Republicans from their more primitive brethren. They'll just have to take care of them-selves while we take care of the country.

But of course there is an easier, safer path of escape for these liberal Republicans trapped behind the G.O.P. line. There's al-ways a light in our Democratic window for the politically homeless or the repentant. There's a warm welcome and plenty of shelter for Republicans as well as independents, and as in the Foreign Legion, no questions asked.

Now, my friends, I shall not argue that it is necessarily fatal to change horses in midstream. But I doubt if it is wise to jump on a struggling two-headed elephant trying to swim in both direc-tions in very rough water.

Man does not live by words alone, despite the fact that some-times he has to eat them. Alas, in this world he sometimes, or per-haps too often, lives by catchwords. Slogans are normally designed to get action without reflection. This one, "time for a change," fits these specifications admirably. This may not be too serious when all that is at stake is whether to buy one cake of soap or another, but I don't think it furnishes a sound basis for deciding a national election.

If we believe in human progress, if we believe with the pioneers that there is a peaceful better life to be found beyond the horizon, then we all profoundly believe that it is always time for a change —a change to something better. "The important thing," as Justice Holmes once said, "is not where we are, but where we are going."

This year the Democratic Party nominated me for the Presidency, a nomination I did not seek. That's the best evidence that the Democrats wanted a change, too. And the Democrat who wanted it most of all was President Truman.

Now, the bitterest enemies of President Truman could never accuse him of being one to run away from a fight. But he knows that change—new men, new blood, new ideas, new methods—is helpful. He has not sought to interfere with the considerable changes in the Democratic Party organization that I've already made. And I could add that no one has made or even proposed any deals with me for any office, or benefit, or favor whatsoever.

Now I think the Republican leaders know this. Yet I hear them attack corruption as if there wasn't a single honest Federal employe and then go on to say that I am indebted to someone, that I would have no freedom, and that I could do nothing if I found dishonesty.

On this subject I want to say, as I've said many times before, that corruption in public office is treason and it's treason to Democrats as well as to the Republicans. Any crooks that I can find in the Government will be exposed and punished as ruthlessly as I've done it in Illinois—Republicans and Democrats alike.

And what's more, my friends, I think I know more about their methods than my opponent because I followed eight years of magnificent Republican rascality in Illinois. I've used an axe on my own party men without fear or favor or hesitation and, frankly, I resent the charges that imply that either my honesty or my fidelity to the public trust would be diminished by election to an office I revere.

I had not expected that from the General. And I will not repay him in kind. But I would thank him to read more carefully what I don't believe he would write himself. Moreover, you'll forgive me if I gag a little when Republican politicians don the ill-fitting mantle of self-righteousness and deliver holier-than-thou sermons on morality.

I've read enough of our history to remember the shameful periods after previous wars, and who was in power then? The Republican Party.

But that doesn't condone the recent revelations of faithlessness. And I don't condone them and never will—either in public life or in private.

Finally, let me suggest to our Republican friends that it's time for a change in that old tired meaningless tune, "It's time for a change." It has been used every four years and it hasn't started any dancing in the streets yet.

What we really believe in, I think, independents, Republicans and Democrats alike—Americans—is not the slogans of people who are out of office and want to get in; what we believe in is the power and the right of peaceful, continuous change for the better.

We believe in it because we, the American people, believe in ourselves. We believe in our ideals and in the necessity for justifying our exalted position in the world.

And finally, we believe that with prudence and patience, with a sense of dedication, and with God's help, we can give enriched meaning to human destiny.

I'm grateful to all of you who have rallied to my support in this vast undertaking. I have learned that the greatest, perhaps the only enduring satisfaction in public office is the confidence and the respect, not the total agreement because it can never exist, the confidence and the respect of disinterested men and women who don't want anything for themselves.

Farm Policy

National Plowing Contest

K A S S O N ,   M I N N E S O T A

September 6, 1952

I am grateful for the opportunity to talk with you about national farm policies. I won't waste your time this afternoon telling you, in the political tradition, all about how I am myself a farmer. I own farm land in Illinois, and I come from a family that has lived in the heart of the Corn Belt for over a hundred years. But I am here today as a candidate for public office—not masquerading as a dirt farmer, but as a politician.

My first venture into public service was in Washington in the old Agricultural Adjustment Administration. That was in the desolate days of 1933, when the American farmer, like everybody else, was flat on his back. I do not want to suggest to anyone that we Democrats are still running against Herbert Hoover, but I am thankful for my AAA experience, because it showed me in a way I will never forget how bad conditions can get on our farms—conditions that must never occur again.

In this spirit, Democratic administrations have developed the farm policies of the last twenty years. As a result, we of this generation, who saw farm conditions at their worst in 1932, have had the happy privilege of seeing them over the last decade at their best. I am proud of the work my party has done in these twenty years to restore the American farmer to a position of equality and dignity in our national life.

For the last three and a half years I have been Governor of a great agricultural state. In this capacity I have worked closely with farmers and farm organizations. With their help and co-operation, we have reorganized our Illinois Department of Agriculture; and, if you will forgive a commercial here at Kasson for a rival show, we have improved our great Illinois State Fair and cut the cost to the taxpayer by two-thirds. I have relied on farmers' advice in

other fields too—notably school and highway legislation. We now
have under way in Illinois the largest highway program since the
advent of the hard road. For the first time a share of our gasoline
tax is going to the townships for the rural roads.

I come to you today as the Democratic candidate for the greatest
responsibility on earth—the Presidency of the United States. I am
running on the Democratic platform. I believe it is a good platform.
I believe its agricultural plank is clear, definite and sound. I can
stand on it without squirming. I feel no need to modify this provision or that, to explain or to reinterpret, to dodge or to hedge.

And I am for this platform, above all, because I believe that its
pledges are not just in the interest of the farmer—they are in the
public interest. I know that the American farmers do not want,
nor will they get through any effort of mine, anything more than
what is justified by the larger good of the commonwealth. We can
all stand on the words of the first philosopher of American agriculture, Thomas Jefferson: "Equal rights for all; special privileges for
none."

A society can be no better than the men and women who compose it. The heart of any farm policy must therefore be the life
of those who work the farms. Our objective is to make that life
full and satisfying. We believe, as Democrats have always believed,
that our society rests on an agricultural base. It is our determination to keep that base solid and healthy. Our farms must grow
more than crops and livestock. They must grow what Walt Whit-
man described as the best bar against tyranny—"a large, resolute
breed of men."

This means that farm policy must focus first on the question of
farm income. This is not because farmers are more concerned with
money than any other group in society. It is because farmers, like
all other citizens, are entitled to a fair return for their labor and a
fair chance in the world for their children. In the past, the labor
of the farmer has remained the same; but his income has risen or
sunk according to the unpredictable fluctuations of the market.
It has been a constant objective of our Democratic farm programs
to maintain farm income—and thereby to assure the farmer that he
can provide food, medical care and education for his family.

The way we have chosen to maintain farm income is to support
farm prices. Our platform lays this out in clear language. Here is
what it says: "We will continue to protect the producers of basic

agricultural commodities under the terms of a mandatory price-support program at not less than 90 per cent of parity."

There are no ifs, buts or maybes about this. And I think it is a policy that most farmers today understand and believe in. I only wish that everybody understood it so well. One place it was clearly *not* understood was at the great fracas in the Chicago stockyards, two months ago, where one of the casualties was the farm plank in the Republican platform. There are, of course, two Republican Parties for agriculture as well as two Republican Parties for foreign policy and almost everything else. The General evidently decided this morning to plow under the Republican platform altogether.

As you all know, the Chicago slaughter finally ended in a cease-fire agreement. According to that agreement—better known as the Republican platform—Republican policy is "aimed"—that is their word—is "aimed" at parity levels. That phrase may have looked good in a smoke-filled room in Chicago. It isn't very clear here in the daylight in Minnesota. There is, and no one should know it better than my distinguished opponent, a vast difference between aiming at a target and hitting it.

How good is their aim anyway? Their sights were a mile off in June of this year when more than half the Republican members of the House of Representatives voted against the law that extended price support at 90 per cent of parity through 1954.

If the Republican candidate says one thing, and the Republican platform says something else, and the Republican members of Congress say still another—how then can anyone tell what a Republican administration would actually do in Washington?

There should be no mystery about price supports. What our program does is to place a floor under our agricultural economy in order to protect the farmer against sudden and violent price drops. What it does is to maintain farm income—and the farmer's purchasing power—in those uneasy moments when there is a temporary glut in the market, or when real depression threatens. By stabilizing farm income, our program maintains markets for the businessman and the worker. The total effect, obviously, is to help stabilize the whole national economy at a high level of production and employment.

I know that opponents of the program claim that price supports raise food prices for housewives. Let us examine this charge a moment. Food prices are high enough today, heaven knows. But supports are not the reason. High employment and strong purchasing power—in short, prosperity—are keeping most farm prices above support levels.

What the support program does do is to encourage farmers to grow more food. You can now plant crops fairly secure in the knowledge that prices will still be good at market time. That is one reason why farm production has increased almost 50 per cent in the last twenty years. The support program thus helps to keep supply up with demand—and that is the way to keep prices from going up.

The price-support program thus does more than assure a decent life and a fair opportunity for most of our farm families. It also improves the life of the boys and girls in our cities. From your farms today food pours in a steady stream to every corner of the country. Think what this means in the terms of human lives! We are feeding thirty million more people than there were in our land in 1932; and we are giving the average American a far better diet. More than that, this better diet costs the average person no greater share of his income after taxes than it did in 1932—if he was lucky enough to have any income, after or even before taxes, in that gloomy year.

I am not presuming for a moment to say that support at 90 per cent of parity is necessarily the permanent or only answer. Economic conditions are constantly changing and I think this program, like all our economic policies, should be constantly reappraised to determine if it is fair to the taxpayer and responsive to our needs. We are all dependent on one another and the only certainty of a stable, prosperous agriculture is a stable, prosperous nation.

The price-support program is doing a good job for the basic crops —corn, cotton, wheat, rice, and the others—for which loan and storage operations are now in effect. The same protection could be accorded to other storable commodities.

For perishable products, however, such as hogs, dairy products, fruits and vegetables, these loan and storage operations do not work well. Yet these products provide about three-fourths of all the income received by farmers.

Our first line of defense for the producers of perishables is, of course, a strong economic policy that will insure, so far as it is humanly possible to do so, high employment and purchasing power.

But behind this there should be protection against unreasonably low prices for those producers of perishables who need it. They should know they can expand production and that the public that benefits will bear part of the risk.

I do not underestimate the difficulty of finding a satisfactory method of doing this. And I can only hope that with continued careful study and close consultation with farmers and their leaders ways will be found to do something both practical and effective.

The farm problem has changed much since the thirties. Once abundance created surpluses because people could not buy what the farmer could produce. Today we seek even greater abundance as we look ahead to a thirty or forty million increase in our population in the next twenty-five years.

Nevertheless, there is the constant necessity to adjust output to need in the short run. We have worked out excellent voluntary methods for doing this.

The Republican leadership would now dispense entirely with production controls. "We do not believe in restrictions on the American farmer's ability to produce," their platform states in one of its rare bursts of clarity. Well, I do not like acreage allotments and marketing quotas myself. I hope—we all have good reason to hope—that a growing population and expanding markets will keep us from again needing controls for staple crops.

But farmers have learned from bitter experience that we need these controls in reserve. I learned how useful they could be in the hard school of the triple-A. Incidentally, there could be no tobacco program at all right now without marketing quotas—as every tobacco farmer knows. I would never favor controls for the sake of control. But I think we have to face a practical problem when we see one.

Price policy is the heart of the farm program but it is not the whole of it. Farming is a way of using our great inheritance of water and land; and it is a way of life. Our effort must be to improve the fertility and productivity of our farms, and to improve the quality and content of life for our farm families. I hope to have a personal part in the continuation and extension of the policies which in the last twenty years have given farm life new strength and new dignity—and so restored it to its old place of honor in the Republic.

We of this generation are the trustees of our soil and water resources for our children and their children. We have an elaborate soil-conservation program. It too should have constant scrutiny to determine if we are getting the maximum value in land improvement out of our conservation tax dollar. We still have far to go in upstream flood prevention and water and forest conservation. And I wish I could say that every farmer was using the best conservation methods to protect his farm—methods such as those demonstrated here at Kasson at this magnificent and celebrated exhibition. With the kind of local leadership you have in the Conservation Service and Districts we see here today, we will get the job done everywhere in time, and I would say very soon in Minnesota.

You may have heard that, where administration is concerned, I am no admirer of mere size. Let us strive for big men, not big government. We must continue to decentralize the management of our agricultural and conservation programs and, if anything, increase farmer participation. I like to think of soil conservation as democracy at work with technical assistance. I think we can go further toward making local administration compact and efficient, and getting dollar-for-dollar value for the money we spend.

Rural electrification is one of our finest national achievements in this generation. It is more than a government program. It is a blessing.

It means electric lights for farm families who have had to live by coal-oil lamps. It means electric power for the farm wife in place of the back-breaking labor of the old-fashioned washtub and the hand pump. It means electric power to grind the farmer's feed, heat his brooder house, and help him with a hundred other chores. You know about this in Minnesota, where the number of electrified farms has risen from 7 per cent in 1935 to 90 per cent today.

The great task of bringing electricity to the farm is now far along to completion. It must be finished, and generation and transmission facilities must be adequate to meet the constantly growing demand for power on the farm, at prices the farmer can afford to pay.

We must also look toward the time when every farm home may be in touch with its neighbors, the doctor and the world through rural telephone service.

The chief agency in this miraculous transformation in country living has been the farmer-owned co-operative. I've been a member of one for years and the co-operative seems to me a wonderful example of people solving their own local problems in their own way. Its effectiveness must not be crippled by hostile legislation.

There is one final part of our farm program which especially concerns me.

Farm ownership and the family farm are the foundation on which our whole agricultural system is built. From 1880 to 1932 we lost ground on farm ownership. In these years—years, incidentally, when Republicans were mostly in power and hadn't yet invented that slogan "it's time for a change"—the proportion of farm owners declined, until by 1932, 43 per cent of all farmers—two out of every five—were either tenants or sharecroppers. That trend has now been reversed; three-fourths of our farmers now own their farms. We have recovered, in twenty years, the ground lost in the previous fifty. I've sold some farms and I've seen to it that they were sold to operators, not landlords, where possible.

Things are not yet as they should be. Many young, vigorous and ambitious men would like to become owners of farms. What is more serious, many farmers cannot, with their existing land and equipment, make a decent living from the soil. In 1950, more than one million farmers had net incomes from all sources including outside employment of less than $1,000. How can a farmer rear, clothe and educate a family on that? We can take pride in our remarkable progress, but we cannot be complacent.

Research, housing, and credit programs particularly must be focused on this problem of rural poverty. No one should promise miracles here; but there must be ways to help the industrious small farmer who wants to help himself. That kind of American is a good risk. And no one knows it better than my running mate, Senator John Sparkman, who has led the battle for them, and who was himself one of eleven children of an impoverished tenant farmer.

This nation faces a stern present and a challenging future. The American farmer has a great role to play in these next critical years of precarious balance in the world. Our national commitment to an expanding economy rests upon the continued growth of our agriculture. Our struggle to strengthen the free world against communism demands the continued and growing productivity of the American farm. A hungry man is not a free man. In the long run, peace will be won in the turnrows, not on the battlefields.

The last twenty years have established a framework of justice and equity within which the farmer can do his indispensable part for the greater strength and safety of our nation. Only in an atmosphere of growth and confidence can the farmer make his necessary contribution to our nation, and our nation its necessary contribution to the worldwide fight for freedom.

If I didn't feel that the party which saw our needs and charted our course in the past is the best custodian of our future I would not be the Democratic candidate for President, and I would not be here on this great day in Kasson asking not for your thanks, but for your confidence.

And now let us get back to the plowing.

The New West

McCormack Junior High School Auditorium

CHEYENNE, WYOMING

September 6, 1952

I usually think of Wyoming, somehow, as a vacation state. I have had a very happy vacation today. It started at 5:30 this morning in Denver, and since then I have been to Minneapolis, to Rochester, to Kasson, to Rochester, to Minneapolis, to Cheyenne. I think I am the only man in history who ever decided to go from Denver to Cheyenne by way of Minnesota.

This restful day suggests to me that I am not running for President of the United States but flying to an insane asylum. But it has given me an opportunity that falls to the lot of few people, to see something of the enormousness, the might and the grandeur of the United States.

I have come in the past four years to know every corner, I think, every crossroad of my State of Illinois, and now I have the privilege that should be everyone's privilege, and, unhappily, is the privilege of all too few, to see—if not every crossroad—at least the principal centers of virtually all of the United States. I can think of nothing that is better calculated to increase one's sense of pride, one's respect for his fellow American and at the same time one's humility.

I have been in Wyoming before. I came here first in 1915, as a boy, and I spent a number of years here in the summer. I even earned my board and keep, working on cattle ranches. I used to tell the folks back home that I was a cowboy, but my recollection—and I think it is accurate—is that I spent the greater part of my time shocking barley, making hay and repairing irrigation ditches. The last time I came here to Wyoming was exactly two years ago, I believe, this week. I went fishing with my three sons up on top of the Continental Divide, at Bridger Lake and around the headwaters of the Yellowstone River. I must say that at that time it never occurred to me that I should be back here two years later fishing again, but this time fishing for votes. I have even concluded, out of the wealth of generosity that is within me, that if you treat me as well as the cutthroat trout did, I will buy a Wyoming fishing license—after November 4th.

I came out here once after college with a classmate of mine. We were on a secret mission; we had solemnly decided that we were going to make our careers in Wyoming, but we weren't telling our parents. The summer wore on and I didn't come home. Then my father ordered me home, and the result was that Wyoming lost a great rancher and the American Bar Association gained a lawyer. I am not sure who came off better, Wyoming or the Bar Association; I have been loath to ask either.

I had an experience on that last journey to Wyoming that perhaps many of you have had. Up on top of the Divide, there is a creek that separates and forms the Pacific Creek, flowing down the western watershed, and the Atlantic Creek, flowing down the eastern watershed. Sitting there on a bright summer afternoon on top of the world, I couldn't help but think of what had happened and the symbolic significance of this lovely spot, there on top of the Continental Divide where the winds blow from all directions. I thought of how the center of gravity in world affairs had moved in the past three thousand years from the valley of the Tigris and Euphrates, to the valley of the Nile, to Athens, to Rome, to Paris, to London, and in our time and in our generation had jumped the Atlantic and had come to the Western Hemisphere, had come to the United States of America.

Somehow, there on top of the Divide, with my feet in the creek— one in the Atlantic and one in the Pacific—I thought that this lovely windswept mountain side was perhaps the center of the center of gravity of the whole world—and just at that moment, in my reverie, I dropped my sandwich in the water. I don't know whether it went east or west but I went hungry for the rest of that afternoon.

I think one of the finest things you do out here is to keep alive the memories of the old West—they are such an important part of the American tradition—memories that are dear to all of us, whether we have ever been here or not. I wish I could have come here in time to see your Frontier Day. I am told that it captures most vividly the spirit of the old times. I used to try as a boy, there on the ranches of the Big Horn, to ride steers. I even tried to ride a bucking horse. Someone told me it took a strong back and a weak mind and I could qualify on at least one count. I hope nobody makes any comparisons with the way I ride the Democratic donkey.

In Minnesota today, the cattle rustlers and the acrobats on horse-back of the motion-picture version of the old West had to take a back seat because my distinguished opponent made off with the farm plank of the Democratic platform—in broad daylight.

You know, what hurt most, however, was what he did to our platform. We don't object to his rewriting the Republican plat-form, but if he wants to stand on our platform, we think it only fair to ask him to take it as it is.

The Democratic platform is strong enough and it is broad enough in its present form to carry all of the progressive Republicans in the land. The trouble is that some Republican candidates seem to be on the platform just for the ride from now until election day. They seem to be only interested in roping votes before the elec-tion, but they won't be doing any branding afterward.

But it wasn't my intention to talk to you about the old West, of course. I want to talk about the new West and only briefly. Of course, the two are closely related; both have evoked the pioneer-ing spirit of the American people. The old West represented the challenge of new and unknown physical horizons. The new West has meant an exploration of less tangible frontiers—the frontiers of science, of technology and of resource development. Beyond these frontiers we can already see the outlines of a thrilling and exhilarating future. We know that increasingly the Western part of the United States is becoming a leading source of American food and fibers, of American power and American industrial might—and the West has always been a schooling ground of American venturesomeness and American ingenuity.

Speaking of the Republican platform, it reminds me of nothing so much as the Powder River. I don't say that the Republican plat-form is a mile wide. But you will be flattering it if you said it was an inch deep. And what is more, it tries to run uphill!

The new West is going to be more and more important to our national future. Every time I have come out here, everything seems to have doubled somehow in size. So far as I can see there are three main components in this staggering growth.

One is the energy and the resourcefulness of the people. Another is the wisdom of the people of the United States in determining that our natural resources be managed for the good of all of the people. A third factor is our free-enterprise system, which releases the creative energy and vigor of a people more effectively than any other economic system thus far devised by man.

People sometimes talk as if government and free enterprise were mortal enemies. In this part of the country you know that they are working together as partners. Land, water and minerals are the bone and the sinew of the West. It takes wise government policy to develop these resources in the interests of all of the people. The Democratic Party knows, as you know, that sound public-conservation policies provide the best foundation for healthy, private enterprise both here in Wyoming and throughout the West.

Now, what are some of the ways in which we have seen this established—proven?

You here in Wyoming have seen that Federal investment in sound irrigation projects will give individual ranchers a chance to own their own land and make a decent living. You have seen power from Federal projects form the basis for greater farm output and new and expanded private businesses.

You have seen sensible and forward-looking public-land leasing policies stimulate the exploration and the development of new oil reserves.

You have seen governmental research work demonstrate that coal and oil shale can be turned into liquid fuel by private enterprise.

These are not the actions of an arbitrary bureaucracy, my friends, seeking any socialization of our economy. They are the actions of a sensible government interested in creating the conditions under which free enterprise can thrive; under which private individuals can have greater opportunities to start farms and businesses, to get better jobs, to earn more money, to provide a more secure future for themselves and for their children. This is the kind of government I think you want to have in Washington. Certainly this is the only kind of government that I am interested in.

Now you might suspect I was slightly partisan, but I am frank to say I don't think the Republican Party can give you that kind of government. Divided, quarreling and disunited, none of the Republicans in either of the Republican Parties has yet offered a single new idea for meeting any of the major issues ahead of this country. They complain, they denounce, they criticize and they fairly burst with self-righteousness. But when are they going to get down to cases?

Here we are, a great industrial nation, seeking to achieve a constructive relationship between employers and workers in the interest of ever-growing production and ever-higher standards of living for us all.

Last week in Detroit I made some specific suggestions for moving ahead in this field. My very distinguished opponent so far has suggested only that we might be able to turn the problem over to a university for study. I suggest that the all-important goal of good labor-management relations is entitled to a higher priority on our action list.

We are likewise a great agricultural nation, seeking to develop farm policies that will give us abundant production with fair prices to consumers and fair living standards for farmers. Earlier today in Minnesota I offered a specific program for moving ahead toward this goal. It is a program which has been written into the Democratic platform and which has been supported by Democrats in and out of Congress. And I can tell you now it will not be realized if we turn the country over to a party more than half of whose members in the House of Representatives voted only two months ago to deny the farmers of this nation firm price supports.

We face real problems—hard problems—in this country. Labor relations and farm policy are only two of many that will not be solved by platitudes or pious good will or extravagant bids for votes. They will only be solved by concrete, specific, practical action. That is what I have been talking about and what I intend to go on talking about. So far, I am sorry to say, we have been getting very little of that kind of talk from our Republican friends.

Even in the field of foreign policy I have been disappointed. There has been much trumpeting by the Republicans to the effect that they were about to unveil a new, a positive and dynamic, streamlined foreign policy. Well, it was unveiled Thursday night by my most distinguished opponent. And what did it turn out to be? Three of the ten planks were "throw the rascals out." And the others turned out to be exactly the foreign policy this nation has been following. It is a good foreign policy. I am glad that the Republican candidate is for it. But does he not realize that this foreign policy has been bitterly fought and obstructed and sabotaged by prominent Republican leaders in the Senate and in the House? Many of the men who have been most indifferent to our allies, who have fought hardest against the Marshall plan, against the Voice of America, and the Point Four Program and the other major pillars of our foreign policy are now running on the same Republican ticket with the candidate who endorses all of these measures.

What with the endorsement of all the social gains of the last twenty years, the adoption of our agricultural platform, and going us one better on this, I am beginning to wonder what sort of a shell game this is—what kind of razzle-dazzle is it? But I guess, after all, there is room for such a distinguished hitchhiker on the Democratic platform. I don't mind it. I welcome it; and so do you. It is just those one-eyed guys with knives in their teeth who are scrambling aboard with him that make me a little uncomfortable.

The Republican candidate on Thursday night repudiated the records of at least half of the Republicans who are running for the Congress, but he does not appear disposed to repudiate the candidates. I think the American people are too smart not to realize that a positive, constructive foreign policy cannot be carried out by a negative, destructive Republican majority in the Congress. I think the people of this country are grown up and I think they can tell oratory from common sense. I think people want serious issues discussed seriously. I think the people of this country know that the problems of war, of inflation, poverty, greed cannot be washed away by saying every day that we are for peace and prosperity. To solve such problems means hard, sweaty, back-breaking labor, pain and anguish and unhappiness. We believe that they can be solved, for we are ready to pitch in with heart and mind and soul to tackle the natural and human difficulties that confront us and stand in our way.

If we do that—if we buckle down to work with the fortitude and energy that our pioneering forefathers showed when they subdued this continent, then we can win through this stormy night to the dawn of a peaceful world.

But, my friends, I don't think I am going to wait that long before I come back to Wyoming to go fishing!

The One-Party Press

Portland Journal *Luncheon for Oregon Newspapermen*

PORTLAND, OREGON

September 8, 1952

It is very pleasant to consider today that I have a group of editors and publishers temporarily at my mercy. I know it won't last long. But, since the press—some of it—keeps describing me as a captive candidate, I particularly enjoy speaking to a captive audience.

In addition, I have had a strange feeling these past weeks that people are following me. They all seem to be friendly, inquisitive and rumpled; they wear hats and keep writing things down on pieces of paper. I cannot drink a milk-shake or put on a pair of shoes without their friendly but implacable surveillance. Given this relentless observation, I find it an agreeable change to stand here and look straight back at such a distinguished group of what I believe are called "opinion molders."

If ignorance, apathy and excessive partisanship are still the greatest enemies of democracy—as I believe Bryce said some forty or fifty years ago—then of course it is up to a free press to help us on all three counts and all the time. Otherwise neither democratic government nor a free press can be sure of permanency.

In short, government—our brand of representative government —depends on you, and, something which I think your profession sometimes overlooks, you depend on government, for the ultimate protection of a free press is in the Constitution.

That is why the rock-bottom foundation of a free press is the integrity of the people who run it. Our press may make a million mistakes of judgment without doing itself permanent harm so long as its proprietors are steadfast in their adherence to truth. I have no doubt whatever that the bulk of owners and publishers and editors are doing an honest job with the news.

I ought to know, because I am straining the impartiality of the press to the limit these days. Yet, as a candidate in a hard-fought campaign, I have been well impressed by the fair treatment accorded me by most newspapers, including most of those aligned editorially with the opposition. I am convinced that nearly all publishers are doing their honest best, according to their lights— even if I must confess that sometimes their lights seem to me a little dim.

I am glad to pay this tribute to the press. It is true, and I think it should be said. I am grateful for the impartiality and fullness of your news columns. Yet I am not recommending complacency. And, from my vantage point, certain defects are apparent. If I were still an editorial writer I suppose I would say that there are some ominous tendencies, or even that these tendencies could weaken the fabric of the Republic.

In my new role in life, I can't help noticing from time to time —I want to put it as delicately as I can—that the overwhelming majority of the newspapers of the country are supporting the opposition candidate. This is something, I find, that even my best friends *will* tell me! And I certainly don't take it personally. In fact, I would have been somewhat startled and unhappy if I received much press support after the reception given my Democratic predecessors, Mr. Truman and Mr. Roosevelt. Some people might even have considered such support an ill omen.

It would seem that the overwhelming majority of the press is just against Democrats. And it is against Democrats, so far as I can see, not after a sober and considered review of the alternatives, but automatically, as dogs are against cats. As soon as a newspaper—I speak of the great majority, not of the enlightened ten per cent—sees a Democratic candidate it is filled with an unconquerable yen to chase him up an alley.

I still haven't got over the way some of our nation's great papers rushed to commit themselves to a candidate last spring, long before they knew what that candidate stood for, or what his party platform would be, or who his opponent was, or what would be the issues of the campaign. I know where a young publisher's fancy turns in that season of the year, and I don't blame them for a moment. But I feel that some of them may yet regret the impetuosity of their wooing now that autumn is here.

I am touched when I read in these papers solicitous editorials about the survival of the two-party system. Now I really can't bring myself to believe that the Republican Party is about to fade away, even if it loses in 1952. If so, it is staging one of the longest and loudest deathbed scenes in history. How can the Republican Party disappear when about 90 per cent of the press for ten or fifteen years has been telling the American people day in and day out that the Republican Party alone can save the Republic? Surely Republican publishers and editors don't honestly believe that they have so little influence!

I am in favor of a two-party system in politics. And I think we have a pretty healthy two-party system at this moment. But I am in favor of a two-party system in our press too. And I am, frankly, considerably concerned when I see the extent to which we are developing a one-party press in a two-party country.

I earnestly wish that the newspapers so highly agitated over the two-party system in politics would contemplate the very real dangers of the one-party system in the press. I don't say this because of any concern over the coming election. My party has done all right in recent elections in spite of the country's editorial pages, and I have a hunch we will do all right this year too.

But, as an ex-newspaperman and as a citizen, I am gravely concerned about the implications of this one-party system for our American press and our free society.

A free society means a society based on free competition and there is no more important competition than competition in ideas, competition in opinion. This form of competition is essential to the preservation of a free press. Indeed, I think the press should set an example to the nation in increasing opposition to uniformity.

What I think I detect is a growing uniformity of outlook among publishers—a tendency toward the trade-association mentality of uniformity of attitude toward the public, the customer, if not toward one another as producers of consumer goods. I doubt if this shoe fits the peculiar function of the newspaper.

I think you will agree that we cannot risk complacency. We need to be rededicated every day to the unfinished task of keeping our free press truly free. We need to work even harder for the time when all editors will honor their profession, when all publishers will have a sense of responsibility equal to their power and thus regain their power, if I may put it that way.

It's not honest convictions honestly stated that concern me. Rather it is the tendency of many papers, and I include columnists, commentators, analysts, feature writers, and so on, to argue editorially from the personal objective, rather than from the whole truth. As the old jury lawyer said: "And these, gentlemen, are the conclusions on which I base my facts."

In short, it seems to me that facts, truth, should be just as sacred in the editorial column as the news column. And, as I have said, happily most papers, but by no means all, do struggle with sincerity for accuracy in the news. Coming from Chicago, of course, I am not unfamiliar with the phenomenon of an editorial in every news column!

What I am saying is that the press cannot condemn demagoguery, claptrap, distortion and falsehood in politicians and public life on the one hand and practice the same abuses on the public themselves, on the other. I know the people are smarter than many politicians think and sometimes I suspect that even editors underestimate them.

The free press is the mother of all our liberties and of our progress under liberty. That's easy to say, but while saying it, it is well to remember what it means.

Having delivered myself of this, let me say a few words about the campaign. It is going to be a tough campaign, and I am not kidding myself about the difficulties. My opponent is a great General, who has served the Army and the nation well. He has behind him a vigorous and active party—a good deal of whose vigor and activity is devoted to the continual scrimmage between the rival Republican teams. Indeed, I wait, breathlessly for each morning's newspaper to see which Republican Party is on top that day. Nonetheless, I would be the last to underestimate the effectiveness or the determination of the professional Republican organization.

But I think we have certain advantages too. One of them is that we are a relatively united party—not just in organization, but, and this may be more important, on our major problems. I do not think the people will install a party which may seem less capable of governing as time goes on. I doubt if this fretful, distracted and divided Republican Party has that capacity. If it cannot govern itself, why should we suppose that it could govern the country?

Another way of saying the same thing is that the Democratic Party has policies. It has a foreign policy, and it has a domestic policy. Some Republican leaders like our policies; most Republican leaders hate our policies; but none of them seems to have any very distinctive policies of their own to offer.

We have policies, I think, because we have ideas. I know, of course, that the Democrats aren't supposed to have any ideas. We are supposed to be stale and weary and intellectually and morally bankrupt—except on the occasions when we are supposed to be so vital and energetic and overflowing with new ideas as to constitute a danger to the Republic—or, at least, to the Republicans. As for myself, I continue to regard the Democratic Party as the party of constructive change in this country. It is always time for constructive change, and that is what I hope we can continue to offer the American people.

In short, I know it will be a hard fight. I hope it will be a clean one. We have had a lot of ground to make up. We have made up some. I figure that we still have a little distance to go. But I think too that we are gaining steadily. As for more detailed predictions, I think I will leave that to you gentlemen!

Of course, the campaign itself bulks large in our eyes today. I would like to conclude with the warning that we must not let it obscure the outlines of the world crisis in which we are involved. This generation has been summoned to a great battle—the battle to determine whether we are equal to the task of world leadership. I am deeply persuaded that the press can be our shield and our spear in this battle. I believe Jefferson said, "If a nation expects to be ignorant and free in a state of civilization it expects what never was and never will be."

We must look largely to the press for the enlightenment that will arm us for this conflict. We should be able to look to the press for much of the sober certainty that will carry us to victory and peace. Our government and our arms and our wealth will avail us little if the editors do not accept this invitation to greatness. The agents of confusion and fear must not usurp the seats of the custodians of truth and patriotism.

In saying this, I want to emphasize my belief that the leadership for this development of a free press must come entirely from the profession itself. Government has its co-operative part to play. It must do everything possible to oppose censorship and to free the channels of communication. Beyond that point, it cannot safely go. The basic job can be done only within and by the free press itself, by you gentlemen. I know you can do it superbly. We have solemn reason to pray it will be done that way.

The People's Natural Resources

Civic Ice Arena

SEATTLE, WASHINGTON

September 8, 1952

If you treat me this well, you may never get rid of me—so, look out. I have read a lot of stories about the time when my grandfather campaigned in the State of Washington for the Vice Presidency, exactly sixty years ago this month. The big issue, I am told, at that time was whether your majestic mountain was to be named Mount Tacoma or Mount Rainier. Apparently, that was the only subject of interest in Washington at that time. Anyway, the views of Seattle and Tacoma were in violent disagreement and it seems that my adroit grandfather solved this difficulty by giving each audience from the rear platform of his train an eloquent speech about the beauties of the mountain, and then went on to say, "And I want everyone to know, all of you good people, that I emphatically agree that this magnificent mountain should be named—" And just then they pulled the whistle on the train and it started with a huff and a puff, and the old man bowed to the audience graciously and they cheered ecstatically.

Well, I tell you that story just to indicate that times have changed in political campaigns and I've got to come clean.

Tonight I find myself at the halfway mark in my first old-fashioned campaign trip. It seems a lot longer than four days ago that we left Springfield, Illinois, where my campaign headquarters, by the way, still are; we left there for Denver, Colorado, where my opponent's headquarters used to be until he suddenly left to find the fountain of truth in New York. Of course, last Friday may seem so long ago to me, mainly because we have covered so much ground since then. I think my party is perhaps the first in history

83

that ever went from Denver to Cheyenne by way of Minnesota. Before I got to bed at Billings, Montana, on Saturday night, I had abused the hospitality of Cheyenne by making a speech after I arrived.

I had some fun at the great roundup at Lewiston, Idaho, on the way; I might say that the other people there also had some fun because I didn't make a speech.

Today I spent with your great neighbor to the south, Portland, and tomorrow we go on to California and then home to Springfield by way of Arizona and New Mexico.

Now, if you don't like to travel, I suggest that none of you run for President, but if you do like to travel around this incomparable land of ours—and I do, whatever the voters may decide next November, I have had a rich and satisfying experience that I wish every single one of you could have. You have to see this country to believe in it and the more I see of it, the more I believe in it.

Although my trip is only half over—this first trip—I think we have in the last few days gone considerably beyond the halfway mark in trying to see what the issues are between the General and myself and what they are not.

In Denver, I pointed out that there is no issue between us in corruption in government; he is against it and so am I, and so far as I know, nobody is running on a pro-corruption ticket. What's more, I was against it in 1948, and that is the main reason the people of Illinois elected me as their Governor.

In Denver, I also said that there is no issue between either the General or myself or President Truman on the question of "time for a change." There could be no issue on this because the Democratic Party is the party of change—change for the better, change in men, change in methods, but not in the forward direction of policies which have produced a better life here at home and raised the hopes of free men for peace in the world at large.

In Minnesota, the General and I both spoke about farm policy from the same platform, a few hours apart. I couldn't but wonder why I had taken the trouble to make that long trip, all the way back to Minnesota from Denver, since I found on my arrival there that the General had been expounding the Democratic farm plank. Evidently, the Republican plank was lost by the movers somewhere between Denver and New York. However, it turned out to be a good thing that I did go to Minnesota because the General had given the Democratic plank such a warm bear hug that he cracked it, and I had to go back and do a little bone setting.

In Cheyenne, on Saturday night, I noted that the General's foreign policy, as he has so far unveiled it, resembles our own in every important respect—except, of course, the Democrats are administering it instead of the Republicans—except in one respect, and that is the early liberation of the enslaved peoples of Europe behind the Iron Curtain.

Now, the General has since been at some pains to say that he didn't mean it just that way. I hope so, but it seems to recur. At best, it may be only a little vote catching, this talk of liberation, cruel as it may be in terms of the illusory hopes it creates, but at worst, it has somber military implications when measured against the hard facts of life in Eastern Europe today. In any event, that is an issue between us and it will stay joined until the counsels of reason really prevail.

Now, I am told, my friends, that when Paul Bunyan reached the Northwest, he retired. The reason is easy to understand; he evidently couldn't stand the competition out here. Everything in the Northwest is built bigger or grown faster or produces more kilowatts than anything anywhere else in the world. At least so I have been confidentially informed by everyone I have met the last several days and I am willing to accept the statistics. I hope you will give the same treatment you have given to me to some of the Republican orators who are glooming around these days saying that the country is coming apart at the seams; I see no evidence of it out here.

The rapid growth of the Northwest is very significant for the future of the United States. It means that what used to be essentially a colonial domain, run by absentee industries, is now coming of age and playing its full part in the progress of our nation. A great part of what is going on here has been due to what my opponents are fond of calling a centralized, despotic bureaucracy, the Federal Government. Year after year we have been told how this ogre has been wasting the taxpayer's money in the Northwest on a series of fantastic projects.

This process of bankrupting the United States by wasting money on the Northwest has had a long history   t ace it at least as far back as 1867 and a certain Secretai,   state who was denounced for being soft toward Russia. At this moment we can hear

—or could if an unaccustomed mood of silence should come upon us—we could hear the whistles of steamers bound north for Seward's Folly. The development of Alaska has meant traffic, commerce, profits, population for the Northwest. Now, if you and I have our own way, Alaska will soon become a State in the Union.

The profligate waste of the taxpayer's money by a spendthrift bureaucracy has paid off. Seward's Folly has become both our wealth and our northern security outpost against the Russians.

Now, I draw a moral from this story, if I may. The moral is that the people who conduct the nation's business sometimes do know what they are doing, partisan assertions to the contrary notwithstanding.

Not far to the east of us tonight is that notorious white elephant, Grand Coulee Dam. Our atomic weapons would not have been developed without the power generated by Grand Coulee and Bonneville on the Columbia and by those other white elephants in the Tennessee Valley. The water stored in Grand Coulee is beginning to make fields and orchards of the barren land in the Columbia Basin.

In some people's view, you will remember, Grand Coulee and Bonneville were not only a waste of the taxpayer's money, they were—and it was still a worse crime—they were an interference with the sacred right of private monopoly to leave a region undeveloped. I will tell you what they were; they were Homer Bone's Folly, Charley McNary's Folly, and Franklin Roosevelt's Folly.

Thanks to the faith of men who could see future cities instead of present sagebrush; thanks, if I may state the blunt fact, to the courage of Democratic politicians, supported by a minority of progressive Republicans who in twelve years of Republican rule after 1920 had broken their hearts in fighting their own party's lethargic and hostile attitude toward Western development, these dams were built. One of them commemorates Senator McNary who, like another Republican Senator from the same State, Wayne Morse, never let his Republican friends stop him from voting for Democratic policies.

Now, I observe that far from diminishing, stifling or crippling private enterprise, these activities of the Federal Government have multiplied, stimulated and strengthened private enterprise in the Northwest and in the rest of the country too, for you cannot enrich one section without enriching all the others.

So I draw another moral. Works like Grand Coulee and Bonneville were beyond the capacity of private enterprise to undertake. If the Government had not built them they would not have been built at all. Hard American common sense concludes that where private enterprise is unable or unwilling to develop our resources, the Government should.

That is what we have been doing, usually against the opposition of the Republican leadership. And that is what we must keep on doing.

The battles in this field are by no means over. There will be opposition in the future as there has been opposition in the past, but the resource development in the West will go on because the people—not just the people of the West—the people of the whole country want it to go on.

When we invest in projects that more than pay for themselves, we act as prudent trustees of the public wealth, and our heirs will profit from our wisdom. But it is public funds we invest. The return on the investment must be real, not hypothetical, and the gains must be national and not merely local.

We must be eagle-eyed and we must be tight-fisted about these expenditures, and the blessings of the local interests are not enough to justify a public project. It must pass the harder test, it seems to me, of comparison—would this money be better spent on rehabilitating eroded farm land in the South or exhausted range land in the West, rather than on reclaiming a desert? And it must pass still another, more immediate test—is the coming fiscal year the one in which to start this investment of public funds at all?

These are hard, practical questions that must be faced. I have faced them in my own State. I know how complicated they are on a nationwide scale. Projects and proposals from all parts of the country compete for public investment. I am not sure that the office of President is well enough equipped, as things now stand, to appraise them with detachment and critical authority. The Hoover Commission has made suggestions for increasing the effectiveness of Executive review; it may be that even better means can be devised, and I propose to find out.

Building a public project, however, is only half the story. Bitter battles have been fought—and many of them are still unsettled—over who gets the good from public investment. There are always plenty of private interests that want to appropriate the benefits for themselves.

There are the examples of power. In an unbroken line from the turn of the century the policy of Congress has been that the benefits of power produced from public funds shall be spread widely, especially among domestic and rural consumers, and shall be sold at the lowest possible rates that will repay the investment with interest. To accomplish this, the laws provide that preference in the sale of public power should be given to co-operatives and public bodies and that public transmission lines may be built where necessary to reach them.

Here in the Northwest you have seen these policies work and work well. Your R.E.A. [Rural Electrification Administration] co-operatives, your public-utility districts and your municipal systems, as well as private utility companies, are tied in with the power-producing dams by the Government's backbone transmission system. Your power rates are low; your homes and farms use two or three times as much power as the average for the nation. Yet these Federal power policies are being fought right now as hard as they were ever fought in the past.

A second illustration is the national forests, whose protection and development by the Federal Government was once fought bitterly as interference with the rights of private enterprise and a waste of public funds. Today, the national forests are a vast resource of virgin timber and reforested areas. They are increasingly valuable to private timber operators, as the last available replacement for logged-out areas, and to all the industries that depend on a supply of forest products. They are of increasing value too for recreation, as the population of the Northwest increases.

Many forest problems remain to be solved; access roads for logging operations, fire-protection roads, trails and access roads for vacationists, loopholes in the mining laws that permit people who do no mining to cash in on timber or recreation. These must be solved, but there is a much bigger problem.

The greatest importance of the national forests is the protection of our watersheds. In many parts of the West, protection of the forests and of the grasslands means the difference between healthy streams and destructive loss of the water, dependable water supplies as against floods, silted-up irrigation systems and dams filling with sediment. That is why we must resist efforts to take away from the public the control of our forest ranges.

These battles for the public interest in our rivers, in our forests and our other natural resources must be won here on the spot and they must be won in the Congress.

We are only at the beginning of a long-term effort to make our resources match our needs. Just recently President Truman's Materials Policy Commission made some careful estimates about how much power, fuel and raw materials of all sorts the nation will need twenty-five years from now when its population is likely to be thirty or forty million larger. Their figures are startling, my friends. They estimate, for instance, that we may need four times as much aluminum as we are producing today and three times as much electric power.

To meet such demands will require our best efforts. We shall have to import from abroad large additional amounts of many materials, and that, incidentally, will have the helpful effect of gradually building a firmer basis for workable economic relationships among nations.

But we will have to do better than we have been doing with the resources within our own borders. Soil and water, fish and wildlife, forests and grasslands, minerals and waterpower—they are all related to one another in nature's order and we cannot separate the problems of one from those of all the others. Our approach must be unified on a wide front by integrated plans, by co-operative effort. This means better administrative arrangements within the Federal Government and intelligent and better co-ordinated action by states, by localities and by private enterprise. Most of all, it means better co-operation among all the agencies, public or private, that deal with natural resources.

I have emphasized these public policies tonight, because I am a candidate for office and I want to make clear where I stand on the problems a President must deal with. But I believe with all my heart that the job of wisely using the resources with which nature endowed the United States is very largely a job for private action. It requires every private landowner, every mine and timber operator, every man in private enterprise, to act with an eye for the public good as well as private gain. Because unto us much has been given, of us much shall be required. And I thoroughly believe that the generality of Americans are men of good will, who put the public good before their own gain.

There will always be selfish people; there will always be groups who try to turn our common inheritance to their private profit, and it will always be the job of government to restrain them. But there is too much talk of conflicting interests. The natural wealth of the United States is our common trust. We must husband and increase it for the future, and our emphasis must be not on rivalry or conflict but on co-operation.

In the United States we have always made our bet on tomorrow. We have always believed that the developing economy would make America steadily wiser and more powerful, and would spread the benefits of a rising standard of living more widely among our citizens. Generation by generation we have won that bet.

Now, in our time we confidently believe that there will be no halt in the process that has made us the richest and the most powerful nation on earth. We must be faithful and wise stewards of the riches we have inherited. We must imagine greatly, dare greatly and act greatly. For on what we do now the future will depend—the future not only of our people but of the whole world.

World Policy

I want to share with you, if I may, a letter from a California lady who knew my parents when they lived here fifty years ago. She writes that after Grover Cleveland was nominated for the Presidency in 1892 and my grandfather was nominated for Vice President, she named her two kittens Grover Cleveland and Adlai Stevenson. Grover, she writes me, couldn't stand the excitement of the campaign and died before the election. But Adlai lived to be a very old cat.

And this, my friends, is obviously for me the most comforting incident of the campaign so far.

As your chairman said, because of my prior service here [at the United Nations Conference in 1945] and because San Francisco is our window to the Far East, I want to talk soberly tonight about foreign policy.

We think and we talk a lot these days about our dangers. We should think and talk more about our opportunities as well.

Victory or defeat for a nation, as for a man, springs, first of all, from its attitudes toward the world. The men who built the West had victory in their hearts and songs on their lips. They were doers, not worriers. They really believed that the Lord helps those who help themselves.

There is something badly wrong, it seems to me, with the perspective of men who call the last ten years the "dismal decade."

And there is something odd, too, in a point of view which at once endorses the nation's foreign policies and promises to save you at the same time from such enlightened bungling.

It was some such curious mixture which was served up in Philadelphia on last Thursday. Now I am reluctant to believe that my honored opponent has been persuaded that bad history is good politics—perhaps he hopes that the Republican Old Guard will swallow his bitter pill of approval of our policies if it is sugar-coated with condemnation of Democrats.

At any rate, however we interpret it, his speech in Philadelphia does not dispose of foreign policy as an issue in this campaign. The General's ten-point foreign program, of which three points were "throw the rascals out," and seven were a recital of the same foreign-policy goals which the "Democratic rascals" have been following for years, does not, it seems to me, contribute much to our foreign-policy discussion.

But foreign policy consists of much more than the setting of goals. Even the extremist wing of the Republican Party will not really argue that peace and prosperity are bad or that the nation does not want allies.

The rub comes in doing anything to make progress toward these goals which we are glad the Republican candidates agree upon. A President can suggest but he cannot pass laws. That's the job of Congress.

And the most powerful and numerous wing of the Republican Party—the wing that would control all of the important Congressional committees—would not support the program which the Republican presidential candidate endorsed last Thursday.

How do I know? Well, because the Old Guard has been fighting that same identical program for years.

Let me illustrate.

My opponent spoke approvingly of foreign trade. Now, among other things, it is not exactly a new idea to Democrats that a thriving foreign trade means better markets for American agriculture and industry and a better balance in world economy.

I don't think even the Republicans will try to take credit for the Reciprocal Trade Agreements program. Certainly the Old Guard won't. It has been trying to wreck that program every time it comes up for renewal—as it does again next year.

I don't think that a Republican President could even get a bill to renew it out of a committee—not, at any rate, without crippling amendments. Or are we to assume that the Republican leaders in Congress have been opposing it in the past not from conviction but just because it was a Democratic program?

I could go on—talking of their attacks on our assistance program, even on the defense budgets, and similar knife work—for the Republican record in Congress is as long as it is wrong.

How, then, can a disunited party unite the country for the hard tasks that lie ahead? I don't think it can. No matter how great their commander, divided and embittered men do not win battles.

America is threatened as never before. The question history asks and which we must answer is whether the idea of individualism— the idea of personal freedom for you and me—is equal to the idea of collectivism—the idea of personal subordination to the state; whether the idea of maximum personal liberty is equal to the idea of maximum personal discipline.

This ancient contest between freedom and despotism, which is renewed in every generation, is acute in ours. And the most important single event, it seems to me, in our history is that it is our turn to be freedom's shield and sanctuary.

I don't think that war is an inevitable part of this contest. Even the most ambitious and ruthless men do not deliberately invite destruction of the basis of their power. They can throw the iron dice, but they know they cannot foretell the fortunes of war.

We who are free must have great strength in order that weakness will not tempt the ambitious. And the measure of the strength we must have is not what we would like to afford but what the adversary compels us to afford.

With 85 per cent of our budget allocated to defense, it is the Soviet Union which now fixes the level of our defense expenditures and thus of our tax rates. The only way to emancipate ourselves from this foreign control, and to cut taxes substantially, is first to develop our strength and then to find the means of ending the armaments race.

And here let me say something to those abroad who may mistake our present wrangling for weakness. We have always had differences of opinion which have produced all sorts of noises and confusion—especially in campaign years! But it is the kind of noise that, to the inner ear, is the sweet music of free institutions. It is the kind of noise that has produced the harmony of firm purpose whenever our people have been put to the test. The costliest blunders have been made by dictators who did not quite understand the workings of real democracy and who mistook diversity for disunity.

No one can predict, and it would be foolish to try to predict, how and when the peaceful purpose of our power will succeed in creating a just and durable peace. But are our efforts conditional upon assurance of prompt success? To answer "yes" would be to accept the certainty of eventual defeat.

Co-existence is not a form of passive acceptance of things as they are. It is waging the contest between freedom and tyranny by peaceful means. It will involve negotiation and adjustment—compromise but not appeasement—and I will never shrink from these if they would advance the world toward a secure peace.

Though progress may be slow, it can be steady and sure. A wise man does not try to hurry history. Many wars have been avoided by patience and many have been precipitated by reckless haste.

In Europe, our efforts to build patiently for peace are meeting with success. The Marshall Plan has brought, as we all know, a striking improvement in political and economic conditions. The North Atlantic Treaty Organization is building a strong system of military defense. Europe is not yet wholly secure against subversion from within or attack from without, but this goal of security is, at least, in sight.

I wish I could say the same for Asia, but there would be no greater disservice to the American people than to underestimate the gravity of the dangers that America faces in this area, perhaps for many years to come.

Now, it's about America's relations with Asia that I should like to talk with you tonight, soberly and realistically.

Across the continent of Asia more than a billion of the world's peoples are churning in one of history's greatest upheavals. All the struggles of man over the centuries—economic, political, spiritual —have come together in Asia and now seem to be reaching a climax.

The causes behind that upheaval are many and varied. But there is nothing complicated about what the people want. They want a decent living—and they want freedom.

The word used most frequently by Asians to describe their aspirations is nationalism.

Nationalism to Asians means a chance to stand on their own feet, a chance to govern themselves, a chance to develop their resources for their own welfare, and a chance to prove that the color of their skins has nothing to do with their right to walk with self-respect among their fellow men in the world. Nationalism to them means the end of a legalized inferiority. It means pride, spirit, faith.

This type of nationalism is not inconsistent with closer co-operation among nations nor with the need for an enforceable peace. The Asians actually regard freedom and national independence as the doorway to international order—just as we do.

Russia's interest in Asia is nothing new.

The expansionist aims of Russia did not change with the passing of the Czars. But today the steel glove of a revolutionary ideology covers the heavy hand of imperialist expansion.

The strategy of communism in Asia is to pose as the champion —the only champion—of the Asian peoples. Communism has not created the cause or the forces behind Asia's vast upheaval. It is attempting to give direction to those forces. It seeks to impose its own label on the multiple revolutions going on in Asia today by identifying itself with the deeply felt needs and hopes of the Asian peoples.

There's an important difference, it seems to me, between communism as we view it and communism as some of the Asian peoples view it. When we think of communism we think of what we are going to lose. When many of the Asiatics think of communism they think of what they are going to gain—especially if they believe that they have nothing to lose.

It's important that we know these things and think about them, for we shall never be able to cope with communism unless we understand the emotional basis of its appeal.

The communists have failed to incite the workers to revolution in Western Europe. They have failed to turn the Western Allies one against the other.

But the communists may well believe that in the aspirations and the grievances of the East they now have the key to world power. They hope, and perhaps even expect, that the West cannot rise to the challenge in the East.

Furthermore, they may not feel the same need for quick and tidy solutions that is felt in certain quarters in our own country. They may believe that they can afford to have a patience equal to the stakes involved.

And the stakes are nothing less than an overwhelming preponderance of power—for with Asia under control, they could turn with new energy and vast new resources in an effort to win a blood-less victory in a weakened, frightened Europe.

These communist expectations define the dimensions of the threat we face in Asia and of the tasks which lie ahead for us— tasks which can be met only by disciplined, resourceful, imaginative, and reasoned effort. It is an effort which has two parts: defense and development.

There is active fighting, as we all know, in Malaya and in In-do-China. Have we given fitting recognition to the hard, bitter and prolonged efforts of the British, the French, the native Malayan and Indo-Chinese forces? These efforts have involved heavy loss of life and great material costs.

What will the defensive task require of us in these areas, and in the Philippines, Formosa, Japan, and Korea? What contributions, what commitments to security in this area should we make and can we make to the emerging system of Pacific defense?

These are some of the questions, the hard, the ugly questions we must face before disaster, not afterward. This is no time, it seems to me, to kid ourselves with press agents' platitudes.

In Korea we took a long step toward building a security system in Asia. As an American I am proud that we had the courage to resist that ruthless, cynical aggression; and I am equally proud that we have had the fortitude to refuse to risk extension of that war despite extreme communist provocations and reckless Republican criticisms.

Whatever unscrupulous politicians may say to exploit grief, tragedy and discontent for votes, history will never record that Korea was a "useless" war, unless today's heroism is watered with tomorrow's cowardice.

On other occasions I have spoken and written much about the solid accomplishments which the Korean war has made possible. Tonight let me say only this:

I believe we may in time look back at Korea as a major turning point in history—a turning point which led not to another terrible war, but to the first historic demonstration that an effective system of collective security *is* possible.

Having failed to defeat us on the field of battle, the enemy there now seeks to defeat us by prolonging the negotiations and by exhausting our patience.

But some men in this country seem to think that if definitive victory cannot be won, we should either take reckless military action or give the whole thing up. Such advice plays into the enemy's hands. The contest with tyranny is not a hundred-yard dash—it is a test of endurance.

This defensive effort in Korea and elsewhere in Asia is building a shield behind which we have the opportunity to assist in the other great task—the task of development.

Listening to the debate over China this past year, I had the distinct impression at times that the very Congressmen whose vocal cords were most active in the cause of isolation and against foreign entanglements were the same ones who were now talking as if they had wanted us to take part in a civil war in China.

The time to stop a revolution is at the beginning, not the end. But I don't recall any pleas from these critics for help for Sun Yat-sen and Chinese democracy back in the twenties. Nor did I hear them demanding intervention by the United States in the mid-thirties when civil war with the communists broke out. Indeed it was not until quite recently, when the Chinese wars were about over, that there was even an audible whisper that we help fight a hindsight war, that we should have given more help to China than we did.

It would seem to me, my friends, that the Republican critics could better demonstrate the good faith of their concern for Asia by doing something about India and Pakistan today rather than talking about China yesterday. I don't think that tearful and interminable post-mortems about China will save any souls for democracy in the rest of Asia, the Near East and in Africa.

India is not caught up in civil strife. It can be helped in a way that is natural to us and best for it; help in the ways of peace and of social progress. India has to grow more food. It has to restore its land. It needs new resources of power. In short, it needs a democratic helping hand in the development programs it has already charted for itself.

The same is true of many other countries.

It is help of this kind that we can provide by sending agricultural experts, engineers and other trained people to these countries, and through programs of assistance to economic development.

By working with each country to expand the production of goods which are needed by other countries in the region, a self-generating and self-financing cycle of trade and development can be initiated, which will reduce and can eventually eliminate the need for American aid. At the same time, we can enlarge our export markets and develop new sources of the products we need to import.

Land reform is, of course, fundamental to the problem of Asia. But in these ways and by this kind of friendly advice and counsel we can help to guide this economic development in ways which will give powerful support to democratic political institutions.

These programs are in accordance, it seems to me, with our best traditions. And I want to assure our friends in Asia that America will never seek to dominate their political and their economic development. We will not try to make their societies over in the image of our own. On the contrary, we respect the integrity of their institutions and the rich values of their cultures. We expect to learn as well as to teach.

These programs are primarily concerned with the material needs and wants of individual men and women. Yet we do not make the mistake of believing that the answer to communist materialism is a different brand of materialism.

The answer to communism is, in the old-fashioned phrase, good works—good works inspired by love and dedicated to the whole man. The answer to the inhumanity of communism is humane respect for the individual. And the men and the women of Asia desire not only to rise from wretchedness of the body but from abasement of the spirit as well.

In other words, we must strive for a harmony of means and of ends in our relations with Asia—and indeed with the rest of the world. The means of our co-operation are primarily material.

If we believe the communist threat to Asia is dangerous to us, then it is in our own self-interest to help them defend and develop, adjusting our policies to the constantly changing circumstances in a world of accelerating change. But we must not, in our necessary concern for the urgent tasks of defense and development, permit the means to obscure the end. That end is the widening and the deepening of freedom and of respect for the dignity and the worth of man.

Some may say to you that this is visionary stuff. To this I reply that history has shown again and again that the self-styled realists are the real visionaries—for their eyes are fixed on a past that cannot be recaptured. It was Woodrow Wilson, with his dream of the League of Nations, who was the truly practical man—not the Old Guard who fought him to the death. And in the fateful summer of 1940 it was the vision of a Churchill that saw beyond Dunkerque to victory.

I say that America has been called to greatness. The summons of the twentieth century is a summons to our vision, to our humanity, to our practicality. If these provide the common purpose of America and Asia, of our joint enterprise, of our progress together, we need have no fear for the future. Because it will belong to free men.

On Political Morality

Town Hall Luncheon

LOS ANGELES, CALIFORNIA

September 11, 1952

I was born in Los Angeles. I have often thought that if my parents concluded to remove me at a very early age that the least they could have done was to endow me with some Los Angeles real estate, which might have been an easier way to earn a living than running for President.

The last time I was in this room was in May of 1942—ten years ago—with my beloved and celebrated boss at that time, Colonel Frank Knox, the Secretary of the Navy. He made a much better speech to you at that time than I will today, and I know because I wrote both of them.

Now, I am persuaded that congenitally, as well as a candidate, I talk entirely too much. I think of those imperishable words of Disraeli when a callow, new member of the House of Commons approached him and said earnestly, "Mr. Prime Minister, do you think I should participate very actively in the debates?" and Disraeli gave him an appraising glance and said to him, "No, I don't think you'd better; I think it would be better if the House were to wonder why you didn't talk, rather than why you did."

Personally, I couldn't agree more, but a candidate has to talk, I suppose, and I think he should talk as plainly as possible about public questions, and admit what he doesn't know and what he can't answer. If he purported to know the right answer to everything, he would be either a knave or a fool. If he even had an answer to everything, he would probably be just a fool. If he had no emphatic views at all, he would probably be just as unworthy, and if he were evasive, he would probably be either cunning or a political coward, of which we have altogether too many. And, finally, if he should arrive at election time with almost everybody satisfied, then you should, by all means, vote against him as the most dangerous charlatan of them all. In other words, you of Town Hall who try to vote intelligently have quite a chore.

From my brief experience in Illinois, I am persuaded that forthright discussion of the real public questions is neither beneath the dignity of political candidates nor above the intelligence of the American people. And it most certainly is the condition precedent to any intelligent choice, except by the faculty of intuition which is by no means infallible in these days of ghosts and press agents.

I wanted to talk to you about politics and I suppose I'm qualified by ignorance to talk about politics because I have been in politics barely four years. There are some politicians who don't think I'm in yet, and others who expect me to be out of it very soon.

Andrew Oliver said in Boston more than 150 years ago: "Politics is the most hazardous of all professions. There is not another in which a man can hope to do so much good to his fellow creatures; neither is there any in which by a mere loss of nerve he may do such widespread harm; nor is there another in which he may so easily lose his own soul; nor is there another in which a positive and strict veracity is so difficult. But danger is the inseparable companion of honor. With all the temptations and degradations that beset it, politics is still the noblest career any man can choose."

Now, I emphatically agree to the hazards and the dangers part of that quotation from Oliver, but how about the honor and nobility. That "politics" and "politicians" have become words of disrepute and abuse, epithets if you please, instead of words of honor and respect is nothing new, but it seems to me paradoxical and very sad in a republic governed by the governed.

More recently than Oliver's comment of 150 years ago, Bernard Shaw said that democracy is a device that insures that we shall be governed no better than we deserve.

Whose fault is it, then, that we get what we deserve in government and that the honor and the nobility of politics at most levels are empty phrases?

Well, having asked you the question, I shall hastily answer it myself by saying that it isn't the lower order of the genus "pol," but it is the fault of you, the people. Your public servants serve you right; indeed often they serve you better than your apathy and indifference deserve.

But I suggest that there is always time to repent and mend your ways. However, you won't mend your ways just by redoubling your resolve to help your favorite candidate for President, including even the Governor of Illinois. No, repentance of your sins is much more difficult than that because there are the little matters of precinct committeemen or state committeemen, state's attorneys, sheriffs, county commissioners, aldermen, councilmen, mayors, governors, congressmen, judges and all the elaborate paraphernalia of our democratic system of popular choice. The whole is the sum of the parts and the whole will be no better than the parts. So I say to you, look to the parts, not just to the major parts, but all the parts in this elaborate mechanism. It will keep you busy a lot of your time, but it will be worth it. You might even end up by getting infected yourself and running for something, and that would be a very good thing indeed.

It seems to me that government is like a pump, and what it pumps up is just what we are, a fair sample of the intellect, the ethics and the morals of the people, no better, no worse.

Well, you say that this sort of pious preaching about better citizenship is grammar-school stuff and that everybody has said the same thing since Plato did, and so they have. And also we have been complaining about government ever since Plato—at least when the human race has dared to complain about its managers. Here and there, now and then, we do something, as you have done in California under your honored and esteemed Governor, Earl Warren. Indeed, I'm optimistic that things are getting better on the whole, especially since we have been slugged in that most sensitive of all our parts—the pocketbook—as never before. But there is a very long way to go.

So I should like to lecture to you a bit about the self-education of voters who want to expiate their sins, if any. I mean if there are any such voters, not sins.

In the London *Times* Literary Supplement, I recently saw this in a review of two American books:

"The cleaning-up of American civic and political life is the prerequisite of any cleaning-up of crime and criminals. It is no use blaming the police for winking at the bookies when the elected sheriff and a whole raft of elected judges are paid from their takings. It is no use blaming the law-enforcement officers if the mass of the people do not respect the law, do not want it for themselves and their families and pay to break it, which is what happens with gambling, slot-machines, liquor in dry States and so on and so on."

I agree with that quote emphatically. You are not going to clean up crime and corruption until you clean up American civic and political life. And who is going to do that? You are, or it isn't going to be done.

In Illinois, I've moved against the slot-machine and local gambling by using the state police where local officials refused to do their duty. The good people applauded, but they went right on playing the slot-machines in their country clubs, lodges, and veterans' posts.

But, my friends, if it is against the law in the corner saloon, it is against the law in the country club, too. And how much respect and how much leadership are the citizens going to have who practice a double standard of law observance? They have stopped their own mouths and tied their own hands, but they still complain about law enforcement.

And what would you think about the banker who complains when you clean up gambling in his town because it reduces bank deposits? Or the real-estate owner who complains that the tenants don't pay as much rent when the restaurant or tavern on the ground floor has to stop gambling? I've had those experiences and many more besides, including all of the varieties of businessmen who will corrupt a state inspector to disregard some law violation. I can fire the inspector if I can catch him, but I can't fire the businessman.

Corruption in government is the only issue in this campaign, according to my very distinguished opponent. I think he means it is the only issue that the various factions of the Republican Party can agree upon, probably. But, my friends, it should be an issue in every campaign for every office from top to bottom of our elaborate political hierarchy, not just this year but every year, because whether you believe in the pump analogy in our political life or not, the responsibility for our moral standards rests heaviest upon the men and women in public life, because public confidence in the integrity of the government is indispensable to faith in democracy. When we lose faith in the system, we have lost faith in everything we fight and stand for. And then there is always that sinister man on horseback waiting in the wings to ride in when we get so discontented that we look for the ultimate solution, and the solution always has its lamentable and inevitable consequences with which we are so familiar, or should be.

As a Democrat, as an office-holder, an aspirant for the greatest office on earth, I do not, I have not, I will not condone, excuse, or explain away wrongdoing or moral obliquity in public office, whoever the guilty or wherever they are stationed. What's more, I have had the satisfaction of firing and prosecuting a good many. One dishonest public official is one too many. A dishonest official is as faithless to his party as he is to his office, and our political parties must never founder on the rocks of moral equivocation.

There have been cases of corruption, of bribery, and of venality involving a minute fraction of all of the tens of thousands of people in Federal service. Many of these cases have been discovered and exposed—I am happy to say, by Democrats—especially by Democratic Senators and Congressmen keeping watch over the spending of the public funds. I need only mention here such names as Senator Kefauver, Senator Douglas, Senator Fulbright, Stuart Symington, your own Congressman Cecil King of Inglewood, Congressman Frank Chelf of Kentucky, and many others. In fact, I induced an old personal friend of mine, Steve Mitchell, who as a public service—one of many—has lately been counsel to the Chelf Committee conducting the investigation of the Department of Justice, to let me nominate him for Chairman of the Democratic National Committee.

And I am reminded of what Justice Charles Evans Hughes said during the Harding era scandals. He said this: "Neither political party has a monopoly of virtue or of rascality. Let wrong be exposed and punished, but let no partisan Pecksniffs affect a 'holier than thou' attitude. Guilt is personal and knows no party."

But there is a great danger in this very healthy public discussion of corruption in government which I hope gentlemen like you do not overlook. The problem of government is the problem of recruiting first-rate personnel. Basically that is the problem, just as it is the major problem in your business. The reward for honest, able public service is too often complaint, criticism, abuse and ingratitude. It would be a tragic disaster if we forgot the tens of thousands of honest, conscientious public servants. Generalities about crime and corruption in government which embrace the many good with the few bad can only make it harder to induce good people to enter public service. We do not lose faith in the

banking system because a few bankers turn out to be embezzlers.
When you realize that American private business is swindled out
of more than a billion dollars each year by its employes, from
clerks to executives, it is not too remarkable, however deplorable,
that government should occasionally be swindled.

For the information of the public and the morale of the multi-
tude of decent, faithful men and women on whom government depends, it is just as important to recognize and support the good as
it is to root out and to punish the bad. It bodes no good for the
public service where recruitment is none too easy anyway, what
with the salary competition of private business, when honest, conscientious public servants quit, because they don't care to be
abused and ridiculed any longer. I know what I am talking about.
I am the Governor of one of the largest States in the Union, and
I have had my recruitment problems.

Only last week a very good friend of mine—a Republican from
Chicago—told me that a revenue agent had been in to audit his
return. He fell into conversation with him, and this able young
lawyer, a recent graduate from a well-known law school who was
doing this work for experience, said, "I am going to quit. I have
been treated by businessmen and taxpayers as though I might be
a thief, not they."

Look at it not alone from the point of view of its mischievous
effect on a gullible public, but also from the point of view of the
consequences to the public service as a whole. I wonder how much
the people know of the stifling, the choking effect of irresponsible
witch hunting, the paralysis of initiative, the hesitancy and the
intimidation that follow in the wake of broad, generalized accusations and inhibit the bold, imaginative thought and discussion
which is the anvil of public policy.

I'm frank to say I get a little confused about corruption in
politics. We tend to think of it as something so simple, in the
unsophisticated terms of graft—of cash on the barrelhead. But its
forms are many, and I think of another which we witness every
day, and to which I have become acutely sensitive in my brief experience in public service.

Perhaps the proper description is not "corrupt," but "expedient" for the legislator, be he in Sacramento, in Springfield, Illinois,
or in Washington, D. C., who will vote for all kinds of special-

interest bills to catch or to hold some votes while he prates piously about economy, and indignantly about waste.

Call that what you will, condone it as you please, even profit from it as you do now and then, its cost to you is infinitely greater than the thievery and rascality that capture the headlines.

Have you ever heard of a candidate who was against economy and efficiency? Of course not. It is part of the standard repertoire. Everybody is for economy, efficiency and honesty, and against waste, sin, corruption and communism. But how about the log-rolling, the lobbying for laws or their repeal to serve the interest of some group at the public expense? To catch some votes, or for fear of losing some, many things are done which seem to me hard to distinguish from outright bribery. Yet, we will condone the one and condemn the other. I have seen many legislators vote for every appropriation during a legislative session, and against every tax, and babble about economy and fiscal responsibility at the very same time, and so have you.

And, what's more, they will be elected over and over again.

In the last session of my legislature in Illinois I presented a very tight budget that called for no tax increases, in spite of all the cost increases in the previous two years. And, I called upon the legislature not to add to that budget without subtracting from it in order to keep it in balance. What do you think they did? They subtracted $300,000 and added $50,000,000. I hope it isn't indelicate to advise you that it was an overwhelmingly Republican legislature in both Houses.

The Republican leader, in that session, sponsored and passed a bill to increase all old-age pension allotments 10 per cent automatically, although we have a system of automatic adjustments in accordance with living costs. The cost of that measure we estimated at roughly fourteen million, but he made no effort whatever to provide any of the money with which to pay for it.

I noted in my veto message that they had omitted from the bill the dependent children and the recipients of general relief—I suppose because they were not organized politically.

I could entertain you at some length with the difficulty I had to get one Republican vote to cut a large appropriation and thereby balance the budget at all, in the previous session. Indeed, if I recounted all my experiences of this kind I am afraid you might get the impression that I am slightly partisan. But I am sure you will forgive me if I say that from where I sit the carefully cultivated impression that Democrats are all extravagant and Republicans are all provident is a fairy tale and part of the phony folklore that a careful citizen will examine carefully.

And perhaps you will also, on closer consideration of the performance—timid, expedient, demagogic, or worse—of a lot of people in public office, share with me the growing confusion about ethics and morals and corruption in our public life. Surely there must be some higher standard and some better test than simple bribery for cash.

But I daresay that the only way that we will attain some higher standard of ethics, and of responsibility and courage in public life will be compounded heavily of forbearance yourselves from exerting pressures for selfish ends, plus some positive applause and tangible support for the guy who is playing it straight, morally and ethically, as well as legally, in spite of the fact that you will probably not agree with him on the merits of issues and actions many times. Indeed, sometimes he may not even bear your party label.

And, bear in mind too, that the special-interest people, especially what we call the hoodlums and the gangsters, are always very free with campaign contributions for the right candidates at the right time.

But, enough of this. Just remember that all that's gold to a politician does not glitter, and that to be good and stay in office he needs a lot of help—from people who don't want anything from him except to be good.

For far too many of us the Presidential election is a quadrennial orgy of absorption in political matters, all centering around the single issue of the identity of the man who will serve as President for the next four years.

It seems to me to contain some subconscious element of expiation for past sins. It is as if that large percentage of us who pay no attention to politics and to government for three years remorsefully seek to repair this deficiency by talking the longest and the loudest in the fourth year about the importance of electing the right man—our man—to the highest public office of all. If the people at large can only be brought to understand the wisdom of what we are shouting, and elect our man, then the nation will be safe for at least four more years; we have discharged our responsibilities as citizens—a little tardily perhaps, but nonetheless adequately and effectively—and can then turn exclusively to other concerns until the time rolls around again when we must once more clamorously assure the national salvation.

Now, I say we must rid ourselves of the easy notion that the right man in one job solves all of our problems. We need to level out this sharp but narrow peak of citizen interest in politics and government in Presidential years with the long and deep valleys of apathy that lie in between.

There are other pitfalls to be found in our traditional habits of thinking about politics and about party leaders. We like to reduce complex issues to simple slogans. Better still, we like to deal in personalities to the exclusion of issues. And, to the extent we must unavoidably get into issues at all, we like to weave them all into a single sort of brightly colored cloak which will cover our man completely and distinguish him clearly from his competitors. This creates the comfortable delusion that we have not subordinated principles to personality, and that we know exactly where our man stands on everything.

Most importantly, it lends itself beautifully to the oversimplified kind of argument we love so much, in which we can throw around freely the short, sharp, fighting—and meaningless—words like "liberal," "conservative," "leftist," "rightist," "socialist," "fascist," "communist," and all of their shopworn and barren brood.

These are all conventions which afflict the laymen as well as the party professionals.

Another conventional belief of politicians is what I call the myth of monolithic voting—the idea that all the votes in a bloc go one way or the other in response to the candidate's willingness to go along with the official positions of the bloc.

I think it's a myth and, if I am right, I believe this to be one of the most hopeful and reassuring elements in our democracy. The myth operates to frighten and to stampede many officeholders into doing things against their own inclinations and their own better judgment. Its exposure is the beginning of real statesmanship for many who have been taken in by it.

Large organizations of Americans simply do not vote uniformly in support of what are represented to be their special interests or predilections. And that is true whatever the nature of the tie that binds the group together and apparently sets it apart from its fellow men, whether it be religion, economic circumstance, geographical attachment or other divisive factors.

The Senatorial election in Ohio in 1950 was a most persuasive demonstration in this important regard.

I had a similar experience in Illinois with the State Federation of Labor in 1948. Last year I vetoed five of the nine bills passed by the Illinois legislature and included within the official legislative program of the Illinois Department of the American Legion. I vetoed special-interest bills of all kinds calling for more than $40,000,000 of appropriation. And I was solemnly warned in every case that I would lose all of the votes of the groups affected.

Probably it's a mighty good thing I didn't run for Governor. I wouldn't have gotten a vote in the State!

Well, my friends, I didn't believe it in 1948, and I don't believe it now, although if I should return to Los Angeles as a private citizen after the first of the year, I should be glad to have lunch with you again—and eat crow.

In any event, and whatever my own fate as a politician, I do know that sound government ends when the leaders of special groups call the tune, whether they represent capital, labor, farmers, veterans, pensioners, or anyone else. And I am convinced that the public servant who does the right thing, no matter whose toes are stepped on, does not lose all of the votes of the hands which go with those toes.

Now, there is something else I should like to mention. The twenty years since the Japanese invaded Manchuria and the Democrats invaded Washington has been a period of change as rapid and as violent as any in our history. The forces that demanded change shattered many societies. We have contained them within the American system of democratic government, popular control, and civil liberty.

There has been no break in the continuity of our institutions. The United States has held to the course of development which it has been following for 150 years. This triumph of stability in a time of world revolution was not accomplished by pretending that there were short cuts to safety, and to prosperity, to freedom, or social justice, or that they could be bought at a discount. And we must not minimize the difficulties or dangers now in the Presidential campaign year.

I say this to you, in conclusion, because I would not have you think that I believe that all there is to good government is honesty and efficiency. These are only means to an end. In the tragic days of Mussolini the trains in Italy ran on time as never before. I am told in their way—in their horrible way—that the Nazi concentration-camp system in Germany was a model of hideous efficiency.

The really basic thing in government is policy. Bad administration, to be sure, can destroy good policy; but good administration can never save bad policy.

So, what I beg of you to ponder in all your governmental judgments is not just how to do a job, but—and far more important—what to do.

And, if you can find a man who knows both what to do and how to do it, well, you are very lucky indeed.

The American Future

Shrine Auditorium

LOS ANGELES, CALIFORNIA

September 11, 1952

Coming to Los Angeles is doubly an occasion for me. This is, first of all, a homecoming—a return, in rather unexpected circumstances and under most agreeable sponsorship, to the city of my birth.

I was afraid that I had lost all claim to your regard by deserting California for Illinois even at the age of five. But the warmth of your welcome, the resolution of the City Council, the affecting ceremony at the home where I was born, today, have touched me deeply and have made me very happy. I am very much your debtor and very grateful.

But more than that, coming back to Los Angeles is a reminder and a most compelling reminder that the central fact of American life is growth. Few communities in our land provide a better ringside seat for this phenomenon of growth than Los Angeles. My memories of this city in 1900, when I first opened my eyes somewhere near West Adams Boulevard, are not exactly vivid or detailed. But I venture that few would dispute me when I suggest that the home town has changed a little in the last fifty-two years. Not only has it spawned new suburbs, new houses, new fashions, new industries, and even new religions, but today I am reliably informed its continued expansion threatens to swallow up most of the territory west of the Rockies, and even a portion of the Pacific Ocean.

Our whole nation has undergone an unprecedented expansion in the past twenty years, but the West has shown the way to the rest of us. During the 1940's, while the total population of the country rose about 15 per cent, the population of the West increased 41 per cent. Industry and agriculture and government have kept pace with the demands of the growing population. And thus we move ahead. The American people—restless, inquisitive, creative—are everlastingly in search of new frontiers. As long as that search continues, so long will we as a nation continue to grow.

I think that that search and that growth will continue for a long, long time. I know there are voices of despair in the land. We are told that the American future is black and melancholy. We are told that our people have grown soft—that they have lost their initiative, their independence, their self-reliance, even their morals. We are told that our economy is so feeble and fragile that it will collapse under the strain of adversity and the strain of growth. We are told that our free government cannot rise to new problems without the people losing their freedom.

And all these wails and lamentations about the future, however they begin, always end by a singular coincidence on a uniform note that the only way to preserve the Constitution and save the Republic and the honor of Americans is to elect Republicans in November. And I mean all Republicans—good, bad and indifferent.

The General doesn't even want one Democrat on his team. I hate, my friends, to think that Democrats are all as bad as that. Perhaps it is heresy, but I am frank to say to you that some of my best friends are Republicans. I have induced Republicans to help me in the Government of Illinois—and I might even need some in Washington. In fact, I think some Republicans are just about as good as Democrats. And, within that very limited category I include the great governor of this, my native state—Earl Warren.

Now, I am beginning to suspect my very old party loyalty in contrast to my opponent's recently acquired loyalty. The whole thing rather reminds me, my friends, of the remark of a recently hired employe of the State of Illinois, who said, "Ever since I have had a State job I have been a Democrat all my life."

There are two respects in which the Republican leadership have a wonderfully consistent record: They never speak well of Democrats—in fact, they don't even speak well of one another any more; and, they have always been afraid of tomorrow. Seldom has there been a bold idea for building America bigger and stronger for the future but that Republican voices say, "You can't do that." The Republican leadership talks big but it acts small. Time after time it has underestimated the needs and the wants and the demands of this country and of its people. We have met great power needs, great irrigation needs, great resource needs in the last twenty years, but each move to meet them has been systematically opposed or attacked, or undercut by members of the Party of the Past—and you know whom I mean. I mean the boys whose elephant cannot figure out whether to follow its trunk or its tail.

Now, of course, I suppose all of this government activity is what they call socialism—creeping or crawling. I am no more in favor of socialism than anybody else, and I particularly dislike things that creep. But if I don't like what they call creeping socialism, there is something else I dislike just as much, and that is galloping reaction.

Let me make one thing forever clear. The Democratic Party has no fear of tomorrow. We have limitless faith in the American future. And we Democrats can take a lot of satisfaction in the record of growth during the last twenty years, but we would not be Democrats if we rested on our haunches, or our laurels. You can't live on laurel leaves. We prefer rather to look forward and see what lies ahead in the next twenty years, and to start now to build for a still greater America.

In the next twenty years the population of the United States will probably increase by more than thirty million persons. This means more than thirty million more Americans who will require food, clothing and shelter; and who will be educated and reared in the tenets of religious belief and the traditions of a free democracy; and who will demand a standard of living far higher than ours— far higher than any the world has ever known. It means that twenty years from now this country must be able to provide nearly eighty million jobs, and that means more people at work than the total population of the United States when I was born here in Los Angeles fifty-two years ago.

This is the challenge of the future. Before we can meet it, we must, of course, resolve our critical day-to-day problems—problems which require immediate decision and action.

But while statesmanship consists sometimes not so much in knowing what to do ultimately as in what to do now, it is the part of natural wisdom to look beyond this turbulent period of history, even as Los Angeles must look beyond its present to its future needs for many things—for water, for example.

What kind of country will this be for our children and our children's children? How can we meet the requirements of the new age? I don't think that we will alter the basic structure of our society. Our national commitment is to a free economy—to the belief that an economic system based on freedom of choice, freedom of opportunity and freedom of decision is more productive and creative than any system devised by man. We will not abandon our free-enterprise system. We will oppose all attempts to limit its freedom whether by centralized government or by private monopoly.

Now, my friends, the foundation of any economy is its natural resources. The new technological era toward which we are moving will make ever-growing drains upon our resources. If we are to maintain our growth we must prepare for the future prosperity of our nation and we must make those preparations today while there is still time—not twenty years from now when it may be too late.

The resources problem is partly a problem of the wise use of the things we know we have and partly the problem of discovering how to use things that have never been useful before. In the last twenty years we have recognized that our land, and what lies beneath it, is a natural patrimony. It is a reserve for all of the people, to be utilized and developed in terms of our national welfare and of the strength and of the security of the free world.

The relationship between industry and resources development grows closer every day. Every day we are learning how the interactions of soil, and fertilizer, and water, and power can grow more and better things that can never be permanently exhausted.

It may not be many years, for example, before you people of Los Angeles can get your drinking water from the sea. Already our scientists have made great progress in turning salt water into fresh. And, there are further miracles in the scientific test tubes—above all the exciting possibilities of new sources of energy. The extraction of oil from shales will soon create one more new industry in the West. Government and private industry both have vital parts to play in these developments which hold for the future possibilities larger and more exciting perhaps than the invention of the steam engine itself.

And that is only one phase of the future. Another lies in our growing control of the power in the atom. As you in the West well know, whole new cities have risen since 1940—Hanford in Washington; Arco in Idaho; Los Alamos in New Mexico—in response to this atomic age, so far only at its dawn.

Should we follow the elephant's tail away from these horizons? Or should we go forward?

This new America will be a healthier America. Our children will have a vastly increased life expectancy. To attain this goal we shall need more medical research, more hospitals, more public-health agencies, more medical schools, more doctors and nurses—and some system of protection against the economic disasters of severe illness and accident, so that adequate medical care will be available for all.

I look forward to more and better housing for our people. In the past seven years more than eight million new homes have been built, and you people in Southern California can believe that huge figure because you can see so many of those new homes with your own eyes. This progress must be continued so that all Americans will have an opportunity to get decent housing—and public housing has a role to play in this problem.

I look forward to an America with improved education. We have made great progress in twenty years which we cannot stop until we have banished illiteracy and enlarged the educational opportunities of all of the boys and girls in this land.

I look forward to an America, my friends, which can take proper care of its aged and its invalids, and which can provide strong and expanding security for all of its workers. I rejoice in the Democratic Party's record in the establishment and the development of social security; and I endorse its pledge of a stronger system of unemployment insurance.

There are those who say that social security and protection against the hazards of life in our industrial society are undermining our self-reliance. And I agree that you can't bring about prosperity by discouraging thrift. But, I don't believe that our public-assistance programs have had that effect. On the contrary, they tend to stabilize our economy, reduce anxieties and lift the level of opportunity.

I look forward to an America united in its national belief in equal rights for all its citizens. We can never stop in the battle against racial and religious bigotry, discrimination and fear. We must ensure equal opportunities of employment for citizens of all colors and creeds. Given our resources, given the productivity of our economic system, given the magic of the new technology, given the undeveloped potentialities of electrical, chemical and atomic power, given the wise use of our wealth in the service of our people, we have within our grasp the possibilities of an un-dreamed-of future.

The American faith has been a faith in the growth of our nation and in a just distribution of the wealth among all of our citizens. And that faith stands today on the verge of its most dramatic realization. We stand on the threshold. The question is whether we have the will to cross that threshold and move into the new era ahead. The struggle between faith and fear will decide the destiny of our nation. Today we stand bewildered and tormented by many fears, some real, some imaginary. There is the fear of war; there is the fear of depression; and the fear of communism; and the fear of ourselves. I would not decry these fears. Without fear we would never act in time to save ourselves, but I would warn with all of the certainty that I possess against permitting fear to seize our mind, to cloud our brain and to paralyze our will.

The fear of war, my friends, is a real fear, but this danger can be met if we recognize that the best deterrent against totalitarian aggression is our strength and our resolution.

I hold out no easy solution to the problem of peace. I reject those who tell you that we can make the Soviet danger vanish by giving one-shot solutions, whether the solution is to retreat behind our frontiers, as one of the Republican Parties suggests, or stir up insurrection in Eastern Europe, which seems to be the doctrine of the other Republican Party. But I do say that the policy of building the strength and the unity of free nations will reduce the haunting fear of war.

The fear of depression is a real fear. But this danger can be met if we have a government determined to pursue a positive policy to prevent depression and to control inflation. I have confidence in the capacity of the American people to steer an ever-expanding economy without running it over a cliff—if their leaders in government are prepared to combat inflation or depression by something more than moans, threats and incantations.

The fear of communism is a real fear. We are confronted, at home and abroad, by a vast international conspiracy. We must, at home and abroad, take measures to protect ourselves. All loyal Americans know today that communism is incompatible with American life. We have driven them out of any places of responsibility that they may have gained in our society. We will expose and identify them at every step along the way.

And then there is the fear of ourselves. I submit to you, it is not a real fear. The real fears of war, of depression, of communism, have stirred up a fantasy of fear in which those who live by the fear of others have had a field day.

Americans do not have to go about in fear and distrust of one another. At least the Democratic Party does not believe so, and I don't think that the rank and file of the Republican Party believes so either. We have, in short, faith in the American people and in the American future.

I do not wish to belittle the towering problems which loom over us at this moment. In other speeches I have described my present policies in some detail; and I propose to continue to lay out these ideas in plain language in speeches to come. We cannot move into the future until we have surmounted the present, but we cannot surmount the present until we know where we ultimately intend to go.

I could not come to the West—the region of the future—and to Los Angeles, the city of the future—without registering my ringing confidence in the capacity of our nation to cope with tomorrow. Stern and exacting moments lie immediately ahead of us. We will be still some time in a dark valley. I cannot promise easy deliverance from the perils of this anguished age.

But I do say to you soberly and sincerely that on the evidence of science, of technology, and of our own common sense, the United States at mid-century stands on the threshold of abundance for all, so great as to exceed the happiest dreams of the pioneers who opened up this vast Western country.

Unless we allow ourselves to be held back by fear, we shall in God's good time realize the golden promise of our future. Let us reject, I say, the prophets of fear and the Party of the Past. Let us move ahead, proud and unafraid—confident of our capacity to meet the challenge of today and to realize the infinite possibility of tomorrow.

Campaign Issues

Fox Theater

PHOENIX, ARIZONA

September 12, 1952

I couldn't but notice, as I walked into this theater that the motion picture playing here now is called, "The Lure of the Wilderness." Well, I am delighted to be the star of this attraction for one afternoon—and if we can but lure enough votes to the Democratic ticket in November, I think we will save the country from a Republican wilderness.

The last time I was in Phoenix I spent my time out somewhere near town in a charming guest ranch, lying in the sun. On this visit I seem to spend my time standing in a spotlight. If you could arrange for me to come back here to lie in the sun again, it will be quite agreeable with me.

There must be something both therapeutically and also politically valuable about that sun, because when I came here today I met an old and dear friend, sprung from a staunch Republican family in Illinois, who has moved to Arizona and joined the Democratic Party!

It reminded me of the story of the little boy who asked his father what a convert was, and the father—evidently a politically minded father—said: "Well, son, if a Republican becomes a Democrat he is a convert." And what, asked the boy, is a Democrat who becomes a Republican. With a scowl his father said: "Why, he's a traitor, of course."

My friends, we are now coming near the end of our first campaign swing through the West. It has been a fine trip. I haven't had a better time for years. Franklin Roosevelt used to say, "I'm an old campaigner and I love a good fight." I'm not an old campaigner—at least not yet; but I must say I have enjoyed every minute of it, and I have traveled on everything except an ox-cart to get here. I have even had to have my shoes resoled!

Now, my ideas about campaigning are simple and probably primitive. It seems to me that the American people want to hear about their problems, and that it is the business of the candidates to talk plainly about these issues. As I said in Los Angeles yesterday, I don't think that real issues are either beneath the dignity of political candidates or above the intelligence of the American voters.

What I had hoped to do was to raise a little debate between the two parties on some of the solemn questions of our national life. Thus far I can't say that I have had very much success. So far as I can see, it is like trying to hold a conversation with a two-headed elephant. One head seems to agree with everything we say, and the other head fumes and curses at everything we say. The best debate of all I suppose, of course, would be between the two elephants.

I have certain warm sympathies for my very distinguished opponent. It must be hard to try to talk sense on issues when half of your advisers tell you one thing and the other half tell you the exact opposite. As a result the Republican leadership has evidently decided that the best thing to do is to use slogans, catchwords and epithets. I think a campaign for the Presidency is worth something better than that, but it begins to look as though the Republicans have decided to file notice of intellectual bankruptcy and to accompany it by a deluge of abuse of their creditors—the people's intelligence.

In fact, their whole campaign so far reminds me of a phonograph record. It sort of monotonously repeats, "I love you, I love you, I love you" and then it adds, "honey chile"—and finally a rebel yell when it goes down South. Now, when you turn the record over it also has a catchy little tune to waltz time. It goes something like, "time for a change, time for a change, time for a change, time for a change" over and over again.

I left Springfield exactly two weeks ago on this trip—one week ago—it seems like two years! We have covered a lot of ground in these seven long days. We went first to Denver. You all know the Denver story. It used to be the campaign headquarters of the Republican candidate for President. I really don't know why they abandoned Denver. Maybe the high altitude was too much for weak hearts; or maybe the closeness of Denver to the Great Divide was too much for a divided party. In any case, by the time I got to Denver, the General and his entourage had decided it was time for a change—and had forsaken Colorado for New York City.

From Denver we went to Kasson, Minnesota, to a plowing contest—or, rather, it started out to be a plowing contest, but after my distinguished opponent had given his speech I began to wonder whether he didn't think it was a plowing under contest. At least he plowed under the Republican platform and adopted ours.

For my part I didn't have to plow under the Democratic farm platform. I could stand on it. In fact, I am perfectly willing to have the General stand on it too, though I wish he would request permission from the copyright owners once in a while.

Someone asked me the other day what I thought the main difference was between the Republican and the Democratic platforms. The answer seems to me easy. The Republican Presidential candidate always tries to run on a Democratic platform. But you will never find a Democrat running on a Republican platform.

Now, I had hoped that we might have a debate upon farm policy at that meeting in Minnesota, but the best debate, as usual, was between the Republican Parties. One of the Republican Parties opposes fixed parity prices at 90 per cent. That party wrote the platform at Chicago. The other Republican Party supports fixed parity prices—and that one wrote the General's speech.

But, when the General proposed that we should go up to 100 per cent, I think he may have misunderstood his audience. I think the farmers of America have too vivid a memory of the Republicans in the House voting against the 90 per cent support law last spring to be impressed by big talk today of 100 per cent.

Moreover, I doubt very much if they like the idea of treating the farm question like an auction in which the farmers' votes would be sold to the highest bidder.

From Minnesota we went to Wyoming, Idaho, Montana, and from there to Oregon and Washington. And, by the way, I think ours was probably the first party that ever went from Denver to Cheyenne via Minnesota.

If you don't like to travel you shouldn't run for President. But I do like to travel, especially around this lovely, rich, fruitful land of ours. We have a great natural heritage in our land, our forests and our rivers. You get an exciting sense of the richness and the variety of this heritage when you travel through the West; and you get an urgent sense of the vital importance of developing this heritage in the interests of all the people of the country, and not permitting it to become a private reserve for special groups to make profits for themselves at the expense of the people.

You here in Arizona well know the importance of our Federal policies of conservation and of reclamation. I have been told that the very first reclamation project in the whole country was in this State. I was especially interested to learn that the original pattern of co-operative membership by farmers in an irrigation district was worked out over here in the Salt River Project. Irrigation and reclamation laws nourished the State of Arizona. Since 1940 farm income in Arizona has increased 386 per cent. And your total income rose or, rather, it leaped some 23 per cent from 1950 to 1951—more than any other State in the Union.

I don't know how to account for this unless it is all these people who are making so much money in this dreadful Democratic era, who come out here to spend it.

Your extraordinary yields of long-staple cotton, melons, grapes, alfalfa and all the other crops contribute to the well-being of all of us. We in Illinois are better off because you are better off. And I might say you are better off because we are better off.

There is another aspect of the conservation problem which was borne in on me both in the Northwest and also down here, and that is the problem of controlling erosion and preventing silt from choking irrigation works and reservoirs. One of the key points in this fight against erosion is overgrazing. I have stated already that I think the public ranges should be used wisely for grazing on a fair and equitable basis, but I am unalterably opposed to turning over control of those lands to private interests. Those lands are public property and they must be managed in the public interest.

So far as I have been able to penetrate the language of the Republican platform, the Republican leadership is interested in giving these natural resources away. "We favor," the platform says —and I quote—"restoration of the traditional Republican land policy"—and we all know, it seems to me, what the traditional Republican land policy is. I would welcome a battle on this issue. I am for conserving the public wealth—the common property of the people—just as I am for conserving the tax dollar.

I hope that some day my distinguished opponent will come to see that both of these questions involve the property of all of the people. He is appalled, as I am, at those public servants who have given away tax favors, but he is apparently willing enough to give away the land, the oil, and the other property of the people.

I talked on these matters in Seattle and Portland because little is more important to American survival than assuring the conservation and the wise development of our natural resources.

Then, from Seattle I flew down the shining Pacific Coast to San Francisco, and there where the Golden Gate looks toward the East I spoke about foreign policy. I said that the question of peace was the most important unfinished business of our generation. I said that our generation can meet the challenge if we but understand the enormity of the threat. I believe peace is possible if we but have the will, the boldness and the patience to conquer it. I believe that we have. I believe this is a time for greatness, and that America has unfathomed resources of greatness.

Then I had a wonderful day whistle-stopping—my first experience with whistle-stopping. I heard and saw everything but whistles, by the way, whistle-stopping through the great Central Valley of California. Yesterday I spoke twice in Los Angeles, after a half dozen miscellaneous speeches. First I had some things to say about corruption. I said that we must be careful not to abuse indiscriminately all of our public servants, because the vast majority of them are as honest and as conscientious workers as any of you. I said that the thieves and the scoundrels—and there have been thieves and scoundrels who have betrayed their trust—must be identified and they must be punished without mercy. And a good many of them have been detected and exposed, I am happy to say, by Democrats.

Yesterday evening in Los Angeles I talked about the fact that sometimes we get so mired down in the problems of today that we forget about the possibilities of tomorrow. I have talked a lot about blood, sweat and tears during this campaign, and I propose to continue talking sternly, because I don't believe that this is a safe or a simple world. But I think too that we must never forget that we are on the edge of a new, scientific, technological age—an age which promises fabulous abundance for a people worthy of it.

We Democrats are not afraid of the challenge of tomorrow. We are the party of faith—faith in America, faith in democracy, faith, if you please, in freedom. We will let the Republicans continue to deal in moans and groans and lamentations and despair—to say that the American way of life is weak and fragile, tottering on the verge of collapse. That is the party of fear—and this contest between fear and faith will decide the future of our country.

While I have been moving around I notice that my distinguished opponent has been active too. The other night in Indianapolis the General gave a chalk talk on team play in basketball and politics. In the course of his talk he made the following admission, and I quote him: "The overwhelming majority of Federal employes," he said, "are among our most patriotic and efficient citizens." Now, I believe this. In fact, as I have said, I know it, and I think that most of the people of the country believe it. We are highly gratified to have the Republican candidate say it in public.

But, some Americans evidently don't believe it. And the most conspicuous of those who impugn the motives and attack the integrity of our public servants are on the General's team. In fact, after last Tuesday it looks as though some of them had been promoted to the first team. One player to whom the General gave his Republican letter—the varsity "R"—on last Tuesday, is Senator Jenner of Indiana. And, according to Senator Jenner, the list of unpatriotic Federal employes is not only practically endless but it is headed by the revered name of General George C. Marshall, our great wartime commander, and General Eisenhower's superior officer. General Marshall, Senator Jenner said on the sheltered floor of the United States Senate, was a "living lie" and not only willing but eager "to play the role of front man for traitors."

Now, I know something about basketball too. I know that you are not likely to get a good team unless the coach and the players are in agreement. And, I am dead sure that this is true of team play in government, because I have been Governor of one of the biggest States in the Union.

The only conclusion I can draw, therefore, is either that the General agrees with Senator Jenner—and this I still doubt—or that the Republican team isn't going to win many games this next few weeks. This is the first time I have ever heard of a party going into battle under the slogan, "throw the rascals in."

What it all gets back to, of course, is the simple and indisputable fact that there is no longer one Republican Party. There are two. It is an ancient political vehicle, held together by soft soap and hunger, and with front-seat drivers and back-seat drivers contradicting each other in a bedlam of voices, shouting to "go right" and "go left" at the same time. I don't envy the driver and I don't think the American people will care to ride in his bus very far.

In recent weeks it appears as though the junior Republican Party is about to be swallowed up by its big, bad, bold brother. I no longer hear the voices which sang with sweet reasonableness for the General before the massacre at Chicago. Someone seems to have muzzled them. It may be because they sounded too much like Democrats.

And now we have the spectacle of the candidate who won the nomination, seeking out his defeated rival and begging for some kind word. I am beginning to wonder who won at Chicago. I am beginning to wonder who our opponent really is. Perhaps there is a six-star general somewhere in the Republican Party.

It occurred to me, flying over here this morning, that the clue to the future of the Republican Party may well lie in the fabled Phoenix after which your city was named. The Phoenix, as we all know, set fire to herself after a 500-year decline, and then rose revitalized from her own ashes. Our opponents may be older than they think. I think they are aging, tired, and querulous. Maybe they should build a fire under themselves and rise again into the twentieth century. I think we would all be glad to welcome them here in the twentieth century.

We Democrats like this century, belong to it and propose to realize its responsibilities to the full. To assure the continuation of progress in the United States, to move toward greater freedom and greater opportunity for our citizens, to fight for peace in the world, there is a broad and proven path, but, of course, as the Democratic candidate, modesty forbids me to tell you which path to follow on November 4th.

The Threat of Communism

National Guard Armory

ALBUQUERQUE, NEW MEXICO

September 12, 1952

This is my last stop on my first major tour as a Presidential candidate; eight states, thirty speeches—good, bad and indifferent. I confess I am tired, but I have been having a lot of fun and I am not ashamed of it. I like people; I even like Republicans, especially if they say they are going to vote for me.

Somebody has been asking me how I was feeling and it reminded me of a story of a man who was shot in the back by Indians in an attack on a wagon train out in this country in the early days. Some time later some troopers came along and found the poor man unconscious with three arrows between his shoulder blades. They revived him with whiskey, and when he could whisper they asked if it hurt awfully, and he said, "It sure does, especially when I laugh."

Well, we Democrats seem to be having entirely too much fun for some of our dour and solemn critics. I have been accused of the hideous crime of laughing a little. I am afraid, my friends, that I have no option but to plead guilty. Politics is a serious business, but I believe in going gaily into battle. I believe that the Happy Warrior has always been a good American symbol, and I am going to go on being myself whether my critics like it or not.

Some people say that I have been going to the left; other people say that I have been going to the right. On the whole, I don't think the average is too bad. But it sort of reminded me of a story I heard long ago about the church that was trying to get a new minister, and they said—the committee said—"Now, we want someone who is not too conservative and not too radical. You know, we want somebody just mediocre."

Well, I am frank to say that I don't look on this political cam-

125

paign as a funeral—at least, I don't look on it as my funeral. And how could you help but be amused when you look at that Republican Party, that two-headed elephant? No matter how solemnly you examine this interesting spectacle, I find it very hard not to crack an occasional smile. One head huffs and puffs and announces that it is fighting mad at the Democrats, while the other head claims credit for all of the Democratic achievements of the past twenty years. I understand the elephant put its two heads together today in New York for a peace conference. They must have eaten crow for breakfast. If they did make peace, I wonder what happened to all those declarations of undying principle we heard from both sides while they were calling each other nasty names in Chicago—names, by the way, that they usually reserve only for Democrats.

Now, after seeing the announcement—or a brief synopsis of the press announcement—I am tempted to make a very profound comment: It looks as if Taft lost the nomination but won the nominee.

But tonight, my friends, I want to speak seriously about some very hard and difficult things. They are issues that present tough choices to the American people. The choice we make will have an effect on the life of every man, woman and child in this country. Our country faces today a crafty and a ruthless foe, as you all well know. It is the purpose of that foe to dominate the life of every person in the world. The modern miracles of aviation and of atomic power have given, or will soon give, this foe weapons with which it can spread destruction everywhere. As the old spiritual has it: "There's no hiding place down there." No one knows that better than you in New Mexico, who live as neighbors to Los Alamos and White Sands.

I want to say a few plain words tonight on this subject of communism. You have heard a good deal about it in these past years, and I suspect you will hear a great deal more about it in years to come. Unfortunately, too much of what we have heard has been shrill and excited or else it has been soft and insidious. If we are going to deal effectively with this disease, it will only be because our approach remains cool, calm and thoughtful.

What is the nature of the threat which communism brings to the free world? It is the threat of an all-powerful state, dedicated to the extinction of individual dignity and individual freedom—individualism, in short. To put it more simply, communism is the death of the soul. It is the organization of total conformity—in short, tyranny—and it is committed to making tyranny universal.

Now, this makes it, first of all, an external threat, the threat of a sullen, aggressive, expanding imperialism, thrusting forth its power in all directions at the points of least resistance. It does not seem probable to me that the Soviet Union desires general war; I suspect it will refrain from any action that it knows will provoke general war. But it has no fear of local war—especially when it can get other peoples, like the North Koreans and the Chinese, to fight local wars for them. And it proposes to extend its power, above ground, under ground, wherever economic insecurity or political chaos or moral weakness or military unpreparedness give it a bridgehead or foothold.

How do we counter this external threat of communism? There is only one sound answer to this, and that is by increasing the strength and the unity of the free world. We can end the conditions which invite Soviet aggression in only one way—by transforming positions of weakness into positions of strength, and this cannot be done by any magic words, by slogans or by radio exhortations. It can only be done by hard, patient building of strength in the free world, enough military strength to deter overt aggression and enough economic and political and moral strength to deter subversion and infiltration. And this means collective strength, that is, strength exerted by the free peoples in concert so that, to an ever-increasing extent, the security of one becomes identical with the security of all.

With these policies, we have already checked Soviet aggression and perhaps saved the world from a third world war. The Truman Doctrine, the Marshall Plan and the North Atlantic Pact have restrained Soviet power in Europe. Our resistance in Korea has checked Soviet aggression in Asia. If we had let Europe fall to the Soviet, if we had acquiesced in aggression in Asia, the Soviet Union would have been emboldened into rasher and rasher adventures. By the time it occurred to the Old Guard of the Republican Party that resistance was necessary, we would have been isolated, a beleaguered garrison state in a Soviet dominated world.

But, my friends, the building of free-world strength does more than just restrain Soviet aggression. Its effect is to make the free world itself—both because of its freedom and because of its strength—a potent counter-attraction to Soviet power. And the emergence of this world, united, powerful, friendly and free, will exert an ever-increasing influence on the captive states within the Soviet Empire.

Now, I say to you in all sobriety, that in this direction is the long-run hope of restoring the independence of nations now under Soviet dominion. We must face the bitter unhappy fact that this is no easy task. It cannot be done, as the Republican opposition has sometimes seemed to suggest, just by secret agents or by parachute drops or by radio propaganda. Harsh language and "cold finality" will do us little good unless we are willing to start a third world war which would end by obliterating the very men and women we seek to liberate.

There is only one way to rescue these peoples and that is through a policy of peaceful and relentless pressure designed to loosen the Soviet grip over these countries. The first requirement of such a policy is the building of collective strength in the free world. Without this, nothing can be done to maintain spirit and hope behind the Iron Curtain. As this is done, we are in a position to intensify political and economic and other peaceful pressures against the Soviet Empire.

This is what we have been doing. This is what we will continue to do. The Republican call for a policy of "liberation" means, in hard fact, either the continuation of the present policy or else it means the initiation of a third world war, but I fear it is neither of these things. I fear it is rather a cynical and transparent attempt, drenched in crocodile tears, to play upon the anxieties of foreign nationality groups in this country. We Democrats are opposed to war. And we are opposed to the exploitation of foreign policy and foreign friends for domestic political purposes.

It is singular to me that Republican leaders, on the whole, do not seem to become much interested in foreign lands until those lands have been lost to the enemy and then of course, it is too late. Today they seem to be concerned about Eastern Europe but not about Western Europe. They are concerned about China but not about the rest of Asia.

We must never forget that the road to the liberation of the slave world lies only through the strength and unity of the free world and that so-called short cuts are all too likely to land us in a third world war.

But I suggest that we would err, certainly, if we regarded communism as merely an external threat. Communism is a great international conspiracy and the United States has been for years a major target of that conspiracy. Communist agents have sought to steal our scientific and military secrets, to mislead and corrupt our young men and women, to infiltrate positions of power in our schools and colleges, in business firms and in labor unions and in the Government itself. At every turn they have sought to serve the purposes of the Soviet Union.

In the pursuit of their objectives, the communists have been ingenious, disciplined, obedient and ruthless. Along the way, they have gained the help, witting or unwitting, of many Americans. The communist conspiracy within the United States deserves the attention of every American citizen and the sleepless concern of the responsible government agencies.

I fear that there are still people in our country under illusions about the nature of this conspiracy abroad and at home. There aren't many American communists—far fewer than in the days of the great depression—and they aren't, on the whole, very important, but they exist, and we should not forget their existence. Some, perhaps, are obstinate and hopeless in their faith. Others, perhaps, can be won back to loyalty to the things that we deem precious in our democratic way of life.

Communism is committed to the destruction of every value which the genuine American liberal holds most dear. So I would say to any Americans who cling to illusions about communism and its fake utopia: Wake up to the fact that you are in an alliance with the devil, and you must act soon if you hope to save your soul. And to those who, in the service of the Soviet Union, would commit acts prejudicial to the safety and security of the United States, I would say: Under me as President of the United States, Federal agencies will deal sternly and mercilessly with all who would betray their country and their freedom for the sake of manacles and chains.

There is only one way for a free society to deal with this internal threat, and that is through the processes of justice. We have tightened up our espionage and security legislation. We have instituted a Federal loyalty system—and we did so, by the way, in 1947— three long years before the Senator from Wisconsin made his shrill discovery of the communist menace. We have prosecuted the communist leadership. Where the law has been violated, the Justice Department has indicted and convicted the criminals. In all this effort, we have had the faithful and resourceful work in national protection of the Federal Bureau of Investigation. Now, I do not believe that any agency of government is wholly infallible, and I think that of all agencies, a bureau of detection should get the most strict and unrelenting public scrutiny.

But, so far as I can see, the F.B.I. is doing and has done an excellent investigation job. To tell you—or to imply—as some do for political reasons that the Government is crawling with communists today is to say that the F.B.I. does not know its business. Moreover, the Department of Justice has now established a new division to deal exclusively with this problem.

We can never relax our vigilance at home and abroad. When I say this, I don't intend to approve all the excesses and the injustices committed in the name of anti-communism. Unfortunately, there are among us men whose hope it is to profit from anxiety, hysteria and fear—to confuse, to blind, to obscure the issues for the American people.

Now, those salesmen of confusion are at work in the field of foreign policy and also on domestic problems. In the field of foreign policy, they tell people that our greatest patriots, men like George Marshall, are traitors. They tell people that, while our soldiers are fighting communist aggression in Korea, our foreign policy is one of appeasement and of coddling communists at home. Men who participated in carrying out our foreign policy, men who served this nation as diplomats abroad, are now trying to sell the people the notion that the United States treacherously "gave away" Poland or "gave away" China to the communists. This is mischievous, this is untrue and this is unworthy of people aspiring to leadership among us.

If there were mistakes, let us discuss them. But let us never confuse honest mistakes, mistakes of judgment, with the insidious designs of traitors. Those who corrupt the public mind are just as evil as those who steal from the public purse.

And let me say too that it is a shabby thing for a man to cry treachery now who only a few years ago said that the only difference between Chinese communists and Oklahoma Republicans was that the latter did not carry guns.

So far as I can see, many of the people most vocal in pursuing communism with words at home are the same people most silent when it comes to supporting the fight in the front lines abroad.

We must recognize that the fight against communism in our own country achieves its purpose only to the extent that it strengthens and does not weaken democracy.

But the excesses of those who exploit anti-communism do not alter the fact that our nation can never for one moment relax its guard. We must take care not to harm innocent people. We must remember that liberals are not communists and that socialists are not communists, and that radicals in the American sense—in the American tradition—are not communists. But where true communists are concerned—men bound to the service and the defense of Stalinist tyranny—we must root them out and give them the consequences of treachery to all America holds dearest.

Now, this region of clear air and broad spaces is the last place any politician should try to dupe people. You can spot a speck on the horizon out here ten miles away. You will not be fooled by men who try to tell you that patriots are traitors and honest men are thieves.

Nor will anyone believe the Republican orators who say that under Democratic administration we have all been ruined by the Government in Washington. A man who could say a thing like that hasn't been around our country lately. Or if he has been around he has been conferring all day with Republicans.

I say look around New Mexico. Cattle which sold twenty years ago for $30 a head now sell for $200. You know that the workers are making twice as much today, after allowing for price changes. You know that your manufacturing output is now twenty-five times what it was twenty years ago. You know that not one cent was lost to anybody last year in federally insured banks. Not one cent.

Let us ask ourselves—who was ruined? Who was ruined when better schools were built for our children; when old folks could afford to stay with their families instead of going to the poorhouse; when forests were saved; when land was irrigated; when oil wells and mines found a market; when electric power was brought to farms and homes?

The Democrats haven't ruined this country; they have vastly enriched it. And the sad thing about it is that the Republican orators know it. Their real complaint is that the only thing the people have lost in the last twenty years is faith in the Republicans.

And why? Why? Because they simply cannot understand that

you can't win elections in this country by fooling people. You win them by a record of service for the people's wants and the people's needs. The Democratic Party has no secret love potion which makes Americans vote for us when election time comes around. Our methods are open and simple. Time and time again in the last twenty years we asked the Republicans to work by our side in the interests of all the people. We told them in plain language that you don't win at the polls with tricky words, with miracle drugs, with slander and with slogans. We told our Republican friends that the way to win an election once every four years is to win it each day by meeting the needs of our times.

But our friends have no eyes to see, no ears to hear and evidently no heads to understand. Or, maybe too many heads with conflicting ideas, or no ideas. These people seem to believe that newspapers have not been invented, that records are not kept and that the tally sheets of votes in Congress are habitually lost. But all these things are available to the public. Americans do read the minutes of the last meeting. And they add up their reactions on election day. If they also add up to another Democratic victory, the Republican leaders have only themselves to blame, even as the Whig Party had before them.

They talk of change. These days they do little else but talk of change. But where were the Republicans when the great changes of these twenty years were made? I'll tell you where they were. They were trying to stop the changes.

Look, my friends, at the things that have meant so much to New Mexico. The Democrats have worked to bring you water. We have steadily supported reclamation measures, as you know. When they had the chance in that famous 80th Congress, the Republicans cut the budget requests for reclamation work so far that some projects had to be stopped in the middle.

The Democrats have worked to provide price insurance for farm crops—cotton, for example. What did the Republicans do? Just this last June—three months ago—more than half of the Republicans in the House of Representatives voted against the law to extend price supports at 90 per cent of parity through 1954 for cotton and for other basic crops.

The Democrats have worked to preserve, to protect the public grazing lands against overuse. We know that protecting the forests and grasslands against overgrazing is essential to protect the watersheds. We want to have the grazing lands used and used to their full capacity. But overgrazing leads to floods and silt, and loss for all.

The Republican platform for this year, if it means anything, means turning over the public grasslands to reckless private exploitation. These are public property, and we Democrats insist that they shall be widely used for the public benefit.

Another example: The Democrats have worked for years to provide a sound system of social security to help the old, the blind, dependent children, those who through no fault of their own cannot fully support themselves. And, where are the Republicans? They say nice things about extending social security to more people, but when they had a chance in the 80th Congress, they took social security away from more than half a million people. Now, do you want that kind of leadership in Washington?

I say that you want instead men who are working for progress and hope and human decency. We have great tasks ahead of us. We must continue with imagination and with implacable purpose the task of building peace in this tormented world. And here at home we must continue to strive for a better living for all of our people. We are united in a single purpose—the great American purpose of freeing men to use their strength and their courage in building a better life. This is the purpose for which the Democratic Party stands, and this, my friends, is the purpose I should like to serve with your help.

The Atomic Future

Bushnell Memorial Auditorium

HARTFORD, CONNECTICUT

September 18, 1952

I am glad to be here in Connecticut. I first came here to school
not far from Hartford about thirty-five years ago as a small boy.
I have always gratefully recalled the warmth with which your
citizens took me in, and also the patience with which my teachers
tried to educate me. Some of them are here tonight and I am
deeply touched by their continued interest in this Democratic
heretic from the prairies of the West. Or should I attribute it to
the fact that the last twenty years have won most of the more enlightened to the Democratic standard!

In recent weeks my distinguished opponent has adopted the singular theory that a candidate for President should support all state
and local candidates on his party ticket—good, bad, indifferent—
and regardless of their views and records.

I believe this is a new theory, even in the Republican Party. It
was not too long ago when Governor Dewey, as party leader, honorably refused to support a Republican Congressman who had distinguished himself by incessant and noisy opposition to vital national policies. But the General's theory is not only novel, it is
dangerous. If the voters of this nation ever stop looking at the
record and the character of candidates, and look only at their
party label, it will be a sorry day for healthy democracy.

Win or lose, I will not accept the proposition that party regularity is more important than political ethics. Victory can be
bought too dearly.

But this exhibition of Republican expediency is not what I
wanted to talk to you about. I wanted to talk here tonight about
something which transcends politics—atomic energy, which is the
new dimension in all our thinking—and also about the relation
of power to peace.

I was moved to select this topic because atomic energy is a major component of our power and because our decisions and actions in atomic energy matters, as they relate to preparedness for both war and peace, will long bear the imprint of our wise and lamented friend, Brien McMahon of Connecticut.

Brien McMahon was among the first to see the great potentiality for good and evil which was opened up by this advance of the frontiers of knowledge. He sought to reconcile the needs for security with the needs for information—both to encourage further scientific advances and an intelligent public opinion. He saw the need for civilian control. He fought to keep the sights of the development program high.

We have already, for example, opened up new fields of medical research. Brien McMahon died of cancer. With luck and the help of atomic research, our children may be safe from this grim disease.

We have already produced, with an atomic reactor, the steam to generate electric power. We are building now—and in a Connecticut shipyard—an atomic-powered submarine. We can begin to dream of electric stations, ships, airplanes and machinery to be powered by the atom. Men are at work today with atomic tools trying to find out how plants convert energy from the sun into food. It is not too fantastic to think that we may, in time, unlock new doors to boundless energy for our homes and industries.

This is a field in which government and industry can work in ever more fruitful partnership. The people of this country have invested more than six billion dollars in atomic development. This work must be for everyone's good, and not just for the profits of some. But more can be done to work out new relationships in this field between government and business—relationships which will safeguard the public interest and yet allow full room for private initiative.

This is the excitement of the future which awaits us. The age of atomic abundance is still far off. And we will never be able to release the power of the atom to build unless we are able to restrain its power to destroy. This is the merciless question of the present—the question of what we should do with atomic power in a divided world.

Here again we face a bitter decision. We shrink from the use of such weapons—weapons which destroy the guilty and innocent alike, like a terrible sword from heaven. The memory of Hiroshima is fresh within us—described in enduring prose by one of the most accomplished of contemporary writers—John Hersey—who, I am proud to say, is head of the Volunteers for Stevenson in Connecticut. But we can't renounce the power which science has given us when renunciation might expose our people to destruction.

In the decision to move ahead Brien McMahon again played a leading role. He demanded that we constantly step up our reserves of atomic weapons. He worked always to keep the sights of the atomic energy program high and its policies bold—and the United States has made a notable contribution to the security of the free world by its rapid development of atomic power.

Yet there has always seemed to me a danger in making the atomic bomb the center of defense strategy. The bomb is but one part of a general system of defense. It cannot be a substitute for such a general system. It cannot be our only answer to aggression. But the bomb remains an essential part of our defense system. Until it is subjected to safe international control, we have no choice but to insure our atomic superiority.

But there can be no solution in an arms race. At the end of this road lies bankruptcy or world catastrophe. Already the earth is haunted by premonitions in this shadowed atomic age. Mankind must deserve some better destiny than this.

Because our Government knew the futility of the arms race, it made its great decision to seek an international system for the control of atomic power. We went to the United Nations and Bernard Baruch, a beloved and wise elder statesman, offered on behalf of the United States to share with other nations the good in atomic energy. In return, we asked that other nations join with us to curb its power for evil.

I think this decision was right—profoundly right. Few things we have done since 1945 have so clearly demonstrated our national determination to achieve peace and to strengthen international order. By this offer, all nations were asked to diminish their own sovereignty in the interests of world security—just as each of us gives up some degree of personal independence when communities establish laws and set up police forces to see that they are carried out.

Unfortunately, as we all know, the Soviet Union has thus far refused to join in a workable system. The reason is obvious. To be effective, such a system would require effective United Nations inspection; and the Kremlin fears to open up the windows and doors of its giant prison. It fears to have the rest of the world learn the truth about the Soviet Union. It fears even more to have the Russian peoples learn the truth about the rest of the world.

And so the negotiations have long been deadlocked. And, in irritation and disgust, some of us have rebelled against the whole idea of negotiation itself. Some of us have even felt that our possession of the bomb makes negotiation unnecessary and, if our allies are alarmed by our uncompromising attitude, so much the worse for them. When we have the bomb as our ally, some of us may say, we need no other.

Such ideas are folly. If we started throwing our atomic weight around the world, no stockpile of bombs could remotely make up for all the friends we would lose. And the irony is that it is our allies who make our atomic strength effective. We built the bomb with the help and co-operation of foreign scientists. Our atomic-production program today depends on foreign supplies of uranium. Our air power would be gravely crippled without foreign bases. Even in terms of the bomb itself, going-it-alone would simply be a shortcut to national disaster.

A year ago some Republican leaders contended that the best way to stop the war in Korea would be to extend it to the mainland of China. In the same vein, Republican leaders today seem to be arguing that the best way to deal with Soviet power in Europe is to instigate civil war in the satellite countries. These are dangerous, reckless, foolish counsels and likely to lead to the sacrifice of the lives of the very people whom we hope to liberate.

And likewise the Democratic Party opposes that weird Republican policy which proposes to reduce our contributions to free-world strength, on the one hand, while it steps up its verbal threats against the enemy, on the other hand. Theodore Roosevelt used to say: "Speak softly and carry a big stick." But these modern Republicans seem to prefer to throw away the stick and scream imprecations.

The Democratic Party will never desist in the search for peace. We must never close our minds or freeze our positions. We must strive constantly to break the deadlock in our atomic discussions. But we can never yield on the objective of securing a foolproof system of international inspection and control. And we will never confuse negotiation with appeasement.

In the long run, the strength of the free nations resides as much in this willingness to reduce their military power and subject it to international control as in the size of their military establishments. This desire and willingness of the free nations to give up their preponderant power and to abandon force as an instrument of national policy in the interests of peace is not only unprecedented— it provides the moral justification for the amassing of great power. And we must never delude ourselves into thinking that physical power is a substitute for moral power which is the true sign of national greatness.

I hold out no foolish hopes. We all know the character of the men in the Kremlin—their fanaticism, their ruthlessness, their limitless ambitions—but we know too that their realism has restrained them thus far from provoking a general war which they would surely lose, and they know that they can have peace and freedom from fear whenever they want it and are prepared to honor their wartime pledges and the obligations assumed when they signed the United Nations Charter. We may hope that the steady strengthening of the free world will increase their sense of the futility of aggression; that the intensification of peaceful pressures against the Soviet Empire will sharpen the internal contradictions within that empire; that, in time, free peoples may lift their heads again in Eastern Europe, and new policies and leadership emerge within the Soviet Union itself.

No one can be certain about the meaning of peace. But we all can be certain about the meaning of war. The future is still open —open for disaster, if we seek peace cheaply or meanly, but open for real peace, if we seek it bravely and nobly.

In any case, let us not cower with fear before this new instrument of power. Nature is neutral. Man has wrested from nature the power to make the world a desert or to make the deserts bloom. There is no evil in the atom; only in men's souls. We have dealt with evil men before, and so have our fathers before us, from the beginning of time. The way to deal with evil men has never varied; stand up for the right, and, if needs must be, fight for the right.

To my Republican listeners I would say: the atomic adventure transcends partisan issues. Win or lose, we Democrats will work with you to follow this adventure to the end of peace and plenty for mankind.

To my fellow Democrats I would close by repeating what Brien McMahon said in his last public appearance. He said: "The way to worry about November is to worry about what is right. If we do not stand for the right, ten thousand campaign speeches will never help us. If we do stand for the right, we will again be asked to lead our country."

The New England Tradition

City Hall

SPRINGFIELD, MASSACHUSETTS

September 19, 1952

I don't know why it is that an American, no matter where he was born or where he lives, has a feeling in New England of coming home. Perhaps it is because this country of yours looks so home-like; perhaps it is because the people and their welcome are always so friendly; perhaps it is because so much of what we are as Americans came out of these valleys and these hills—our habit, for example, of making up our own minds in our own way, and saying what we think—our habit of respect for each other, and for ourselves—our habit, if you please, of freedom.

At all events, I have felt very much at home today in Massachusetts, and yesterday traveling through Connecticut. I hope I feel equally at home up here after November 4th. Maybe I feel particularly at home in Springfield because I, too, live in Springfield, albeit some two hundred years younger than your Springfield, but equally famous.

Now, my friends, I have thought that the proper way to conduct a campaign was to discuss the issues, and by that I mean the choices that people have to make between alternative courses of conduct. It has been a little hard for me to get a discussion of the issues in this campaign. Our Republican friends, to be sure, are in favor of throwing the rascals out, but they are also in favor of throwing the rascals in. While approving everything that has been done for the past twenty years by the Democrats, they say that the country is headed for perdition and they call us all dreadful names.

Indeed, to keep this campaign on the highest possible level worthy of its significance, I have been tempted to make a proposal to our Republican friends: that if they would stop telling lies about us, we would stop telling the truth about them. Which reminds me that about the only place where they have really taken issue with us seems to be on the subject of humor. The Republicans are against it. And those of us who have found a certain friendly amusement in the antics of the two-headed elephant have been rebuked—an elephant, we are given to understand, is no laughing matter. Well, for myself, I can't think it a hideous offense to believe that the American people have a sense of humor. We used to call Al Smith "the Happy Warrior."

In fact, he was given this name by another happy warrior, Franklin Roosevelt, who got his title "the Great Humanitarian," by the way, in this city of Springfield, Massachusetts. In the midst of the terrible years of the Civil War, Abraham Lincoln—and the Republican Party still claims him—at least at election time—said of humor:

"If it were not for this occasional vent, I should die."

It is a far cry from Lincoln to these solemn individuals who want to banish it from American public life. I have about concluded that what G.O.P. really means is "grouchy old pessimists."

Maybe this feeling about a little humor to enliven our lives goes far to explain the General's remark last week about Oliver Cromwell. I found myself somewhat puzzled when he announced that Cromwell was going to be the model of the Great Crusade. Why should he have chosen Oliver Cromwell? Obviously it could not be because Cromwell sent his Roundheads on a bloody crusade against the people of Ireland with religious persecution, starvation and the sword as his weapons. It could not be because Cromwell led his army into the House of Commons to seize control by force of the Parliament of England. But now I think I know why the General admired Oliver Cromwell. Whatever else you may say about Cromwell, you can never accuse him of having cracked a joke.

I suppose we must not be too critical. To be surrounded by the Republican Old Guard night and day would be a melancholy fate for anyone and I can understand why it is no laughing matter for the General. In fact, Senator Taft seems to be getting most of the amusement. When he walked out of the General's house in New York with the surrender in writing I have never seen such a contented smile since the cat swallowed the canary.

I have been wondering sometimes what that brutal battle in Chicago last July was all about.

I am glad to note that not all of the crusaders who marched

into battle against Senator Taft so gallantly are prepared to follow their leader in his inglorious retreat.

Let me say to the good Republicans of New England: there is always a light in the Democratic window and a warm welcome awaiting you in the Democratic Party. We know how to make people feel at home, and that's why we win elections.

Let me further say that if I should be elected President in November, I will be President, and I will not be honorary head of a regency.

Now, my friends, you all know how this country has been transformed in the last twenty years. The Democratic Party took over when the nation was almost in a state of receivership in 1933. Fortunately, we had a great and revered leader—Franklin Roosevelt. Under his leadership the Democratic Party dedicated itself to improving opportunity and security for all of our citizens. In the last twenty years we have restored and reconstructed the nation. Where there was once poverty, there is now prosperity. Where there was once anxiety, there is now security. Where there was once discrimination, we now have opportunity. Democratic administrations have produced the great social reforms of our era. We will defend these reforms against all of those humorless people who haven't been happy since the days of William McKinley. And, we will defend these reforms and this free society of ours—we will defend them against those on the extreme left, the admirers of Lenin and Stalin, who would bind all of us to the service of an omnipotent and all-powerful state.

It is the Democratic administration in Washington, assisted by many good Republicans, who followed in the train of Arthur Vandenberg, which has rallied the free world against communism in the last seven years. Indeed, if it had not been for the wisdom and the courage of our national leadership, Europe might have by now fallen to the communists. If it had not been for the wisdom and the courage of our national leadership, communist aggressors would by now have swallowed Korea and swarmed over all of Asia.

The fight for freedom and for security takes place on many fronts. You of New England, by the way, have been waging your own battle in recent years—a battle to maintain the economic health and the vitality of this region.

A few days ago in a report to the President by the Council of Economic Advisers, I found this comment about New England—

I think many of you are familiar with it. It said: "Its people are noted for their independence and self-reliance. They seem to look less to the Federal Government for help than do the people of any other region."

Now, if I were a New Englander, I would be mighty proud of this compliment.

I want to say to you here in New England what I have said elsewhere. I believe the Federal Government must not hesitate to do those things that are necessary for the country's welfare, which the people of the states and the localities cannot do for themselves. Decisions on Federal expenditures must not be made simply in response to local or regional pressures, or the demands of particular pressure groups. Such decisions would reward those who bring the most pressure, and at the expense of those who bring the least. We must see that modesty is never penalized.

I am also conscious of the things that disturb New England—the textile mills and the shoe factories that have been closing or moving south; the unemployment in some mill towns when jobs elsewhere have been plentiful; and the fact that any drop in business hits New England with special severity. The relatively slight recession, even of 1949, was keenly felt in many New England communities.

Now the Federal Government must never seek to impede the growth of one part of the country to help another. Nor have I ever heard any New Englander suggest that the salvation of New England lies in blocking the advance of the South or of the Midwest. But government can work toward fair standards of competition between regions. We know that Massachusetts pioneered not alone in manufacturing, but in a decent and dignified life for the men and women who work in industry. Your standards of unemployment compensation, of accident compensation, protection for women and children, have always been high. Unions in New England are strong and alert to the interests of their members.

Competition which derives its advantage from lower wage standards, less protection for workers, or lower living standards, is not always healthy competition.

We must have, it seems to me, reasonably uniform wage and hour standards. We must have reasonably uniform standards of social security throughout our country. That has been the policy of the Democratic Party, as I understand it, during these past twenty years. New England's greatest resource is in its people, its unparalleled supply of skilled labor, its experienced and thrifty management, its knowledge of how to produce to the highest standards of workmanship. Any region with such a resource is assured of a great future. In the next twenty years we shall have in the United States an increase in population of over thirty million persons. New England is certain to be called upon to supply many of the needs—from fine textiles to grinding wheels—of this expanding population. Of that there can be no doubt.

The success of New England in meeting this challenge of a growing population with a rising standard of living will depend in the future, as it has in the past, on New England brains, initiative and leadership. You haven't been waiting here in this section of the country for Washington to tell you how—and there is no danger that you will.

There are some ways, however, in which the Federal Government can help. Some of them are immediate. Your new industries —and many of your old ones—produce things that are vital to our national security. The small New England manufacturer and the firm that is new in its business must get a fair break on Government orders. Orders must be guided to communities where men and plants are idle. It is poor economy indeed to pay unemployment compensation and provide public assistance in one place while defense orders go where labor is scarce.

There is also here the problem of power. I am told that the power rates in New England are nearly twice as high as for the country as a whole. This means higher production costs in factories, higher costs and smaller use in homes and on the farms.

You still have an important resource in water power that awaits development. The decision both on our power development and on flood control on your streams is a decision that belongs to the people of New England. And the Federal Government, my friends, should stand ready here, as in other parts of the country, to help local people develop resources which they cannot develop themselves.

In many parts of the country, New England has resources that are better known than its factories. The farms of the Connecticut valley looked good even to a man from Illinois, and that is saying something. Also you take care of our insurance out in this part of the country. You educate a lot of our children and you seem to do them much good. I can testify to that because I was educated here myself and so have all of my boys learned something about the rigors of New England climate, and also its classrooms! You are the custodians of some of the greatest monuments to our past and of some of the finest scenery in our land. The day will surely come when every American, at least once in his lifetime, will come up the Connecticut valley, will go over to visit Lexington and Concord, will go on to Boston, and then go on for a vacation somewhere in the Green Mountains or the White Mountains or the coast of Maine. I wish I was up there myself!

I am sure that New England has a brilliant future—a future to match its brilliant past. Men and women who trace their ancestry to Ireland, to Italy, to France, to Poland, and a dozen other lands have joined their traditions and energies with those who first landed here in New England to build the New England way of life.

I have said many times during this campaign that we have hard, heartbreaking tasks ahead of us. I don't minimize them, but I say to you that we will win through, and we will win through, my friends, with the Democratic Party—I hope!

To the Young Marines

Commissioning Ceremonies
United States Marine Base

QUANTICO, VIRGINIA

September 20, 1952

[*Adlai E. Stevenson III received his commission as a Second
Lieutenant, United States Marines, at this ceremony.*]

You know something about the life of a candidate for high office in this country. You know what happens to him, what is expected of him. He is supposed to have something to say about every sort of issue to every kind of audience. He does his best to put his beliefs, his convictions, into words so that the people who listen to him can think about them and judge for themselves. His whole concern is to find the right words, the true, faithful, explicit words which will make the issues plain and his position on those issues clear.

Well, there are times when the words are very hard to find and this is one of them.

Let me just say that I am proud that my son and each one of you has achieved the special distinction of a commission in the Marine Corps. I am proud that my country has a military unit with the spirit of the United States Marines.

You are being trained to fight, and if you are called on, you will fight as Marines have always fought. Yours is a great tradition. You are part of the shield of our Republic in a time of peril. Do not underestimate the effect that you, and others like you in all our armed forces, are having in the hard and painful work of creating peace.

In one way or another each generation has to fight for its freedom in the conditions of its time. Our times are hard—as hard as any in our history. We, your fathers, have asked you to make ready to fight so that you and your children may walk upright and unafraid.

146

Your country does not accept the inevitability of world war. But the way to peace is essentially a work of construction, by far the largest we have ever undertaken. It is nothing less than the rebuilding of a ruined world and the establishment of conditions in which free government can take root and grow elsewhere, as it has long since taken root and grown here in America.

Marines have always manned the places of great peril, and also of great honor. Your job, wherever you are sent, will be the first line of defense or assault to halt aggression before it gains ground and momentum. More than that, you will be ambassadors to men in other lands whose hopes for freedom are dimmer than ours. Understand them and their hopes. You may have many a chance to compose the differences and to ease the conditions that provoke wars.

You carry with you not alone the hope, the prayer and the love of the people who gave you birth. You carry the same hope, the same prayer, and the same love of people around the world who do not know your names, but who do know you by your cause and your great tradition. Not alone America, but all free men winced when the flag was lowered on Wake Island. Not alone America, but humanity was vindicated when the flag was raised again on Iwo Jima. Our fate rides with you.

I know something of the massive threats you face. But I know, too, something of the mighty heart of your Corps. I've seen it, face to face, in the steaming jungles. And I shall never forget it.

But with all that, I know full well that I have not yet answered the question in the hearts of many of you. It is a question which your presence here asks of us all.

Why must you defend your country when your country seems to lie in peace around you? Is it because of some mistake made in the past by those older than yourselves—some failure of foresight or decision? Is it for that you must offer the sacrifice of the young years of your lives?

Certainly there have been failures and mistakes. The course of human history is a record, in tragic part, of things done which should not have been done, things not done which should have been done. Our own history is like the rest. But of one thing I, for myself, am certain and I think you also can be certain.

It is not to make good the errors of the past that you are here but to make good the promise of the future. The fighting in which we are now engaged in Korea is fighting undertaken in the name of the common collective security of the great majority of the nations of the world against the brutal aggressiveness of one or more of them. It is fighting which might, conceivably, have been avoided on that particular battlefield had we acted otherwise than we did—though, as to that, no man can surely say. But it is fighting which must inevitably have been faced, somewhere in the world, so long as the Soviet Union pressed its purpose to subjugate the free peoples of the earth, and so long as the United States and the free peoples of the earth retained their purpose to resist.

We and our friends found the courage to resist two years ago. It is to press that courage home, to affirm and to establish the faith that a peaceful world can in truth be built, that you and the thousands upon thousands of young men like you have been asked to serve your country with the hope and promise of your lives.

I guess it is just that simple. But the verities are simple. I hope you understand. I hope every man in your commands will understand.

I wish you God speed and all good fortune.

The New South

Mosque Auditorium

RICHMOND, VIRGINIA

September 20, 1952

I was reminded that my grandfather, then a candidate for Vice President, spoke here in Richmond exactly sixty years ago this week in the old Academy of Music. According to the newspaper account, the audience responded "enthusiastically" to his "exposure of the iniquities of the Republican tariff system," and he took his seat amid "deafening applause."

For the deafening applause his grandson is prepared to await the conclusion of his remarks, and meanwhile any reference to Republican iniquities will be wholly unintentional!

Here in Richmond tonight, in Virginia, rich both in history and in the knowledge of its history, I am moved to talk for a few minutes of the past.

This is not an idle task. We can chart our future clearly and wisely only when we know the path which has led to the present. A great American philosopher has said that those who can't remember the past are condemned to live it again.

The South is a good place to take our bearings, because in no part of the country does the past—a past of great nobility and great tragedy—more sharply etch the present than in the South. It is a good place to think of the grim problems of war and peace which weigh so heavily on all of us today. For here we can best learn the lessons suggested by the peace of 1865, made when the great voice of moderation had been stilled. (I have been privileged to live for four years in Springfield, Illinois, the home of Abraham Lincoln.) The victor's settlement permitted the South to keep its charm, its mockingbirds, and its beaten biscuits. For himself the victor retained only the money and the power.

It took the South decades to recover. During these bleak years, from 1865 to 1912, the Republican Party was constantly in power,

149

except for the two discontinuous terms of Grover Cleveland. In one of them my grandfather was privileged to serve as Vice President. And, again, between Woodrow Wilson and Franklin Roosevelt, the Republican Party had another long term of rule. The Democratic Party, therefore, had the dubious distinction of wandering in the desert for a longer time than the Children of Israel after their flight from Egypt.

For the South this period was a desert without an oasis. But, however hard it was to bear at the time, we in the more fortunate present can view it with a semblance of charity. For the Republican leadership did not neglect the South and other Democrats simply because you were Democrats. In its frozen impartiality it also neglected Republican farmers, small businessmen and working people. Men earned the neglect of the Republican leaders not by their political affiliation, but by being small and poor. And this is why so many people have shifted to the Democratic Party.

The Republican leadership did not merely treat the South with arrogant and massive neglect. It did more. It shackled the South, and millions outside the South, through its control of Congress; its control of money and banking; its favoritism to powerful interests; its espousal of high tariffs, high interest rates and unfair freight rates.

In the larger sense you became colonials of an empire which, if it was not alien, was at least absentee. Yours was primarily an agricultural economy, depending for cash income largely on cotton and tobacco. Of these you produced far more than could be consumed at home.

You paid exorbitant rates of interest for mortgage and crop loans. Nobody consulted you about freight rates. You just paid them. Crops sold for what they would bring because farmers could not hold them for higher prices. Bitterly they witnessed prices rise only after their crops had gone out of their hands.

It is interesting to recall that more than half a century ago Southern and Western farmers pleaded for government warehouses where they could hold their crops for better prices in exchange for certificates at 80 per cent of the market value. The plan was denounced by Republican leaders as socialistic, a phrase they evidently never get tired of. But now, since the Democrats have enacted essentially the same plan, the Republicans approve enthusiastically. Indeed, bidding for the farm vote up in Minnesota the

other day, the Republican candidate for President pulled the
Democratic platform right out from under me!

But to return to the past. When you marketed your crops abroad,
you sold in free markets for the going price. But when you bought
manufactured goods at home, Republican tariffs compelled you
to pay through the nose. You have been protesting this injustice
since at least the year 1828.

Of course the Republican tariff wasn't all bad. It generously
permitted Americans to worship at duty-free altars; eat from duty-
free tin cans; import duty-free yachts; be hanged with duty-free
rope; and admire duty-free paintings in museums.

The Republicans were still at their old game only a little while
ago, and I wish we could be sure they would not return to it if
they have a chance. Over the protest of over a thousand American
economists, they enacted the Smoot-Hawley tariff that raised rates
to an all-time high. I need not tell Virginians, or your tobacco-
growing and tobacco-processing neighbors, what that did to tobacco exports. Nor need I remind Southern cotton growers and
cotton manufacturers how they were harmed; or say that this tariff
was a turning point in precipitating the worldwide depression of
the 1930's.

But I am not going to talk about the depression when the
average yearly income of the families of one Southern state was
$500. I have said—and I repeat—that I am not running against
President Hoover. Indeed, I think all of us have reason to be grateful to him for the work of the Hoover Commission. And the fact
of the matter is, I don't know who I am running against, but I
strongly suspect it is Senator Taft after all.

But I most certainly am running against the unchanging and
apparently unchangeable attitudes of the Republican leadership.
Presidents come and go. But attitudes remain. For a political
party, as a man, is the sum total of its inheritance, environment,
experience and attitudes.

Thus, for example, when the depression was coming on, the
Secretary of the Treasury was Andrew Mellon. What was his formula for dealing with the depression? How did he propose to act
when the magnificent promise of American life seemed at a shabby
and ignominious end? Mr. Hoover, in his recently published
memoirs, tells us. It was: "Liquidate labor, liquidate stocks, liquidate the farmers, liquidate real estate."

That is certainly one way to deal with a depression—the grave-yard way. But somehow the American people were less than enthusiastic about it, and they turned to the Democratic Party which held out the prospect of life and hope.

The Democratic Party of today was born, then, of the sufferings of the people. It is neither all-wise nor all-knowing, for these are not man's gifts, but God's. But it is now—as it always has been—compassionate, merciful, humane; no stranger to human needs and wants and fears.

The task of striking off the shackles of the South, begun by Woodrow Wilson, has brought you to your rightful place in the Union, not as a matter of charity, not as a sectional matter, but because a happy, purposeful people in a strong, prosperous country is the democratic goal. The Southern states, too, it seems to me, have played a large part in liberating men's creative energies and reaching these goals.

Everywhere this liberation of man's powers during the Democratic decades has brilliantly succeeded, but nowhere has its success been more marked than in the South. Here has come the richest flowering of a great region our nation has witnessed. A new vitality and creative energy is apparent in every aspect of Southern culture, material, intellectual and spiritual. Your colleges are crowded. There is a keen interest in the arts.

Some years ago a famous American critic said that the South was the wasteland of the mind. Yet at that very moment, I am told, so many of your housewives had novels simmering with the soup—among them *Gone with the Wind*—that many husbands had to wait for supper. And men—in an effort perhaps to keep up with their women, among them your own Ellen Glasgow—were writing books and plays, too. So it was that the Nobel Prize for Literature came to the Mississippian, William Faulkner, a prize that he accepted in an exalted address, extolling the unconquerable spirit of man.

If this means much to the nation, it also, I am sure, means much to you. Your way has often been hard. Yet you have always held that civilization is something more than the bending of the resources of nature to the uses of man. Man cannot live without bread, but his spirit cannot live by bread alone.

In the course of this resurgence, I hope that it may be possible for us to keep all that was good of the Old South, while embracing all that is good of the New South. Technicians can make a country, but they alone cannot create a civilization. There are riches in your inheritance which are sometimes overlooked—riches which the rest of the nation could borrow with great profit. I believe it was Gladstone who said that no greater misfortune could befall a people than to break utterly with its past.

Among the most valuable heritages of the Old South is its political genius, which in many respects was far ahead of its time. Even today some of the finest products of Southern governmental thought are only beginning to win the general acceptance which they have so long deserved.

A classic example, it seems to me, is the Constitution of the Confederacy. Scholars of constitutional law have long recognized it as a sound and most thoughtful document. It contained some brilliant innovations, including the so-called item veto—authorizing the President to disapprove individual items in an appropriation bill, without having to veto the entire measure.

This inspiration of the Confederate statesmen has since been incorporated into the constitutions of about three-fourths of our states, including my own state of Illinois.

Is it too much to hope that our Federal Government may soon adopt this priceless invention of Southern statesmanship? I hope not, because it is a most useful tool. It has enabled me to veto more appropriations, involving more money, than any Governor in Illinois history. And, by the way, forty-six other states had higher state tax burdens than Illinois in relation to the income of their citizens last year.

In other fields, I am glad to note, the Southern talent for government has won the recognition which is its due. Many of your states are among the best governed in the land. Southern diplomats have earned wholehearted respect in Asia and Europe. In Congress Southern leaders once again give wise and distinguished service to the nation, especially in the all-important area of foreign affairs. I am proud to have one of them, Senator John Sparkman of Alabama, as my running mate. And I am also proud that other such leaders—each himself a candidate for the Presidency—have given me their support—Senator Kefauver of Tennessee, and my distant kinsman, Senator Richard Russell of Georgia.

Just as the governmental contributions of the South sometimes were not fully appreciated in the past, so too, I suspect, some of the problems of the South have not been fully understood elsewhere. One of these is the problem of minorities—a problem which I have had occasion to think about a good deal, since my own state also has minority groups.

One thing that I have learned is that minority tensions are always strongest under conditions of hardship. During the long years of Republican neglect and exploitation, many Southerners —white and Negro—have suffered even hunger, the most degrading of man's adversities. All the South, in one degree or another, was afflicted with a pathetic lack of medical services, poor housing, poor schooling, and a hundred other ills flowing from the same source of poverty.

The once low economic status of the South was productive of another—and even more melancholy—phenomenon. Many of the lamentable differences between Southern whites and Negroes, ascribed by insensitive observers to race prejudice, have arisen for other reasons. Here economically depressed whites and economically depressed Negroes often had to fight over already gnawed bones. Then there ensued that most pathetic of struggles: the struggle of the poor against the poor. It is a struggle that can easily become embittered, for hunger has no heart. But, happily, as the economic status of the South has risen, as the farms flourish and in the towns there are jobs for all at good wages, racial tensions have diminished.

In the broad field of minority rights, the Democratic Party has stated its position in its platform, a position to which I adhere. I should justly earn your contempt if I talked one way in the South and another way elsewhere. Certainly no intellectually dishonest Presidential candidate could, by an alchemy of election, be converted into an honest President. I shall not go anywhere with beguiling serpent words. To paraphrase the words of Senator John Sharp Williams of Mississippi, better to be a dog and bay the moon.

I should like to say a word about the broader aspects of minority rights.

First, I utterly reject the argument that we ought to grant all men their rights just because if we do not we shall give Soviet Russia a propaganda weapon. This concept is itself tainted with communist wiliness. It insultingly implies that were it not for the communists we would not do what is right. The answer to this argument is that we must do right for right's sake alone. I, for one, do not propose to adjust my ethics to the values of a bloodstained despotism, scornful of all that we hold dear.

Second, I reject as equally contemptible the reckless assertions that the South is a prison in which half the people are prisoners and the other half are wardens. I view with scorn those who hurl charges that the South—or any group of Americans—is wedded to wrong and incapable of right. For this itself is an expression of prejudice compounded with hatred, a poisonous doctrine for which, I hope, there will never be room in our country.

So long as man remains a little lower than the angels, I suppose that human character will never free itself entirely from the blemish of prejudice, religious or racial. These are prejudices, unhappily, that tend to rise wherever the minority in question is large, running here against one group and there against another. Some forget this, and, in talking of the South, forget that in the South the minority is high. Some forget, too, or don't know about strides the South has made in the past decade toward equal treatment.

But I do not attempt to justify the unjustifiable, whether it is anti-Negroism in one place, anti-Semitism in another—or for that matter, anti-Southernism in many places. And neither can I justify self-righteousness anywhere. Let none of us be smug on this score, for nowhere in the nation have we come to that state of harmonious amity between racial and religious groups to which we aspire.

The political abuse of the problem of discrimination in employment, the exploitation of racial aspirations on the one hand and racial prejudice on the other—all for votes—is both a dangerous thing and a revolting spectacle in our political life. It will always be better to reason together than to hurl recriminations at one another.

Our best lesson on reason and charity was read to us by Robert E. Lee. It was not the least of his great contributions to the spirit of America that, when he laid down his sword, he became president of a small college in Lexington—now the splendid Washington and Lee University. There he remained the rest of his life; unifying, not dividing; loving, not hating.

As the autumn of 1865 was coming on, General Lee, in one of the noblest of American utterances, said: "The war being at an end, the Southern states having laid down their arms, and the questions at issue between them and the Northern states having been decided, I believe it to be the duty of everyone to unite in the restoration of the country and the re-establishment of peace and harmony . . ." Later he said: "I know of no surer way of eliciting truth than by burying contention with the war."

We have great need of Lee's spirit in this hour of peril to our country, when voices of hatred and unreason arise again in our land. As free men we shall always, I hope, differ upon many things. But I also hope that we shall never be divided upon those concepts that are enshrined in our religious faith and the charters of our country's greatness.

No one could stand here in Richmond without reverence for those great Virginians—Washington, whose sturdy common sense was the mortar of our foundations, and Jefferson, that universal genius who, proclaiming the Rights of Man when few men had any rights anywhere, shook the earth and made this feeble country the hope of the oppressed everywhere. And so it is today after nearly two centuries.

Fortunately for us all, the Southern political genius still lives. It flamed not long ago in Woodrow Wilson. It burns steadily to-day among Southern members of Congress, and among many of the leaders of your states.

Good politics make good government. In this campaign I shall not try to minimize the tasks which we confront. That we shall pass through these troubled times I am sure, not by grace alone, but by faith, intelligence and implacable determination.

In my travels about the country of late in quest of your confidence I have felt that determination, that indomitable spirit. But nowhere more than here where I suspect it is as strong today as it was in the spring of 1865, when the Army of Northern Virginia returned to their homes. They found a wasteland of burned houses and barns, fences fallen and ditches caved in, weeds, and sorrow brooding over the fields.

That was in April. But by June a crop was growing. The next year the crop was larger, and the next year it was still larger, and so, painfully and slowly, with no help except their hands and the benison of God, the South started on its long march from desolation to fruitfulness.

This is part of your great heritage. And if I could speak for all Americans as I now do for myself, I would say that it also is part of the great heritage of America.

The Role of Labor

The Convention of the American Federation of Labor

NEW YORK CITY

September 22, 1952

This convention has followed the American tradition of giving a hearing to both parties to an argument, and I am glad to take my turn.

You have been transacting your business here for eight days. And I would think it was high time for a little humor. But I fear that there may be some people listening who don't like the light touch, although—well, they don't seem to mind the heavy touch, as long as it is a Republican and not a Democrat. But, gentlemen, there is business before your house and I propose to get right to it, obeying, as far as I can, what seems to be known as the Republican law of gravity.

I have been told that I should try here today to make you roar with enthusiasm. Why, I would not do that even if I could. After all, you are the responsible leaders of organized labor, which, if it does not act responsibly, could do the nation and the working people infinite harm. And I, in turn, am a candidate for the most important individual responsibility in the world. If I were more comforted by your cheers than your thoughts I would hardly merit the confidence of responsible men.

So you will, I hope, understand that what little I have to say, or rather to add, to the many speeches you have dutifully listened to, is intended for your heads and not your hands. And, if I don't start any cheers, I hope at least that I shall not stop any minds.

First I should like if I may to dispose of this matter of the Taft-Hartley law.

The Democratic platform says that the Taft-Hartley Act is "inadequate, unworkable and unfair," and should be replaced by a new law. I developed, on Labor Day, the five basic respects in which the present law seems to me defective and I outlined some five principles to guide the writing of a new one.

How to get a new one? The method, whether by amendment of the existing law or replacement with a new one, has, frankly, seemed to me less important than the objective. But, because the required changes are major changes, because the present law is spiteful, and because it has become a symbol of dissension and bitterness, I urge, therefore, as I did on Labor Day, that the Taft-Hartley Act be repealed.

The Republican platform commends the Taft-Hartley Act because among other things it guarantees to the working man, and I quote, "the right to quit his job at any time."

To this deceit they add the insistence that the real issue here is whether the present law should be "amended" or "repealed." This is not the real issue. The real issue is what changes should be made in the law of the United States. But, if repeal were in itself the issue, I would remind Senator Taft that he himself has publicly recognized twenty-three mistakes in his favorite law, and it seems not unreasonable to recommend that a tire with twenty-three punctures and five blowouts needs junking and not a recap job—and especially a recap job with reclaimed Republican rubber.

There has been, too, the usual barrage of intemperate name-calling. Why is it that when political ammunition runs low, inevitably the rusty artillery of abuse is always wheeled into action? To face the facts of labor relations is to be accused of "captivity," and of "turning left." Now these are words without roots, weeds which grow in darkness and wither in the sun. But the sun is sometimes slow to rise—especially during campaigns. And I am reminded of the saying that a lie can travel around the world while the truth is pulling on its boots.

Now the final Republican maneuvers were executed [by General Eisenhower] on this platform last Wednesday. I am grateful that it was the Republican, Senator Morse, who revealed so masterfully how all of those explosions we heard were only blank cartridges.

It is proposed now apparently to change the Taft-Hartley Act in just two respects: by removing what the speaker called the union-busting clauses, and by making employers, like union leaders, swear that they are not communists. The tinkling sound of these little words was unfortunately smothered in the thundering silence of what was left unsaid.

And on only one point was there anything even approaching a joining of the issues.

It was charged that I had "embraced," and I quote the words, "the principle of compulsion" by asking for the power as President to "compel" arbitration of disputes which threaten the national safety. Now, after that great reunion with Senator Taft on the love-seat at Columbia University, I must say I respect the General's authority on the subject of embraces. But if he wrote what he said, he had not read what I said.

My proposal was, and is, that if Congress sees fit to direct the President to intervene in a labor dispute it should give the President authority to try, among other things, to have that dispute referred to arbitration. I did not say that he should be given the power to "compel" arbitration. I recommended a flexibility of procedures, all built around the mediation process, to replace the present requirement that in all of these cases the collective-bargaining process be stopped—stopped dead—in its tracks, by a court order.

Now what my distinguished opponent would do I cannot determine. If that was his purpose, by the way, he succeeded. He says he is against compulsion. Yet he seems to support the present law, which compels men to work under court injunction for eighty days on terms they have rejected. I find it hard to see where there can be a greater compulsion than this. And if I read what he says as fairly as I can, I gather that in fact he recognizes this too and agrees with me, and with you, that the labor injunction is not a fair or effective dispute-settling device.

He cites with approval the Norris-La Guardia Act which was passed, so he said, under his party's administration in 1932. Now this will all seem a pretty broad claim to those who remember that the House of Representatives in the Seventy-second Congress was safely Democratic, and who can't see much resemblance between Republicans like George Norris and Fiorello La Guardia, on the one hand, and Senator Taft and Representative Hartley on the other. He didn't mention the fact that that act virtually outlawed the labor injunction in the Federal courts or that it had been seriously cut down by the Taft-Hartley Act. I wonder if by any chance Senator Taft deleted such frankness from the General's text.

But the General in his talk to you did recognize squarely that issuing injunctions, and I quote him, "will not settle the underlying fundamental problems which cause a strike." That is one statement we can all agree with. The trouble is that the Taft-Hartley Act was written by those who don't recognize that squarely.

But enough of the labor relations law. There are other problems of equal concern to American labor.

When many of you first came into this business, the only job of American labor—and it was a tough one—was to organize workers and to bargain with employers. This is still perhaps your main job. But you also have greatly expanded your interests and broadened your horizons.

One of the most significant developments in our national life is that the American labor movement is today much more than an instrument of collective bargaining. It has become a vital agency of a working democracy. Your purposes extend to making America strong in a free and a peaceful world, and to seeking all the democratic goals to which the Government of this country is dedicated.

I should like, therefore, to discuss with you how we can best make this relationship work—this partnership, if you please, between government and an independent organization like the American Federation of Labor, both devoted to the same ends.

We recognize, to begin with, that in this partnership no partner can be allowed to dominate the other. Labor unions, like all private persons and organizations, must maintain an independence from government. Government, including political parties, must be independent of any private bodies.

As spokesman for the Democratic Party, at least for the moment, I put this in plain language, not because you of the A.F. of L. misunderstand, but because others try to misrepresent. I am glad that the Democratic Party and the American Federation of Labor have both been guided for a long time by the same stars—stars that have led us toward the realization of human hopes and desires.

But our functions are different, and our responsibilities are different to different groups, even if these groups possibly overlap. The Democratic Party is the party of all the people. Were it otherwise, it would be false to democracy itself.

We seek then a pattern for full co-operation, but one which recognizes our mutual independence.

And what are the specific things we can do in moving toward the human goals we hold in common?

We can start, because the opportunity is so obvious, by making the Department of Labor a more effective service agency. To mention a few specific responsibilities here is to suggest many others:

1. Given sufficient funds, the Bureau of Labor Statistics could, it seems to me, better perform its essential service as keeper of the people's budget, and serve a much broader function than it now can.

2. We should consider a labor counterpart of the Agricultural Extension Service to help train the men who make democracy work in the labor unions and around the bargaining tables. And

3. By retraining men who are replaced by machines and directing them to new jobs, where now we simply pay them unemployment compensation, we could save both manpower and tax money.

4. Again the National Labor Relations Board, operating outside the Labor Department but in this same field, must be staffed to process cases in half the time it now takes, for in this field particularly "justice delayed is justice denied."

5. Then there is the problem of the migrant farm laborers, over a million Americans who move north and south with the sun and the seasons, their lives often bleak cycles of exploitation and rejection. It certainly invites our compassionate attention.

Strengthening the Labor Department is an old subject. Advocacy is always easier than action. But I lay what I hope is not immodest claim to at least a journeyman's qualifications. My apprenticeship was served in getting, and assisting to get, at least a partial labor program—over fifty bills—through a Republican legislature in Illinois.

It will also be an important development in democracy when men and women will come in ever-increasing numbers from your ranks to positions of key responsibility in government.

What you have to offer, in all of our essential governmental programs, has been perhaps best proven by the contribution that labor has already made on the international front.

Your effective fight against communism goes clear back to the time it was called bolshevism. You have licked it in your own houses, and you have gone after the roots from which it grows.

I join with my distinguished opponent in saluting you for these accomplishments. One wonders why his party forgot them when, in 1947, they singled you out as peculiarly suspicious characters and required your taking a special oath of loyalty. I hope you don't misunderstand me—I am neither courting nor embracing—when I acknowledge and applaud the job you have done, not only through the International Labor Organization, the Economic Co-operation Administration, the Department of State, but through your own offices in rejecting the communist World Federation of Trade Unions; pressing the case in the United Nations against forced labor in the Soviet Union; supporting free trade unions in Europe and Asia and in South America; helping build up popular resistance wherever the spiked wall of Russia throws its shadow over free men and women. Where men's minds have been poisoned against democracy, many will learn that America is free, and they will only learn it as they hear it from you when you say that you are free. To the workers of other nations, yours is today perhaps the clearest voice that America has.

I am proud, as a Democrat, that a Democratic administration has recognized this and I hope that more and more union leaders will be called upon to serve their country abroad. I think we need diplomats who speak to people in the accents of the people. Ambassadors in overalls can be the best salesmen of democracy.

There are other tasks ahead, many of them here at home. President Truman listed the biggest among these jobs in his message to this convention, the priority jobs in making America still stronger and ever more healthy.

How well we meet these problems together will depend upon, it seems to me, these three things:

First, that we understand each other, and

Second, that we exercise our powers always with firm self-restraint, and

Third, that we hold fast to the conviction that only people are important.

The understanding which flows between the party for which I speak and the enormous group you represent requires no detailing here. To remember the loneliness, the fear and the insecurity of men who once had to walk alone in huge factories beside huge machines, to realize that labor unions have meant new dignity and pride to millions of our countrymen, human companionship on the job, and music in the home, to be able to see what larger pay checks mean, not to a man as an employe, but as a husband, and as a father—to know these things is to understand what American labor means.

Franklin Roosevelt knew these things. Harry Truman knows

these things. But they are the imponderable human elements that some among us, unhappily, have never understood.

Now—as to the exercise of our powers.

The Democratic Party has been entrusted for twenty years with the awesome responsibility of leadership in governing the United States. During these years, the labor unions have become strong and vigorous. So American labor, too, has enormous power today and enormous responsibilities. "Uneasy lies the head that wears the crown." It is cause for very real humility. It is the whole history of mankind that power lacking the inner strength of self-restraint will be eventually cast down.

It is the history of the Republican Party that it supported, and was supported by, those interests which believed that freedom meant the right to exercise economic power without restraint. And that party was cast down.

It has been the basic belief of the Democratic Party that only human freedoms are basic and that economic power must be exercised so as not to curtail them. We hold, too, that the power of government must be restricted to the point that government stands never as master and always as a servant.

It is no less essential to the future of democracy that American labor walk wisely with its power. Your awareness of this has been shown in many practical ways. There is, most recently perhaps, the forthright and heartening manner in which you have attacked the problem of jurisdictional strikes. Your joint-board procedure in the building trades and your prohibitions upon picketing in support of jurisdictional claims are examples of sound self-regulation directed against the abuse and, therefore, the corruption of power.

You have expressed your willingness to accept procedures which recognize the priority of the public interest in national-emergency disputes. You today accept the fact that, in the private free-enterprise system which we all recognize as basic to our liberty and our prosperity, employes can prosper only as their employers do, and that irresponsible demands are only self-defeating.

Yet American labor, like the Democratic Party, faces new and uncharted tomorrows. You, as we, will be challenged anew to measure up to the demands of both freedom and power. The future of democracy, perhaps the future of our world, depends upon the exercise of power by America's private and public bodies alike with that self-restraint which separates power from tyranny and order from chaos.

American labor's role, its whole purpose has been to restore to people the status and dignity they lost when the sprawling factories reached out to engulf them. Hence, for example, your insistence that there be a community law of job rights—seniority rules—to stand beside the law of property rights.

Equally has the Democratic Party drawn its strength, I think, from the people. We have built our program on their hopes, stood by them in adversity and found the measure of our accomplishment in their welfare. We have written the laws of twenty years from pictures in our minds of men and women who are tired after a day's full work, who are defeated if a week's wages don't buy a week's food, who are out of a job, or who are sick or have finished a life's work. We believe in a government with a heart.

Yet we are told that we have gone too far.

What do they mean? Are they saying that our people are too well fed, too well clothed, too well housed? Do they say that our children are getting more and better schooling than they should? Have we gone too fast in our efforts to provide equal opportunities to working men and women of all races and colors? Are the 62,000,000 workers of America too healthy, too happy? Should fewer of them be working?

The Republicans say they want a change. Well let them, then, speak out: Which of these things do they want changed?

With mutual understanding, with a humbling sense of our power, with belief in our masters, the people, we shall see to it, my friends, that these things are not changed.

I want, if I may, in closing to salute a tradition of leadership which embodies all I have been trying to say here today. The foundations of that tradition were laid by Samuel Gompers, and they have been built upon by William Green. You have held, sir, if I may say so, to the ideal of democratic leadership—the leadership which seeks the good of all, the leadership of him who wants only to serve.

The Control of Inflation

Fifth Regiment Armory

B A L T I M O R E ,   M A R Y L A N D

September 23, 1952

I find myself tonight tempted to stray from a path I have followed now for a month.

Day after day, night after night, I have tried to talk about public questions: international policy, farm policy, labor policy, civil rights, atomic energy, and many others.

This road has led me through some twenty states from coast to coast. It has been lined with great numbers of people, friendly people, people who nod encouragingly when you try to talk to them intelligently and straight from the shoulder.

But, strangely enough, the road itself is lonely—for I never meet anybody coming the other way.

The temptation tonight is to talk not about more issues, but about this road itself, about our campaign—how it is going, how high our spirits are. For I know now, with the beat of my heart no less than with the certainty of my mind, that this is going to be another victorious year for those of us who believe in the positive principles of the Democratic Party.

We know now that we face, in the party of the opposition, a sadly divided command. The G.O.P. elephant has two heads nowadays and I can't tell from day to day who is driving the poor beast—Taft or the General. The sad thing is that the elephant doesn't know either! As Americans first and political partisans second we find no satisfaction in this state of affairs in a year when our country faces choices of leaders, choices of attitudes and choices of policies of such enormous consequence.

Instead of confident, positive purpose, there is indecision, uncertainty and compromise in an effort to reconcile the irreconcilable, the internationalists and the isolationists, the liberals and the reactionaries. The end product is loud denunciation, epithet and

165

abuse of the Democrats, which seems to be the only thing they can agree upon. But that will lift no hearts, and feed no hungry minds, and win no elections.

And so each day their statement of position moves in like a new fog bank.

America will not entrust its future, its hopes, to the masters of a house divided against itself, to men so divided in their own thoughts that they cannot, or will not, tell us where their party stands on America's pressing problems.

And about the only place they appear to stand is squarely on the Democratic policies. There is hardly room for us Democrats on our own platform! But at the same time they say the authors and executors of Democratic policies are rogues and rascals, or timid and stupid men who should be thrown out and promptly replaced by the Republicans who fought all these very same programs.

But I shall yield no further to temptation. There are still issues to be faced. I have tried as best I can, from city to city, to discuss them one by one and to express my views forthrightly, not confident I am always right or even wise, but certain that you are entitled to know my views, right or wrong.

Tonight, here in Baltimore, I want to discuss another and a very important issue—inflation. In plainer terms it is the issue of whether we are going to be able to pay our grocery bill, and keep up with the mortgage or the rent on the house.

Whether you have a boy of draft age, or one in Korea, the problem of peace is first in your mind and in your heart. But this problem of prices is another ominous cloud which hangs heavy over our thoughts. As far as the Government is concerned, it must give both problems top priority.

I want to talk particularly to whoever in your family does the shopping and keeps the budget. I am thinking especially, too, of those family budgets where only one of the two ends ever moves— because all the income is from savings or pensions. White-collar workers and schoolteachers also face a special problem here.

If our question, then, is what we are going to do about inflation, we must first be sure we understand what causes it.

Those who let their politics impeach their honesty tell you that inflation is the product of governmental waste and mismanagement. Whether this is legitimate politics I shall not presume to say. But as an explanation of the causes of inflation, it is pure poppycock. It's like a husband coming into the kitchen, seeing one potato peeling that is too thick, and exploding that now he knows why you can't make ends meet. I'm for the Government's peeling its potatoes with a sharp knife and a miserly eye. And I've done some sharp and miserly peeling in Illinois myself. But I'm not going to fool myself or you that meeting a nation's inflation problem is that simple.

Prescribing a patent medicine with a good taste for a growth which may become malignant is dangerous practice. This is a kind of politics which places party victory above national welfare and assumes that the people are fools. I shall do neither.

The causes of inflation can, I think, be made plain. Let's stay in the kitchen a minute longer. It is as though we were making bread, and while we answered the phone, an evil neighbor dumped a whole cup of yeast into the bowl. That's the inflation story. In fact that *is* inflation.

We have inflation today—not disastrous, but serious—because the gods of war, working through their agents in the Kremlin, have dumped a barrel of yeast in the bread of our economy.

American industry has been suddenly called upon to make tens of billions of dollars' worth of guns and planes and tanks and bombs. This is the yeast which causes inflation.

These unexpected demands mean that the prices of steel, aluminum, machine tools and the like—as well as labor—go up, unless something is done about it, because the supply of these things is limited. Those who have them to sell can demand more for them because the Government must have the end products. The supply of consumer goods is diminished, because factories which made roller skates are now making gun assemblies.

The other side of this picture is that those who buy have more to buy with and will therefore pay higher prices. The manufacturers have orders for guns, so they can pay higher prices for steel and for labor. Consumers, you and I, have had increases in our incomes, so we will pay more for the roller skates we can find.

If this then is our problem, what can we do about it? Do we have to just sit back and let prices and wages keep chasing each other on up?

If I sense rightly the mood of people today they are ready to say "we want these increases to stop—and we mean business."

And if we do mean business, I say that we can get results.

Telling you what I have in mind is going to be a little dull—for I haven't any trick ideas up my sleeve. This job takes courage and it takes common sense. It has to be a partnership job—with the people and the Government working together.

Let's not talk generalities. There are four things I think the Government has to do.

First there is the necessity to cut the Government's non-essential expenditures to the bare bones of safety. It is the biggest spending agency in the country and every dollar it spends adds to the inflationary pressure. It must spend every penny as though it were a five-dollar bill; and it must not spend a single penny for anything that is not needed right now.

This is going to mean a strict auditing of every payroll in the Government and slashing every piece of administrative fat. I've been through this process in Illinois and I know what it means.

This is going to mean no pork-barreling while our economy is in its present condition. If your principal interest in life is getting a new federally financed boondoggle for your state you had better vote for somebody else. I've vetoed more appropriations in Illinois than any Governor in our history.

We will have to make most of our savings in the military departments. About 85 cents out of every dollar the Government spends goes now for paying the costs of past wars and preventing another one. I know one can't buy national security at a bargain counter. And I emphatically reject the idea that national security must be adjusted to a tax ceiling rather than taxes to national security. For that is to say that we propose to continue free and independent—if it does not cost too much. But I don't believe either in the theory that military budgets are sacred and untouchable.

I warn you, however, that the tightest-fisted government economy conceivable won't meet this problem. Despite the Republican propaganda, our budget is determined more by the Russians than by the "bureaucrats." We are going to survive even with sacrifice rather than perish cheap.

The next thing the Government has to do is keep itself just as close as possible to a pay-as-we-go tax standard. When we pay for these guns by borrowing money we contribute to inflation. When we collect taxes to pay for them we help stop inflation.

I don't like taxes. I shall do everything I can to reduce them. But I will make no promises I know I cannot keep. We must spend to be safe and taxes are better than inflation. I would not favor reducing taxes until we are getting in a dollar to cover every dollar we spend. And I'll bank on the American people, even in an election year, to understand straight talk and the need for a balanced budget.

In the last six years, since the end of World War Two financing, the Government's net receipts have been four billion dollars more than its expenditures. We have reduced the Government debt by eleven billion dollars. No man in the United States has worked harder for a pay-as-we-go policy than President Truman, or received, I think, less credit for his achievements on this front.

The Republicans in Congress have, on the other hand, fought this pay-as-we-go program every inch of the way. In 1951, for example, the Republicans in the House of Representatives voted three to one against raising more money to pay our current war-production bills. Those were votes for inflation, for they meant borrowing to pay those bills. It is hypocrisy for these men to present themselves now as the defenders, or even the friends, of your dollar.

The third thing the Government must do is to prevent excessive private borrowing, for that can be just as inflationary as excessive Government borrowing.

Some buying on credit is all right—like buying a house and paying on the mortgage instead of for rent. Some of it is necessary to keep business active. But some of it can go too far. I shall hope to be able to work out with the Congress a set of restraints upon excessive private credit which will keep the money market on an even, noninflationary, keel.

Finally, there is the matter of direct controls—on prices and wages and rent. I don't like them; not many people do. But if the alternative is a steady rise in our food, clothing, rent and other living costs, then we must have them.

The present price, wage and rent control laws are, I think, in pretty bad shape. They are pock-marked with loopholes, loopholes bored by special-interest groups so that they could feed and fatten on inflation. Yet I am convinced from what I know of the situation, and I make no pretense of being an economist, that these laws are operating as essential brakes upon an economy which could otherwise get out of hand.

I shall favor retaining the controls we now have until prices stop going up, and if they don't stop before January first, I think the situation should be re-examined and Congress should take further steps to stop them.

This will mean, if it has to come, tighter wage controls as well as tighter price controls. I don't know whether the wage and price increases which came out of the steel case this year were required by what had happened elsewhere in the economy or not.

But I do know that many people see in that case a further impetus to inflation. It brings into sharp focus the question of whether the price and wage loopholes aren't becoming bigger than we can afford. We just can't be either pulled or pushed any further into the twisting cyclone of inflation.

I have a deep belief in a free economy. I look forward anxiously to the time when these casts on our economy—these price, rent and wage controls—can come off. I cannot tell you when that will be, for I can only guess as to the Kremlin's future course of conduct or misconduct. I can only say to you that I believe, with the modern doctors, that a healthy, but temporarily fractured economy, like a healthy patient, should get out of bed and get active again as quickly as possible.

I wish I could tell you how my position on this matter differs from that of my distinguished opponent. But I cannot; I do not know. He has, however, permitted the astonishing statement to be made for him that he agrees with Senator Taft on all matters of domestic policy. And Senator Taft's record as the leader of the inflationary shock troops in Congress is clearly written.

The great majority of Republicans in Congress voted to end rent control. They voted, too, to end controls on steel, copper, aluminum and other vital defense production materials. Four times, a majority of the Republicans in both the Senate and the House voted to end controls on all things consumers buy.

This is the Republican position on inflation.

This is the record the Republican candidate has bought. It is a record the nation refused to buy when it was being made. This is a record the Republican Party refused to buy in Chicago last July.

We offer you, in place of this record, a four-point program of strict government economy, of a tax program kept as nearly as possible on a pay-as-we-go basis, of restraints on excessive private credit, and of direct price, wage and rent controls as temporary pontoon bridges between abnormal and normal times.

I think such a program, supported in good faith by both the Congress and the Executive, can stop inflation without stopping the healthy, normal growth of our economy.

The people must, however, do their part of this job. If this system of ours works as well as you and I think it does, the battle against inflation will be finally won, not in the bureaus of government, but in the fields, in the factories, in the union halls, in the stores and in the homes of America.

The ultimate defense against high prices is more production, more production of food and houses and steel, and of everything we buy.

Our production capacity today has been so increased that when our defense production levels out, we can turn to a full production of consumer goods which will provide the fullest defense against inflation. And we'll use that production, too, all of it.

In the meantime, we all face questions which we can, as individuals, answer either for or against inflation.

This is true of the directors of a manufacturing company when they vote on a proposal to expand their plant's capacity.

It is true of the members of a labor union when they vote on whether to demand a wage increase or on what it is to be.

It is true of the storekeeper when he is deciding whether to go through his shelves and mark up his prices.

It is true of the housewife as she debates in her mind whether to save or spend what is left from last week's pay envelope.

It is a dangerously wrong feeling that what individual people do on points such as these won't matter. America's decisions are made this way—in millions of little pieces.

There is one other thing for us to do as individuals. Inflation feeds on fear of inflation. We know what scare-buying does.

We must remain on our guard. What this job takes is just common sense, calmness and courage.

I have approached this subject with you tonight as straightforwardly and as seriously as I know how. Inflation will not be driven out by campaign orators flapping their arms at it like scarecrows.

I am convinced and I think you are, that when the Republican leaders, after sabotaging every anti-inflationary measure in Congress during the past two years, reach out to put a consoling arm around the American housewife and whisper in her ear that this is all the Democrats' fault, they won't deceive her.

Most of us are people of small or at least modest incomes. We could be hurt badly, a lot of us, by just a very little more inflation. Our interest in stopping rising prices is as real as tomorrow night's supper and new overcoats for the children this winter. We are not fooling and we are not going to be fooled.

The time has come for us to draw a line and say to the forces of inflation, "You cannot cross that line." With your help I'd like to do just that.

Economy in Government

Indiana State Fair Grounds

INDIANAPOLIS, INDIANA

September 26, 1952

These gracious introductions always remind me of a Hoosier who had a more direct way of introducing himself. He used to say:
"I'm an Indiana farmer and I want it understood
That I make an honest living and my reputation's good."
I am hopeful that my own reputation is reasonably good in Indiana, because I've been a close neighbor for a long time. I feel perfectly at home here. As you may have guessed, I'm here on a political errand, and I know that politics comes as naturally to Hoosiers as plain speaking.

We could use a lot more plain speaking in this campaign. And on some rare occasions when my distinguished opponent, the General, has ventured to talk plainly, he has advanced some startling ideas: the idea, for example, that people should vote this fall for all Republican candidates, whatever their character and ability. He wants us to elect them all: good, bad and outrageous.

Until a few days ago, I had believed this was a new theory of politics. I am told, however, that it actually is an old and familiar tactic in certain Republican circles. In 1925, for example, no less than the Chief Justice of the Indiana Supreme Court advised the young people of the state to "Vote the straight Republican ticket, regardless of the qualifications of the candidate even though you know a man to be incompetent . . . even though you know him to be immoral, vote for him because he represents the Republican ticket."

But this kind of barefaced political cynicism has never won much favor in Indiana or anywhere else. And I don't think it will be successful this year.

My opponent said the other night—and I must say I was surprised that he of all people should say it—that men are known by the company they keep.

Well, the company I like to keep in Indiana, or anywhere else, is the company of men like my old friend, Henry F. Schricker— and I shall never know a gentler, kinder, wiser man than the great and beloved Hoosier who governs this state, Governor Schricker.

I have a special feeling of kinship for him. He's the man who put my name in nomination. But we are still friends! You know in America any boy may become President and I suppose it's just one of the risks he takes! As Governors of neighboring states, we have been wrestling with the same problems. These are problems which face every governor in our times—problems of economy, of efficient administration, of states' rights, and of integrity in government. I want to talk to you about some of these things tonight. It's not the most exciting thing I could talk about, but it's one of the most important.

In particular I want to talk to you about economy in government. This is a subject on which I have passionate convictions and so does Governor Schricker. Bankers usually do. I am certain that economy in government—the most rigorous and searching economy—is vital to the health of this Republic just as it is to our states.

I think Indiana is a good place to discuss this subject. The Hoosier has always been a hard man with a dollar—his own dollar or anybody else's. I think of a Hoosier as a down-to-earth, prosperous, rather generous, neighborly fellow—but one who knows where every stray piece of string is in the pantry. He is a hard-to-beat man. And he's hard to fool. I remember saying down in Vincennes at the 150th anniversary of the Indiana Territory, which included Illinois, that probably shrewd Hoosier business deals were too much for the Illinois suckers so they broke away and set up their own territory.

And so tonight I want to talk a little sense about government economy.

Like Governor Schricker, I have had practical experience with this problem. In Illinois we have lived within our means these past four years without increasing taxes except to restore our worn-out roads. Taking into account our needs and the increased cost of everything, it has not been easy. And I had to live with a Republican legislature, but, strange to say, we got along pretty well, and more than once I was reminded of the words of your Hoosier philosopher, Abe Martin, who said: "Now an' then an innocent man is sent to the legislature." I could add—even a Republican, now and then!

But during the last session of the Illinois legislature, what do you think they did to the thrifty, closely balanced budget I presented to them? They cut out $300,000 and added $50,000,000! But I vetoed most of it; I vetoed more appropriations than any governor in Illinois history. So you will understand when I say that I think the carefully cultivated legend that all Democrats are wasters and all Republicans are economical is the bunk. I think this is a time for bare-bone economy and the Republican legislators in Illinois can tell you I mean what I say.

We tightened up our spending in Illinois in other ways, too. We rid ourselves of political parasites. We stopped graft. We overhauled the highway and building-construction and the purchasing systems. We enlisted the services of excellent men and honest men who knew their jobs. And if I have earned any respect for the administration of Illinois in the past four years, it is due to them.

As a result, we saved money where it could be saved, and we were able to spend money where it needed to be spent. We were able greatly to increase state aid to common schools, enlarge and improve our facilities for the care of the mentally ill, increase public-assistance grants, etc., etc.—and all without any increase whatever in general-purpose taxes. The current biennial budget I submitted was actually lower than the preceding one. The cost of state government in Illinois in relation to the income of its citizens is one of the lowest in the country.

I think the methods we used in Illinois will work in Washington. I want to give you five concrete rules—rules I know from my experience will work. I emphasize that they require action, not just words. It is cheap talk to say we must spend less and tax less. We have heard such talk in abundance. You always hear it loudest and oftenest at election time.

To manage the public purse efficiently and economically is a brutal job and let us make no mistake about it. I have served my apprenticeship and I tell you the man who says he can move in and work miracles with a meat axe—or with mirrors—is either kidding the people or revealing his own inexperience. Nomination to public office and a round of speechmaking do not automatically qualify anyone as an economical administrator.

First, saving money in government requires, above everything else, hard-headed, tight-fisted, vigorous leadership by men who are passionately concerned with getting the job done at the lowest possible cost—men who will instill a deep feeling for thrift in all branches and at all levels of the public service. I have found such men in Illinois and managed to persuade many of them to take on the exacting tasks of government.

In Washington, civilian leadership is most important in relation to the military because that is where the great bulk of our tax dollars are spent. We must make sure that wastage of our silver is not a privilege of our brass.

In this connection I am obliged to say that I think the Republican suggestion that a General can best cut down on military waste at least deserves examination. I call as witness the bi-partisan Senate committee now investigating our preparedness program under the chairmanship of Senator Lyndon Johnson, of Texas. These Senators, both Democrats and Republicans, have concluded: "It is not an easy task to change the deeply ingrained attitudes of military men who, for centuries, have operated on the theory that cost is not a compelling consideration."

The present civilians in charge of the Department of Defense, and the President, have saved literally billions of dollars in our present defense program. Secretary Lovett testified that he and the President saved nineteen billion dollars in this year's budget by cutting down the requests of the military services. And please don't mistake my admiration for the generals and the admirals, with whom I worked in great intimacy for three years during the war. Some of them, even the Republican ones, are among my best friends. But from what I have seen I am not persuaded that either their education or experience or inclination is the best insurance of thrift with public funds.

Rule one, then, is to get strong-minded, economy-minded civilians in top jobs. Rule two is to give them the authority to manage their departments efficiently.

This means carrying through the work of government reorganization so ably started by the Hoover Commission. Incidentally, while I do not regard economy in government as a partisan issue, I was interested to learn that a majority of Republican Senators

voted against fifteen of the nineteen reorganization plans submitted by the President that have come to a vote in the last four
years—often overriding the direct recommendations of their former
President, Herbert Hoover.

The present reorganization law expires next spring. I shall certainly ask the Congress to extend it. Improvement in organization
is a job that has to be worked at day in and day out.

Efficiency in government also requires that we reward people
who find ways to save money, and that we promote supervisors
on the basis of their ability to get the job done at minimum cost
and with the fewest subordinates. I think also we need some improvement in our civil-service system, to make sure the strong safe-
guards we need against arbitrary or unfair discharge do not strangle
our ability to hold employes to strict standards of efficient performance.

The third method for saving money in Washington is to improve the machinery for scrutinizing appropriations, so that the
Budget presented by the President and the money bills voted by
the Congress will be based on cold fact and not hot air. As a
candidate for the Presidency, I am disturbed by the knowledge
that there are now several hundred people in the Pentagon preparing the military budget for next year, and only thirty-eight
people in the President's Bureau of the Budget to review those
estimates. The Republican candidate, incidentally, had some harsh
words to say the other night in St. Louis about replacing the present staff of the Bureau of the Budget. I think he would have been
better advised to recommend enlarging that staff—a step that has
frequently been proposed by the President but blocked in the
Congress.

Last week, in Virginia, I suggested that the President be given
the item veto—the power to disapprove individual items in an
appropriation bill, without having to veto the entire bill. The
President could then wield a sharp scalpel against special interests without bringing the machinery of government to a stop.
Three-fourths of our states, including my own, have long since
adopted this useful tool and I think it is time the Federal Government adopted it too.

The Congress, too, needs more help on appropriations. Until
recently, the House Appropriations Committee has had only
twelve busy Congressmen, assisted by a four-man staff, to comb

through the staggering figures of a fifty-billion-dollar military budget. The Congress just this year voted itself some more help, which should enable more Congressmen to be sure they know what they are talking about when they propose cuts in appropriations.

A fourth step for saving money is to establish more effective means for controlling expenditures after the Congress votes the money. This is the problem of getting a dollar's worth of value for every dollar spent.

Here, too, the problem is hardest in the Defense Department, where the need for speed in obtaining results must be constantly balanced against the costs of hurrying. The North African air bases are fresh in our minds. We needed those bases and we needed them fast. But surely in this case we paid a high premium for speed.

Let no one think, however, that improvement can be accomplished just by good intentions. It takes hard, patient, steady work. It was only three years ago that the Defense Department was established on its present unified basis. Much has been accomplished in these three years. Where the Army, Navy and Air Force used to compete with each other in buying medical supplies, food, lumber and many other items, there is now centralized buying for all three; where each military service used to run a separate air-transport system, there is now one for all; where the three services used to buy hundreds of different sizes of nuts and bolts, they are now standardizing on a few.

These are only a few examples of the improvements taking place month by month. Some save a few dollars; others save millions. It is no criticism of the present management of the Defense Department to say we need to go much farther, as fast as we can.

I know something about what can be done, as well as what has been done. I spent a good deal of my time in the Navy Department during the last war on the problems of organization and the economy of manpower and money in naval commands and installations. But it can only be done by relentless action. Republican oratory never saved a nickel!—or Democratic oratory, for that matter!

My fifth and last method for reducing Federal spending requires action not by the Federal Government but by States and localities and plain, ordinary citizens.

We can do much more to make our smaller units of government strong and vigorous and efficient. I have put considerable
sweat, and some tears, into this endeavor in Illinois, and so has
Governor Schricker here in Indiana.

I have never believed in states' rights when they are used as a
cover for states' wrongs. But I firmly believe in states' rights when
the states assume the responsibilities they ought to. As I said over
at the Illinois State Fair in August, I hope you will sweep me
into Washington in November, but I hope you will not sweep any
more responsibilities to Washington that the states can handle.

In addition, I think it is time for a kind of national stock-
taking and a good deal more self-discipline in what we ask our
national Government to do for us. Perhaps you have heard about
the Chamber of Commerce that sent off two letters to a Senator
in the same mail. One demanded an immediate and drastic reduction in the Federal budget. The other demanded a ten-million-
dollar appropriation for a harbor improvement for the home town.
(I'm sure nothing like that ever happened in Indiana!)

You know how it is; anything that helps the other fellow is
"extravagance"; anything that helps you is a "necessity." An Iowa
farmer may be tempted to think it wasteful for the Government
to construct a petroleum experiment station in Pennsylvania. And
a New Jersey businessman may think building a dam in Oregon
is fantastic. What each of us must do is to stretch our minds and
look at these things the way the President and the Congress have
to look at them—from the standpoint of the whole nation.

These five points are the framework I propose for a real economy
drive—one that seeks results, not headlines: first, get tight-fisted
executives; second, give them the authority to run their organizations efficiently; third, scrutinize appropriation requests with a
cold and penetrating eye; fourth, spend appropriations frugally;
fifth, don't do in Washington what can be done in Indianapolis,
and don't ask Uncle Sam to bridge Catbird Creek if you can help
it. Simple rules. Nothing spectacular. But I know they work on a
smaller scale in Springfield, and I believe they will work on a
larger scale in Washington. At least I would like to try them—
which will take a little help from you!

Let no one deceive himself. Pinch every penny as best we can,
our Federal budget is still going to be large—much larger than we
would like.

And why is this? It is because about 85 per cent of our present budget—sixty-nine billion dollars of our seventy-nine billion—is going for national security, including the cost of past wars.

You know and I know that we are confronted with a hostile, inscrutable and ruthless enemy. To deter that enemy and to defend ourselves, we must have what it takes, and quickly. We are building an air force of 143 wings, and it is going to cost us billions. No honest man can say how long we shall have to maintain it, but you can be sure it is likely to be for a long time to come. If I told you anything else I would be deceiving you or myself. Deceit may win elections now and then but it will never win wars or save civilizations.

I will leave deception to the Republican orators. They have been practicing it day and night. They promise one day they will cut your Federal budget by ten billion, or twenty billion, or forty billion, depending upon which one is talking and to whom. And the next day they say they are going to increase America's armed might.

This is nonsense. It is worse than that—it is the oldest and cheapest of political tricks. Cut taxes but spend more money—in the name of common sense, have we not outgrown such childishness?

The only way you could cut tens of billions from our budget now would be to disband our armies, renounce our friends abroad, quit buying airplanes and guns, cancel our present defense orders, and, presumably, crawl into a cave to await destruction.

Well, I don't think the people are prepared to surrender to communism. And I don't think we will be fooled by irresponsible demagogy about the Federal budget. We know that what is involved is nothing less than war or peace. And we know the billions we spend to prevent a third world war are but a drop in the bucket to what we would have to pour out in dollars and in lives to win it if it came.

There is but one way you can cut those tens of billions—and that is to get the foreign assistance and the defense job done and tip the scales against the communist tormentors of the world and toward peace. That is the direction the Democratic Party has charted, that is the way I want to go, and that is the way I think you want to go.

Korea

Memorial Auditorium

L O U I S V I L L E , K E N T U C K Y

September 27, 1952

While I feel very much the uncomfortable politician trying to beguile your votes here tonight, I do not feel at all like a stranger in Kentucky.

My great-great-grandfather and great-great-grandmother were married here in Kentucky. In fact some historians say that their marriage is the first recorded marriage in Kentucky. They built a home near Danville more than 150 years ago which is still standing.

My Grandfather Stevenson was born here before his parents moved to Illinois 100 years ago this year. He was a student at Centre College where he fell in love with the President's daughter —always a sound policy for a struggling student—and thus I acquired a Kentucky grandmother also.

So you will forgive me, I hope, if I claim a very close kinship to Kentucky. But if that's not enough, I'll also claim kinship with Alben Barkley—the greatest Kentuckian of them all.

And I also have Kentucky to thank not only for my ancestors but also for Wilson Wyatt—once the Mayor of this great city and now my campaign manager.

So, my fellow Kentuckians, I want to talk to you tonight about the war in Korea.

When I entered this campaign, I expressed my hope that Democrats and Republicans alike would regard this election year as a great opportunity to educate and elevate a people whose destiny is leadership. I hoped that both parties would talk sense to the American people.

But I have been increasingly disturbed about the tone and spirit of the campaign.

181

Last Monday the General spoke in Cincinnati about Korea. He said that this was a "solemn subject" and that he was going to state the truth as he knew it, "the truth—plain and unvarnished." If only his speech had measured up to this introduction! And since he has tried, not once but several times, to make a vote-getting issue out of our ordeal in Korea, I shall speak on this subject and address myself to the record.

We are fighting in Korea, the General declares, because the American Government grossly underestimated the Soviet threat; because the Government allowed America to become weak; because American weakness compelled us to withdraw our forces from Korea; because we abandoned China to the communists; and, finally, because we announced to all the world that we had written off most of the Far East.

That's what he says—now let's look at the record.

First, the General accuses the Government of having underestimated the Soviet threat. But what about the General himself? At the end of the war he was a professional soldier of great influence and prestige, to whom the American people listened with respect. What did he have to say about the Soviet threat? In the years after the war, the General himself saw "no reason"—as he later wrote—why the Russian system of government and Western democracy "could not live side by side in the world." In November, 1945, he even told the House Military Affairs Committee: "Nothing guides Russian policy so much as a desire for friendship with the United States."

I have no wish to blow any trumpets here. But in March, 1946, I said: "We must forsake any hope that the Soviet Union is going to lie still and lick her awful wounds. She's not. Peace treaties that reflect her legitimate demands, friendly governments on her frontiers and an effective United Nations Organization should be sufficient security. But evidently they are not and she intends to advance her aims, many of them objectives of the Czars, to the utmost."

My opponent's next point is the question of demobilization. We know how self-righteous the Republican office seekers are on this question today. But what were they saying at the time? In the 1944 campaign, the Republican candidate of that year accused President Roosevelt of deliberately delaying demobilization and promised that the Republicans would do it quicker. "I believe," he said, "that our members of the armed forces should be transported home and released at the earliest practical moment after victory." Although the General warned against too rapid demobilization, he later said—in September, 1946—that: "Frankly, I don't think demobilization was too fast."

Demobilization did go too far and too fast. But it would have gone farther and faster if the Republicans had been in power—and it is nonsense to pretend otherwise.

Next, take the question of the withdrawal of American forces from Korea. The General acts as if this were the result of some secret White House decision. I would call his attention to the fact that while he was Chief of Staff of the United States Army, the Chiefs of Staff advised that South Korea was of little strategic interest to the United States, and recommended withdrawal of the United States forces from the country.

Next, my distinguished opponent has recently begun to parrot the charge of some of his recently acquired political tutors that the administration abandoned China to the communists. He did not talk this way once; but then he has changed in a good many respects of late. Maybe he's competing for the title of Mr. Republican as well as Mr. President. But he still must know in his heart, even if he does not choose to admit it, that in the past six years nothing except the sending of an American expeditionary force to China could have prevented ultimate communist victory. Did he propose that; did any of the Sunday-morning quarterbacks on the Republican team propose that?

Distinguished American military men—including at least one Republican—have testified that the Chinese Nationalists did not lose for want of supplies or American support. Their armies were larger and better equipped than the communist armies. They had every physical advantage.

Has my opponent forgotten the wise words of the most responsible Republican of them all, Senator Vandenberg? Here is what Senator Vandenberg said in December, 1948, on this subject of China:

"The vital importance of saving China cannot be exaggerated. But there are limits to our resources and boundaries to our miracles . . . I am forced to say that the Nationalist Government has failed to reform itself in a fashion calculated to deserve continued popular confidence over there or over here . . . If we made ourselves responsible for the army of the Nationalist Government, we would be in the China war for keeps and the responsibility would be ours instead of hers. I am very sure that this would jeopardize our own national security beyond any possibility of justification."

So spoke Senator Vandenberg and his view was shared by intelligent and responsible men in both parties. Now who talked sense about China: Senator Vandenberg or the General?

Then there is the question of "writing off" Korea. The General condemns the Secretary of State's excluding Korea from our defense perimeter in 1950. But the General fails to point out that this defense perimeter was a line developed by the military authorities themselves. Surely it is a gross and discreditable distortion to say that the Secretary of State took the lead in this matter. Twice in 1949 General MacArthur, then our top commander in the Pacific, defined our defense perimeter in the terms later used by the Secretary of State. It was on the recommendation of our military authorities that Korea and Formosa and mainland areas were not included in a direct military commitment.

And I am, frankly, astonished that my great opponent stooped at Cincinnati last week to the practice of lifting remarks out of context. Why did he quote only a part of what the Secretary of State said—why did he skip the Secretary's pledge that, if there should be an attack on these countries, "the initial reliance must be on the people attacked to resist, and then upon the commitments of the entire civilized world under the Charter of the United Nations"? The United States Government thus clearly announced its determination to seek United Nations action against aggression. And that's exactly what we did.

The true significance of the Secretary's remark, therefore, is that the military situation made it necessary for him to do what he could diplomatically to give some assurance of our interest in the security of the Republic of Korea. Why does the General not only skip this but distort the whole meaning of these developments? And how does he honestly square this campaign-time charge of writing off Korea with his own statement in July, 1950, that "when our Government guaranteed the Government of South Korea, there was no recourse but to do what President Truman said and did."

I deeply regret the necessity for this recital. I was prepared to ignore the political license and false charges of extremists and reactionaries. But I cannot ignore them now when they are uttered by the Republican nominee himself, a man personally identified with and presumed to be intimately informed about the recent course of our foreign affairs.

Nor do I list these mistakes in judgment and errors of prediction in order to lay any personal blame on the General. I would never have brought these things up had he not pointed the accusing finger. Many Americans of both parties made the same mistakes. Better we refrain from competing in denouncing each other in a scramble for votes, admit our common mistakes—and get on with our business.

Let's talk sense. Let's admit that mistakes were made. America did demobilize too rapidly and too severely. America did allow the Russians to develop an undue superiority in conventional arms and in ground forces. Perhaps this country should have given a direct military guarantee to the Republic of Korea. And it might well have been wiser if American forces had not crossed the 38th parallel in the fall of 1950.

There is another curious example of my opponent's uncertainty that is worth noting.

At Abilene, Kansas, on June 5th, shortly after his return to this country, he said that: "There has been built up behind the Yalu River a very definite air strength that would make very dangerous any attempt to extend the war at this moment, until we have a bigger build-up of our own."

Three months later the General says this: "I have always stood behind General MacArthur in bombing those bases on the Yalu from which fighter planes are coming . . ."

What kind of straddle is this? On one occasion he is against bombing across the river. And a little later he is for it. I confess I am bewildered.

This seems to me to be too serious a matter for such wandering opinions.

But enough about the past, and even about the past inconsistencies of my opponent. I have always agreed with Winston Churchill that if the present tries to sit in judgment on the past, it will lose the future. The important thing is to draw the right lessons from the past and to get on with the job.

One lesson which I had hoped that most of us had learned from the past is an understanding of what the present threat to our freedom really is. I thought that my distinguished opponent, of all Americans, would agree that this threat is the threat of world communism.

But it develops that he has now adopted the theory of Senator Taft, who unsmilingly states that the greatest threat to liberty today is the cost of our own Federal Government!

It is surely fundamental to the making of wise policies to decide whether the threat to the United States is internal or external. Either the threat to our security is world communism or it is not.

This is surely more than the "differences of degree" which, according to Senator Taft's statement following the peace conference on Morningside Heights, are all that separate him from the General on foreign policy matters. It is not a question of degree whether we measure our defense by an arbitrary budget or measure our budget by the needs of survival.

If we should follow out this theory that the threat is internal, we would undertake the deliberate and systematic weakening of ourselves and our allies. And such a policy of national weakness and international weakness can lead to a single result: that is, to invite the expansion of Soviet power.

By adopting this theory, the Republican candidate has reversed the advice of Theodore Roosevelt to speak softly and carry a big stick. The new advice is to talk tough and carry a twig.

You saw this policy proposed a year ago for Asia when some Republicans wanted at one and the same time to cut the defense budget and expand the war. Now you see it proposed again for Europe by those isolationists who would reduce our aid to our allies and our own defense appropriations and simultaneously speak with "cold finality" to the Soviet Union. This is the policy of tougher words backed up with smaller armies.

I wonder if the General realizes the full implications of the agreed statement issued by Senator Taft. Senator Taft has evidently reassured him by saying that their differences in foreign policy are just differences in degree.

Differences of degree, indeed!

Is it a difference of degree to be for or against the North Atlantic Treaty?

Is it a difference of degree to blame the Korean War on Stalin or on our own President?

Is it a difference of degree to be for or against the strengthening of our allies?

Such differences of degree may well turn out to be the difference between success and disaster—between peace and war.

Tough talk about communism will not deter the Soviet Union from new adventures. The thing which will save the world from war is American strength, and real strength need not be loud or belligerent. Nor is it just a matter of our national strength alone. It is equally the strength of the free world—the strength of the nations which stand between us and the Soviet Union.

Strength is the road to peace. Weakness is the road to war. This is the simple truth of peace and war in our times. The Democratic Party has been consistently the party of strength—and thus the party of peace. With equal consistency, the opposition has been the party of weakness—the party which persists in the dreary obsession that we must fear above all, not the Kremlin, but our own Government. And as the party of weakness, it gives evidence of pursuing, once in power, a policy of weakness which would demoralize the free world, embolden the Soviet Union to new military adventures, and, in the end, pull down the world into the rubble and chaos of a third world war.

Let's talk sense to the American people. Peace is far more important than who wins this election. Whichever party wins, the American people must be sure to win. Let us not place victory in a political campaign ahead of national interest.

And let's talk sense about what we have gained by our determination, our expenditures, and our valor in Korea.

We have not merely said, we have proven, that communism can go no further unless it is willing to risk world war.

We have proven to all the peoples of the Far East that communism is not the wave of the future, that it can be stopped.

We have helped to save the peoples of Indo-China from communist conquest.

We have smashed the threat to Japan through Korea and so have strengthened this friend and ally.

We have discouraged the Chinese communists from striking at Formosa.

We have mightily strengthened our defenses and all our defensive positions around the world.

We have trained and equipped a large army of South Koreans,

who can assume a growing share of the defense of their country.

We have blocked the road to communist domination of the Far East and frustrated the creation of a position of power which would have threatened the whole world.

We have asserted, and we shall maintain it, that whenever communist soldiers choose freedom after falling into our hands, they are free.

We have kept faith with our solemn obligations.

These are the values won by the fidelity and prowess and the sacrifices of young men and women who serve their country. We have lost many of our beloved sons. All Americans share in the bereavement of so many mothers, and fathers, of wives and sweethearts. The burden lies heavily on us all. We pray God that the sacrifices and the sorrows will soon end.

I would say one thing more about the great debate over our foreign policy. My opponents say the threat to our liberty comes from within.

I say that the threat comes from without—and I offer the fate of the enslaved peoples of the world as my evidence.

My opponents say America cannot afford to be strong.

I say that America cannot afford to be weak.

I promise no easy solutions, no relief from burdens and anxieties, for to do this would be not only dishonest; it would be to attack the foundations of our greatness.

I can offer something infinitely better: an opportunity to work and sacrifice that freedom may flourish. For, as William James truly said, "When we touch our own upper limit and live in our own highest center of energy, we may call ourselves saved."

I call upon America to reject the new isolationism and to surpass her own glorious achievements. Then we may, with God's help, deserve to call ourselves the sons of our fathers.

First Fireside Speech

Radio and Television Studio

C H I C A G O ,   I L L I N O I S

September 29, 1952

I am grateful to the Volunteers for Stevenson for affording me this opportunity to visit you in your homes as nearly as may be—perhaps I should say returning your visit, because so many of you were good enough to come out to see me during my recent travels around the country.

First let me say that I suppose some of you have been curious about the presents that I have given some of my associates as Governor of Illinois. I am frank to say, immodestly perhaps, that I am very proud of what we have accomplished in the state government of Illinois in these past four years. Most of the daily newspapers of this state—preponderantly Republican, of course—who have followed our work in Springfield, have expressed their approval. I cannot, much as I should like to, detail everything that has been done in Illinois during these past four years, but I should have no reluctance in matching our reforms and our progress in all of our state services in the same interval with any other state in the Union. While running for President I shall not deprecate my opponent's great services to his country as some Republican governors are now attempting to deprecate what we have accomplished in the State of Illinois. I am content with the record, and I am beholden for it to men of both parties whom I induced to work for the State of Illinois when I came into office.

In my inaugural speech in January, 1949, I said: "It is obvious to all that many of the senior positions in the state's service do not pay enough to support, let alone attract, the quality of management and leadership these positions demand and the people deserve, except upon a basis of unselfish sacrifice. And too often, as many have noted, the reward for sacrifice in public service is not

189

gratitude in lieu of dollars but abuse, criticism and ingratitude.

"Government cannot, will not and should not attempt to match the salary scales of private business, but government can and must, if it is to be good government, pay salaries which are not an invitation to carelessness, indolence, or even worse, corruption."

Some of the men I brought into the state government did so at great financial sacrifice. Pending better salaries, I made gifts of money to a few of these men on my immediate staff from political contributions. At least four of these men, while serving me in Springfield, have had offers in private employment of double or more their state salaries. Some have had financial worries known to me. None ever asked me for help, and none could have been improperly influenced by these gifts, because I gave them and I appointed them to their jobs and I could have discharged them at any time. Two of them have left the state service long since—one to become vice-president of the Federal Reserve Bank of Chicago, and the other is now a justice of the Illinois State Supreme Court.

I do not consider this public curiosity either a smear or a Republican plot. It was never a secret. Indeed, I discussed the difficulty of getting competent people into state service frequently and publicly. Actually I think the public interest in the compensation of government servants is very healthy. It is a problem that perplexes everyone who holds major public responsibility in either elective or appointive positions. I am glad that I have been of some help to a few of the people who have been of tireless help to me in a job of great difficulty to which I have given everything that is in me for the past four years. To attract and employ better people in state government is never easy. It has been my greatest satisfaction in Illinois. You will only get good government from good people. But I have no brief for the means I used except that I had no other. If it is wrong to give money to people in appointive jobs which could not influence them, then it must be wrong to give money to people running for elective office which *could* influence them. Yet, we give political contributions to candidates every day in the week.

It is no simple question. But I hope I have not discouraged anyone from contributing to the Democratic Party! However distasteful, public service makes you public property, and I have long felt that candidates for high office should make a full disclosure of their personal finances so that there can be no misgivings about their connections and independence. But it should be possible to do this through some confidential means without invading a man's legitimate privacy. No such machinery being available to me, I have made my income tax returns for the past ten years public, and Senator Sparkman, my running mate, will provide similar information. Actually, as few people seem to realize, President Truman proposed more than a year ago in a message to the Congress that high officials in all branches of government should place on record each year full information concerning their income from all sources as a step toward insuring the integrity of public service and protecting government officials against false charges.

But I don't want, and must not spend all evening talking about the intricate and all-important problem of getting better men into government service. To get back to the campaign and to your choice for President and Vice President in this fateful year. I have traveled now through some twenty states from coast to coast. I have expressed my views as clearly as I could on a great variety of public questions, not that I am confident that my views are always right, or that I am particularly wise, but because I think you are entitled to know what my views are. I could not expect everyone to agree with everything—and there are many who say that too much candor is a dangerous way to campaign—that it is better to talk in generalities, capitalize discontents and leave solutions cloudy or uncertain. But I said when I accepted the Democratic nomination in Chicago that it would be better to lose the election than to mislead the people. So, I have talked about the cost of living, labor problems, farm policy, conservation—about civil rights, corruption, and economy in government, and about the overshadowing issues of war and peace.

I have expressed my views as best I could. I have done the best I could to keep my promise to talk sense to the American people. I had hoped that my opponent would also state his position on the issues so that we could debate them out in the American way. But he has chosen instead to insist that he and his running mate are the only candidates of sufficient integrity to assure the nation clean government during the next four years. I think that the object of opening the mind, as of opening the mouth, is to shut it again on something solid. But what the General now believes on most of the big questions that trouble us, I do not know. There is one exception, however—agriculture—where the General has jumped off of his platform onto ours. But he knows that the Republicans in Congress won't follow him.

While talking a lot during this past month, I have also done some listening, and some reading from the thousands of letters that come to me. Among things that evidently trouble people most seem to be these four questions: Korea; how serious is the communist danger in this country; is our prosperity in danger; and how can we get the highest integrity and efficiency in government. Now let us work backward up this list.

A number of people have written in to ask, in effect: "You and your Republican opponent both say that you will give us an honest administration. How do we know?" It is a fair question. One kind of answer comes from a lawyer in Kansas who fills five pages of single-space typewriting indicting the graft, the thievery and the corruption under state and national Republican administrations during his lifetime. Everything he says is true, but this is not answer enough. No approach to the problem of corruption in government is good enough if it ignores the deeper problem of corruption in men—of men. We do not say that a bank is corrupt because the cashier embezzles. The problem of corruption—of graft, in its simplest form—is a problem of individual morals, public and private.

Behind every crooked tax collector is a crooked taxpayer. Although I have done so before, and on many occasions, I think this topic is evidently important enough to talk about it again at length, and I propose to do so. In that speech I will outline some ideas for a program of action. Tonight I would only remind you that the Democratic Party is the party of Senator Kefauver, Senator Douglas, Senator Fulbright, Congressman Chelf of Kentucky, Congressman King of California—men who have distinguished themselves in the fight against evil in and out of government. With the help of men like these, and many more like them, I have no doubt that we can keep the Federal service clean.

Now I want to turn to the question of whether this country is heading for runaway inflation, or for depression, or whether we can look forward to a continuation of the prosperity we have been enjoying for some years.

Driving through Connecticut the other day, an older man came close to the car and said to me this: "Why don't you just tell people how good they have it and how bad it used to be?" And a little later, as we passed a mill town a man waved one of those home-made signs you see so often, reading, "If you can't stand prosperity, vote Republican."

There has been a real temptation to base this campaign on the plain and pleasant fact that the Democratic Party has been in control of this nation and has led it out of an awful depression into the greatest prosperity it has ever known, and through a world-shattering war and a great wave of social reform. It is a great temptation to point out that the Republican leadership has opposed us almost every step of the way. And now, while adopting everything and proposing to repeal nothing, at least publicly, their orators still sneer at everything we now have and shout about socialism. They call our lives of pride and dignity, "cradle-to-the-grave rides through the welfare state."

Moreover, the Republican candidate has agreed to agree on all domestic matters with the Republican Old Guard. I don't know whether the Old Guard would take it away if they could, but I do know, on the basis of the record of the past twenty years, that if they had been in the saddle they would never have had it to take away.

I think we can keep production and employment high in this country, and I think we can and must arrest inflation—the rising prices which make it so difficult for many.

In Baltimore last week I outlined a program to stop inflation—a pay-as-you-go tax policy for the Government; the strictest possible control of all government expenditures; restraints upon excessive private borrowing; and closing the loopholes in the present wage-and-price controls if these other measures don't work. I think if we have the guts to do it, this program will do the job. But it will be carried out only if you send to Congress men and women who have the courage to force through these measures over stubborn opposition. We will stop rising prices and wages which just eat each other up if you will do your part. We have laid out the lines of defense and you must support them if you really mean business about these rising costs of living.

Now, about the questions regarding communism, especially communists in government, I think I will devote a whole speech to this, perhaps next week, but I will give you a brief answer right now. These mortal enemies cannot be permitted to get close to the bloodstreams of America, particularly its Government. I don't believe oaths and affidavits are much good, for a real communist never hesitates to lie, nor is catching and punishing communists after their treachery enough to end the hazard.

I think generally that close screening of government employes and the quiet professional work of the F.B.I. is the best way to turn over every stone in this country to see what lies beneath it. This is a job for professionals, and I think it can be done without slandering innocent people. I distrust those who have made political capital out of broadside charges discrediting hundreds of loyal government employes. I do not believe that we can jettison our processes of justice without endangering freedom for every American.

Beyond this I say to you that the battle against communism in America is an infinitely tougher and harder battle than most of the Republican leaders have ever admitted or evidently even understood. Why is it that these politicians that scream loudest about communism in America have fought hardest against every Democratic program to fight communism itself? They criticize our efforts to block the communist invasion of Korea. They have opposed our efforts to make the people of Europe and of Asia secure enough to reject the false gospels. They have opposed making the people of America secure enough so that they will never turn again, as some did in the thirties, to the false prophets.

The F.B.I. figures show that we have in this country now only a fraction of the communists we had twenty years ago. The point is that we have got to fight communism, not just communists. We have got to see to it that the soil is so healthy that communism just can't grow and survive in it, and that means the creative and constructive work of assuring good jobs, decent homes, good education and free political institutions.

These are some of the things I should like to talk about further.

Finally, now, peace and war. You know the kind of letters I receive; so many of you have written me about Korea and about your soldier sons. Every one of us knows in his heart why we have to stand up and fight in Korea. We all know that when the communists attacked across the 38th parallel that was the testing point for freedom throughout the world. The men in the Kremlin thought that they would be unopposed, and if they were, the whole question of the future could be settled in one blow. If they had been allowed to conquer free people in Korea, they could have picked away at the free world and engulfed more millions, piece by piece, one by one. Sooner or later we would have had to fight, and the later we made our stand, the bigger and the harder the war would have been. Stopping the enemy in Korea before Japan was threatened and before East Asia with all of its resources of manpower, rubber, tin, oil, etc., fell to the communists was received with enthusiastic shouts of approval by the majority of the American people and even by the Republican leadership.

Now, however, they attempt to make you believe that it was almost an act of treason, but what do you think they would be saying now if we had not stopped the enemy in Korea, if Japan was threatened and if East Asia was falling bit by bit to the enemy? Would they not be saying now that Harry Truman and Joseph Stalin were boyhood friends in Outer Mongolia?

And another thing the Republican leadership is now telling us is that the danger to this nation is from within, not from without; the danger lies not with Moscow but in Washington; your enemy is not Joseph Stalin but Harry Truman—or even possibly Adlai Stevenson.

A campaign addressed not to men's minds and to their best instincts, but to their passions, emotions and prejudices, is unworthy at best. Now, with the fate of the nation at stake, it is unbearable; with the darkest evil, the mightiest force ever gathered on earth arrayed against us and our friends, this is no time for such talk. It is not for me to stand in judgment upon the men who pilfer truth and say such things, but for your sake and for mine—for the sake of my sons and your children, and the future of millions of our friends overseas, and the future of our nation, and for those who languish imprisoned behind the Iron Curtain—we must know the truth and come to grips with the facts of life, look them in the face and stare them down, and in so doing, triumph over them.

We are not, I take it, a race of whimpering adolescents who can't face the truth, but a race of men and women, proud, courageous and unafraid. I shall state the facts as they appear to me from some years of experience, not only in domestic affairs but in foreign affairs. The Republican leadership blows thin drafts of crafty words down your neck, but it fails to tell you the following things.

Eighty-five per cent of the Federal budget goes for past wars and for preserving our present and our future liberty. The world has been at war almost continuously now for forty years. The intervals between the wars grow shorter; the wars increase in dimension and in destructiveness. The last war was man's first true world war. The revolutions of our times are manifold revolutions; their flames burn from one end of the globe to the other. The intercontinental airplane makes counties of continents; it makes lakes of oceans. In the words of the song, "There is no hiding place down there." Much of mankind is changing its entire outlook upon the world; whatever was, is cast out; whatever is, is questioned. Mankind and its hundreds of millions is on the march, toward what goal and with what destruction on the way no man can foretell. Whole nations have sunk out of sight behind iron curtains; whole peoples have disappeared from view.

Today there is less communication between great groups of men than there was in the roadless world of a thousand years ago. We can no more communicate with half of mankind than we can raise the dead. The while the anti-Christ stalks our world. Organized communism seeks even to dethrone God from his central place in the Universe. It attempts to uproot everywhere it goes the gentle and restraining influences of the religion of love and peace. One by one the lamps of civilization go out and nameless horrors are perpetrated in darkness. All this is done by an enemy of a kind that we have never faced before. He is primitive but he is also advanced. He goes with a piece of black bread in his hand, but in his mind he carries the awful knowledge of atomic energy. He is careful, cool, calculating, and he counts time, not impatiently as we do, not by the clock, but by decades, in terms of centuries. Much of what he is trying to do today his ancestors were attempting to do four hundred years ago.

The problems of a tortured, convulsive humanity stagger the nation. Unprecedented times demand of us unprecedented behavior. The task that confronts us will try our souls. It will exact a high price in discipline of mind and in austerity of spirit. It will determine whether we are worthy of our high place in the world, whether we are worthy of our forefathers who converted a wilderness into a country, fair and free, and left to us all the riches, material and spiritual, that they wrought in pain.

Long ago we asserted a great principle on this continent: that

men are, and of right ought to be, free. Now we are called upon
to defend that right against the mightiest forces of evil ever assem-
bled under the sun.

This is a time to think, a time to feel, a time to pray. We shall
need all of the resources of the stubborn mind, the stout heart, the
soul refreshed, in the task that confronts us.

It is the most awesome task that any people has ever faced. For
we are become the leader and mainstay of one great wing of humanity in conflict with another wing of humanity. As such, we
must play the principal part in saving ourselves, our friends, and
our civilization.

Whose task is this? It is inescapably your task. You and you
alone will decide the fate of your family and your country for
decades to come. You will decide whether you are to be slaves or
free—to live gloriously or perish miserably. You may seek comfort
at the feet of false leaders who, like medicine doctors, beat drums
to ward off evil spirits. You may listen to false leaders who tell
you that there is an easy way; that all you have to do is elect them
and thereafter relax in a tax-free paradise—the political equivalent
of sending ten cents to cover the cost of postage. You may, fearing
to face the facts squarely, be distracted by phony issues that have
no bearing upon the life-and-death controversy of our times. But,
so deluded, you run the risk of being beguiled to destruction, for
there is no easy way.

What is the lesson of history and of all human experience?
What is the primary law of life? You struggle and you survive—
you fail to struggle and you perish. The ways of the world are
marked with the bones of peoples who hesitated.

Your salvation is in your own hands; in the stubbornness of
your minds, the tenacity of your hearts, and such blessings as God,
sorely tried by His children, shall give us. Nature is indifferent to
the survival of the human species, including Americans. She does
not weep over those who fall by the way.

I repeat, then, that the task is yours. Yours is a democracy. Its
Government cannot be stronger or more tough-minded than its
people. It cannot be more inflexibly committed to the task than
they. It cannot be wiser than the people. As citizens of this democracy you are the rulers and the ruled—the law-givers and the
law-abiders—the beginning and the end. Democracy is a high privi-

lege. But it is also a heavy responsibility whose shadow stalks you although you may never walk in the sun.

I say these things to you not only because I believe them to be true, but also because, as you love your country, I love my country and I would see it endure and grow in light and become a living testament to all mankind of goodness and of mercy and of wisdom.

(The following two paragraphs were omitted from the radio speech due to lack of time:
If telling you the truth about the world as I see it should cause you to cast me down, and revile me, and with me the Democratic Party, I should still tell you the truth as I see it. For no office within your gift—including the Presidency itself—is worth the price of deception.

I say we must know the truth, for the truth alone will make us free. What American is content to chew the cud of comfort in fancied security? What American—I ask you—blessed as no other man in history, would blind himself to the ancient wisdom; the wisdom which tells us that much shall be asked of him to whom much is given?)

How long can we keep up the fight against the monster tyranny? How long can we keep on fighting in Korea; paying high taxes; helping others to help ourselves? There is only one answer. We can keep it up as long as we have to—and we will.

That is why we cannot lose, and will pass from darkness to the dawn of a brighter day than even this thrice-blessed land of ours has ever known.

Social Gains and the
Public Welfare

Franklin County Memorial Auditorium

COLUMBUS, OHIO

October 3, 1952

This is my first campaign visit to Ohio, the residence of Senator Taft, whose team lost the Chicago game, but he won the breakfast game in New York single-handed. They're planning to play the third game in the White House in Washington—unless, of course, they are rained out on November 4th.

The Republican Convention reminded me of the story of the two fellows from Straddle Ridge who swapped mules—or should I say elephants?—and then fell to bitter quarreling, each accusing the other of skinning him. When a bystander asked why they didn't trade back and settle the fight, another witness of the battle said: "I reckon they're both afraid of getting skinned again!"

Well, it sort of looked to me as though the G.O.P. had swapped elephant drivers at Chicago and half of them were skinned, and so they traded back again, and now the other half are skinned.

Anyway, I am glad to be in Ohio and pay my respects to the uncrowned boss of the Republican Party—Senator Taft. At least you know where he stands, even if you don't know how he stands.

I've tried in this campaign to talk about all the specific public questions that concern you and your Federal Government and I've tried to make my views clear on them, one by one, because I think you're entitled to know my views as a candidate for President, even if you can't always agree with me.

Tonight I want to talk with you about the most precious thing in the world. I want to talk about people—about you and your children and your father and your mother. I want to talk about the family problems of a democracy: such things as seeing to it

199

that children are fed and educated, that there are hospital beds for those who are sick, that there is dignity for those who have done a life's work, that the scars of slums are removed from America.

I chose tonight to speak of these problems because this is Democratic Women's Day. It marks the occasion, thirty-three years ago, when women first took their places in the directing councils of the Democratic Party. The following year our party won for women the right to vote; no Democrat has ever had reason to regret it—and we don't think we will on this November 4th.

Understanding human needs is half the job of meeting them. I think we Democrats understand them. We have learned how important it is to approach the writing of laws, themselves cold things, from clear, warm pictures in our minds: of a family sitting around a supper table; of a rent bill coming due when there has been sickness in the family; of a child going off to school dressed differently from the others. We think we understand the feeling someone has when he is denied a job he knows he would have gotten if his skin had been of a different color. We think we know the feeling of an older man and woman who do not want to move in with their children.

It is upon this understanding that we have built the laws of twenty years.

First of all, we have been working for better housing. Twenty-four million families now own homes of their own—an increase of ten million in two decades. The job has been accomplished in the American way, through private enterprise and local responsibility, with the Federal Government providing the means to bring down interest rates to reasonable levels, plus the help necessary to build homes for low-income families.

What the Republican position is on housing we do not know. The Republican platform has no housing proposals at all.

While we have been building homes we also have been bringing to our farm people most of the comforts of city life. We have banished the hand pump, the kerosene lamps and battered zinc washtubs which once made life so hard for our farm women. These relics have been replaced, on nine farms out of every ten, by electric lights, running water and all the other conveniences which the magic of electricity makes possible. By these improvements we are encouraging young people to remain on the farms, where there is a shortage of labor, so that they may participate as their fathers and mothers have, in the feeding and clothing of our nation.

Here again we have done the job in the American way, working through farmer co-operatives which are locally organized, locally owned and locally managed. Your own Ohio Farm Bureau Federation, under the far-sighted leadership of Murray Lincoln, has pioneered in developing these Rural Electrification co-ops under Federal sponsorship.

I hardly need to remind you that these things have been accomplished in the teeth of implacable and relentless opposition of Republicans in Congress. Year after year, decade after decade, each social advance meets with shouts of the old refrain, "socialism," as if the American people could be frightened like children on Hallowe'en. I sometimes secretly suspect that the Republicans haven't caught on to the fact that we have free public education in this country and have had for quite awhile. We know more than they think, and we know it isn't socialism to give a veteran a chance to buy a home of his own. We know we are not softening the moral fiber of America when we help a farm woman put a washing machine in her kitchen.

We know, too, what the Republican leaders plan to do if they ever get the chance The junior Senator from this state of Ohio made that quite plain when he spoke to the Chicago convention. "The last vestiges of the New Deal . . ." he said, "must be destroyed."

That is a shocking statement, unless, of course, the people of Ohio don't take their junior Senator seriously. But do you dare take a chance when so many of them echo the same refrain of contempt for all that's been accomplished?

Let us take a careful look at what it is they want to destroy. Here in Columbus you are now building a million-dollar health center; I am told that it has been badly needed for many years. The Federal Government is paying about one-quarter of the cost. Throughout the country 1,500 such hospitals are going up, or have already been completed—most of them in farming areas which have never before had any kind of hospital service.

Is this socialism? Is this something we can permit the Republicans to wipe out to the last vestige? Of course not.

The hospital-construction program is only a sound beginning toward meeting the medical needs of all our people. I am just as much opposed to socialized medicine as any doctor in this country, just as I would be opposed to socialization of my own profession of the law. I never want to see our physicians on a government payroll, and I'm sure you don't either. You and I know that the United States already has the best system of medical care in the world, but we also know that it is not yet good enough.

Many small towns and rural areas still suffer from a dangerous shortage of doctors and nurses. Unhappily it looks as though private support is not enough and that it will take Federal aid to help support the medical schools necessary to turn out enough doctors and nurses.

And so far we have found no way to cope with the problem of catastrophic illness, which may spell economic disaster for a whole family. No matter how thrifty, few families can ever protect themselves completely or endure the crushing cost of the accident which disables the father for life, or the case of rheumatic fever which puts a child in the hospital for months or years. We await the recommendations of the President's excellent Commission on the Health Needs of the Nation, which is now holding hearings throughout the country and will make its report in December.

With the advice of that Commission and with the guidance and co-operation of the medical profession we must find the means of solving our health problems in a constructive spirit and without, I hope, abuse and ill temper and misrepresentation.

Now let's talk for a moment about children. Did you ever wonder what happened to the old-fashioned Orphan's Home? Twenty years ago nearly every town had one—a mournful institution, sheltering lonely youngsters whose fathers had died and whose mothers could no longer keep the family together. Today these institutions have almost completely disappeared—and do you know why? Because the Democratic Party, thinking in terms of human needs, wrote into the Social Security Act a provision to bring help into homes where a father is disabled or dead.

The youngsters we are raising now have never had to wander hungry and homeless, riding the freight cars and sleeping under old newspapers in the hobo jungles. They don't have to leave school for want of clothes. There are more children attending school today than ever before, and they are staying in school longer.

What I have been able to do, as Governor of Illinois, in building up our school system has been one of my most satisfying experiences. Many of our schools were and some still are in pitiful shape—insufficient teachers, underpaid teachers, classrooms overcrowded, buildings in ill repair, and Illinois was one of the lowest in state aid to education. One of the first things I did was to ask the legislature to increase vastly the state's contribution to the common-school fund. Now it is almost double what it was four years ago. We have set up a permanent commission to study the needs of our schools and take them and their appropriations out of the area of lobby and logrolling. Teachers' salaries have been raised and our common-school system is healthier than it has ever been. And we have not raised taxes either!

We have not solved all of our school problems in Illinois, and the nation hasn't yet found a final answer either. We pursue our folly of paying the lowest salaries in many communities to those who handle, not our goods, or even our garbage, but our children's education. We have far too few school rooms for the vast increase in school children that is ahead of us. Too many areas, especially in the South, lag behind in education, because they produce more than their relative share of the nation's children and get less than their share of the nation's income.

These are real problems, hard problems. The Democratic platform spells out a program of action to meet our needs. We mean what it says.

And again the Republican platform is entirely negative, offering no program at all for better education. And they mean that, too.

We hear those who would push aside Federal action with the usual cries of "socialism" and "regimentation." But there has been Federal help for education ever since 1785, when the Government set aside one section in every new township for school support, and we are no closer to Federal control of our schools than we were then. The Democratic platform says squarely that "The Federal Government should not dictate or control educational policy." And we mean that, too.

And now of our deep concern for our "senior citizens," which is a new name for our older people. For millions of Americans, old age once meant charity, or the county home, or a life as an unwelcome burden on their children. We're proud, as Democrats, that today—thanks to Social Security—these people can pass their evening years in dignity, security and independence, not with handouts, but with the proceeds of insurance earned by a life of hard work.

Splendid as it is, our Social Security system has room for improvement. It should be extended to many workers not now covered. Benefit payments should keep up with living costs to accomplish the purpose for which they were intended. The present law should be changed to encourage people who are still alert, able-bodied, and eager, to keep on working even after they are sixty-five. Our country needs every hand and brain we can give it and enforced idleness is good for no one.

What are the Republican views on social security? The General once told us what he thought about it, when he blurted out—thoughtlessly, I hope—that the best place to find security is in prison. The General talks differently now; in fact, he seems to change his mind not infrequently these days. But the Republicans in Congress have written a record that can't be changed. When they controlled the Eightieth Congress, they took social-security protection away from more than a half million people. Now they say they want to extend it. What should we take them at—their word or their deed?

The American people want no retreat on these issues. We want to advance, to improve, to carry forward our efforts to provide better housing, better health, better schools, better security. These are not "vestiges" of the New Deal that we mark for destruction. They are part of the fabric of our life, part of the progress we have been making toward human dignity and human freedom, part of the promise of our future.

The voters of our nation will not be fooled by the Republican leaders who have arched their backs and been dragged, protesting, through these years of advance in human welfare—who even now are saying, on the one hand, that all these hard-won social gains are now "above politics," and, on the other, that they want to destroy, to go back, to tear them down.

The strange alchemy of time has somehow converted the Democrats into the truly conservative party of this country—the party dedicated to conserving all that is best, and building solidly and safely on these foundations. The Republicans, by contrast, are behaving like the radical party—the party of the reckless and the embittered, bent on dismantling institutions which have been built solidly into our social fabric.

I had a letter the other day from a man who said that I evidently wanted to put the word "candid" in candidate, which seemed to be a novel and appealing idea. Well, I never thought of it just that way before, but I do want to do just that. I think candidates for high public office have a responsibility to deal in fact, not fiction, in truth, not fancy, transcending any responsibility to their party to get elected at the price of guile and deceit. This is a democracy, the most difficult form of government there is, requiring the most informed and discriminating electorate. Who but candidates appealing to the electorate for support can set the standards?

In short, I've decided that I could have no better epitaph than "the man who put 'candid' in candidate." And in that spirit, I owe it to you to say that I think of our social-security system and our Democratic Party's sponsorship of the social reforms and advances of the past two decades as conservatism at its best. Certainly there could be nothing more conservative than to change when change is due, to reduce tensions and wants by wise changes, rather than to stand pat stubbornly, until, like King Canute, we are engulfed by relentless forces that will always go too far.

But change for the sake of change—even in national administrations!—has no absolute value. The changes in our society and national life to meet changing times and needs must be first studied, weighed, evaluated. The radical shouts "change!" The conservative says "change wisely."

Even more important, candidly, than immediate further advances, such as I have sketched, is our national solvency. It is not just that a program is desirable; the question is also whether we can afford it without endangering something else, or, indeed, everything. The top priority now is defense and inflation control. Social gains at the price of peace or a healthy economy, on which the whole world depends, will not be gains but frightful losses.

Our directions, our party purposes, our new social horizons are clear and I am proud to bear the Democratic standard in this fateful campaign. But I would not earn that epitaph of candor if I shamelessly promised immediate delivery of what we either could not deliver at all, or could deliver only at too hazardous a price.

We stand at a perilous moment in a perilous century. The false prophets of communism would offer us security without freedom. The false prophets of reaction would offer us freedom without security. Every day these false prophets—both the communists abroad and the Republican Old Guard at home—tell us that freedom and security are incompatible.

But we know they are wrong. We have proven that a free society is strong enough to take care of its own without losing its freedom. We know now that freedom and security are indivisible and that any society which chooses one loses both.

We have made a new society here in America. We have given democracy a new dimension. We have given our men and women a new strength. We are moving toward a spacious future—a future in which our children's children will be born in freedom, work in dignity and live in peace. This is our faith and our passion, and in that faith and with God's help, we shall make our own the promise of the future.

A Whistle-Stop

Michigan State Normal University Campus

Y P S I L A N T I ,   M I C H I G A N

October 7, 1952

Mr. Dawson was good enough to say that I have attempted to talk sense during the campaign. I have, and I attempted to just a little while ago over in Saginaw, but in the hall there were some very young people who shouted, "I like Ike," every few minutes while I was attempting to speak. It reminded me of that wonderful remark of Bernard Shaw—some of you will recall it—that youth is such a wonderful state, it is a pity it has to be wasted on young people.

But the fact of the matter is that I like this business of kids wearing Ike buttons who wave at me as I go through the streets or shout at me. After all, I think many of us here—the older ones at least—will recall that their first political consciousness came from national campaigns of this kind. This is, after all, perhaps the last country in the world—or pray God it isn't the last—just one of the last countries in the world where we can enjoy healthy differences of opinion at all ages.

Do you remember the remark of that wonderful old Quaker —his name was Rufus Jones—who was addressing a school graduation class one time, and he looked at them and he said, "Seeing all of you happy boys and girls here this morning reminds me of the time when I too was a happy boy and girl." I feel a little that way myself.

However, I am now a candidate for the most austere office in the land, and I needn't tell you how proud I am that I head a ticket which includes men like Senator Moody, like Governor Williams, and like your candidate for Congress, John Dawson.

After all, you don't need to clap when I say things like that, Governor Williams!

Each of these people in his own way, I think, illustrates the fact that the Democratic Party constantly changes itself. It always draws into its ranks men of new vitality, of new courage, and men of new vision—all of them dedicated, however, to the same old end of making democracy work.

I believe democracy has been the main work of Ypsilanti for a hundred years. For it was exactly—I am told—a hundred years ago this year that this University, Michigan State Normal, was established as the first Teachers' College west of the Allegheny Mountains. That interests me a great deal for very personal reasons. It was my own great-grandfather who founded Illinois State Normal University, the first teachers' training college in the State of Illinois.

A VOICE: Oh, yeah!

I suppose she is going to tell you that she is an alumna of its first class. But that, my friends—and particularly my feminine friends—was in 1856, just four years after this University was founded. Since then, thousands of men and women who lived here have gone out to prepare the minds of the young everywhere for the rights and the duties of citizenship in a democracy. A democracy, by the way, as many of you know and are learning here in this University, is not only the best but the most difficult form of government that the mind of man has ever contrived; difficult because you have to think for yourself and no one is going to do it for you, unless, of course, you listen to some politicians who have an approach that does not always bear a relationship to what we call "sense."

It is unfortunately the case, however, that our teachers and our school system generally throughout our country have suffered from public indifference, I think. The other night in Columbus, Ohio, I said that we pursue the folly of paying the lowest wages, the lowest salaries in many communities of our country—if not all— to those who handle not our goods, not indeed our garbage, but to those who handle our children's education. I could say something very similar about the ministry in this country and the salaries we pay to the people who look after our souls. We have also been inclined to indifference about the quality of our common-school teaching and about the sort of buildings in which our children are taught.

I faced this kind of a situation in my own State of Illinois when I succeeded a Republican administration. Illinois, one of the richest

states in the union, had one of the lowest ratings for state aid to
common-school education in the whole United States. The revival,
the strengthening and the doubling in four years of the State's
contribution to our common-school distributive fund was one of
the most satisfying experiences I have had in my regime as Governor of the State of Illinois. We set up a permanent commission
to study the needs of our schools, to take school affairs out of the
area of lobbying and logrolling. Teachers' salaries were raised, and
our common-school system is now stronger than it has ever been,
and we did this, my friends, without raising general-purpose taxes
in the State of Illinois.

(A remark from the audience, not audible)

Thank you. I thought for a moment that there must be an
Illinois taxpayer in the group.

The nation, as a whole, has by no means found the final answer
yet to the countrywide school problem, but the progress is impressive. Nationally we Democrats have shown our will to find a solution. Non-school attendance by children of school age has been
reduced from nine out of every one hundred to two out of every
one hundred, while college attendance, as you know, has doubled.
(A noisy airplane passes overhead.)

Republican pilot, no doubt!

But we know that our education problems are going to become
more acute and not easier. Within the last twelve years, there
has been a tremendous shift in population, due, among other
things, to the building of new industries for national defense. You
here in Ypsilanti know how this taxed your own resources when
the vitally important Willow Run plant was built nearby during
the war years. We must expect these population movements to
continue, with all of their strains on our local communities' facilities. In addition, by 1960 we will have an increase of some 50 per
cent in the number of youngsters of school age.

Our party looks ahead to this as it does in all other fields. We
have spelled out in our platform a program of action to meet our
present and our future educational needs, but it can only be done
consistent with our national solvency and with a sound national
fiscal policy, and we explicitly declare that the Federal Government should not dictate or control educational policy. And we
mean that. The Republican platform is entirely negative; it offers

no program at all for better education. And the Republicans mean that too.

Now, it seems to me—if I can be faintly partisan for a moment—that there are two basic things on people's minds as this election approaches. One is peace and the other is prosperity.

And it is clear, too, that the position of the two parties on these issues is exactly the same as it has been for the last twenty years. The Republicans say that they are for peace and prosperity—but they don't want to do anything about it. The Democrats are for peace and prosperity too, and we have been doing something about it and we are going to go on doing something about it.

Hurriedly, let me only say of the foreign-policy issues in this campaign that they boil down to this difference: the Republicans say—and their record confirms it—that the threat to this country is internal, not external; the first job is to cut taxes rather than to increase defenses. But that policy, my friends, leads to weakness and weakness leads to war. The Democratic position is that we and our friends and our allies must be strong, still stronger than we are today, for in our strength is our one guarantee that the warlords of Russia will not plunge this nation and this world into war again.

Whenever I hear one of these Old Guard leaders on the other side talking about cutting taxes, when he knows it means weakening the nation, I always think of that story about the tired old capitalist who was driving alone in his car one day, and finally, he said, "James, drive over the bluff; I want to commit suicide."

I think you know what the Democratic Party stands for on the domestic issues. Our convictions are written into the statute books of the nation. They are written into our lives. They are written into your jobs, into your system of social security, into your housing, into your education, into the abundance of opportunity that confronts you.

And you know too what the Republican Party has stood for historically. It stands for a bitter and unrelenting opposition to every important measure of social change during these past twenty years. It stands for a hands-off attitude toward the economic engine. It stands for letting the economy boom and bust at its own wild speed, first into inflation and then into depression.

Twenty years ago, after eight years of Republican do-nothing and care-nothing policy, this nation was flat on its back. The system was running down; it was running down like a broken clock or a broken body. The Republican administration was dispirited and battered.

Then a great Democrat became President, and this nation will never forget what it owes to that peerless leader, Franklin Roosevelt. The American people began their long, hard climb out of the pit of despondency. Government at long last was warm and vigorous and decisive. Government at long last cared about the people of the country. And, because it cared about the people, it released the people's energy.

In twenty years the people have built a new America—a strong and friendly America—big enough to take care of its own, productive enough to assure steadily rising living standards, and fair enough to fight for equality of opportunity for all.

Some people think that now that we have these things it doesn't much matter which political party holds the country's reins. That kind of attitude reminds me of the old boss of a wrecking crew in Chicago. He said, "I can easily wreck in a day what it takes a year to build."

I think it is now abundantly clear to any objective witness that my distinguished opponent, the General of the Army, has accepted the principles of the Old Guard of the Republican Party lock, stock and barrel. And that is certainly the most distinguished wrecking crew in American political history. Even in the past five years they have voted almost a straight ticket in Congress against the people. They have voted against farm-parity price supports which mean security for the farmer. They have voted against a fair collective-bargaining law which means security for American labor. They have voted against social-security changes which would mean fuller security for more of our older people. They have voted against inflation controls which mean security for all of us against inflation—an enemy as inscrutable and as sinister as Stalin himself. They are always against everything and for nothing. It is the same old do-nothing, hear-nothing policy.

And their candidate? Well, he has given the Old Guard a first, a second and a third mortgage on every principle he once had.

You might think I was against Republicans the way I talk. The fact of the matter is I am really not. Some of my best friends are Republicans. And I would trust them with anything I've got—I would trust some of my Republican friends with anything, except public office. You know, the unhappy fact of the matter is that

I'm a half-breed myself. My father was from an old, staunch Democratic family, and he was a Presbyterian. My mother was from an equally old and staunch Republican family and she was a Unitarian. And somehow, when I became conscious, I found that I was a member of her church and his political party. I guess I was just a compromise to begin with.

Our Democratic program for America isn't complicated. We stand for the people. Our programs grow from what we think are people's needs—and I don't mean just a few people—I mean all of the people. And that means equality of opportunity for all, regardless of race and color or creed. Most of all today we stand for peace —not for another war to end all wars, but for peace without war. We are not making the promises that the Republicans are, and we don't play politics with promises we know we cannot keep. We are trying to talk straight to the American people. We are recognizing that the course ahead of us is a stern course; that there are no easy, cheap solutions for communism, for want, for hunger, for all of the miseries that torment our world. But, we believe with all of our hearts that if we make this nation strong we can keep good times at home and avoid that war that would destroy the world.

It is toward this purpose that we direct our best energies and our efforts—and, my friends, it is just possible that we might need your help on November 4th!

(*Presentation of necktie*)

CHAIRMAN: I am very happy to present to this group Mrs. Olendorff, who has a little gift which she wishes to present to Governor Stevenson. Mrs. Olendorff had seven sons in the Second World War and still has two sons serving now. Mrs. Olendorff.

MRS. OLENDORFF: The Democratic women of Washtenaw County would like to present you with this token. This is from your personal friends.

GOVERNOR STEVENSON: Well, thank you very much, Mrs. Olendorff. I might say that what I perceive here is a necktie adorned with six baby donkeys. That is an abnormally large litter, by the way, and I think this obviously is a significant political omen!

May I thank you from the bottom of my heart and express to you what I know is the heartfelt gratitude of everyone here for your infinite contribution to the welfare of our country through your sons and also through your own splendid citizenship.

Safeguards Against Communism

Masonic Temple

DETROIT, MICHIGAN

October 7, 1952

I've been trying in this campaign to talk about all the public questions that affect your welfare as Americans, sanely, sensibly, and forthrightly. I hear it said, now and then, that I am talking over the heads of the people.

Well, if it is a mistake to appeal to intelligence and reason, instead of emotion and prejudice, then I plead guilty to the charge.

Besides that, I would rather be charged with talking over your heads than behind your backs.

People are smarter than some may think—"There's still a God's plenty left in people of the little red schoolhouse and the tall white steeple."

So you'll just have to forgive me if I go on trusting your intelligence.

I want to talk to you tonight about a disease. It is a disease which may have killed more people in this world in the last several years than cancer, than tuberculosis, than heart disease—more than all of these combined.

It has certainly killed more minds, more souls, more decent human hopes and ambitions, than any corruption—including the darkest days of Hitler.

I want to discuss with you the ways that communism has attacked this nation—and the ways in which this attack has been met.

This subject is swathed in fog and confusion. Most of this has been created by the communists themselves, seeking under confusion's cover to advance their evil purposes. But some of it has

213

been created by political demagogues, who are hunting for votes much more than for communists.

I propose tonight to do what I can to penetrate this fog and dispel this confusion. I propose to make precisely clear the record and the position of the two political parties on this problem. Unhappily facts sometimes get smothered in falsehoods.

These are the facts:

Twenty years ago the most serious threat of communism this country ever faced—a threat arising from poverty and despair, following, as it happens, twelve years of Republican administrations—was stopped by a Democratic administration.

For twenty years my party has helped the people of America to build that economic strength and that faith in freedom which make communism impossible—and every step we have taken has been opposed, ridiculed and sabotaged by the Republican Old Guard.

For years your Government in Washington has been desperately rallying and strengthening the free peoples of the world against communism, and leading the way in building the collective strength which is the only bulwark against communist expansion—and this, too, over the bitter protest and unrelenting opposition of the Republican Old Guard.

Again, Democratic leadership has built an elaborate internal security system to protect this nation against communist subversion —a system which has put the leaders of the Communist Party in this country where they belong—behind bars.

Let's look at the record a moment.

Agents of Soviet communism first began making headway in this country in the 1920's. The administration, you will recall, was Republican at that time. A month ago the junior Senator from Wisconsin quoted what he said was a Department of Justice document to prove the existence of communists in the State Department. It is true that he found the quotation in a Department of Justice document. But he neglected to say that it described the situation in 1928, and that what it proved was the existence of a communist plot under the Presidency of—Calvin Coolidge.

But, as I have said, the great communist conspiracy had its first real chance when the Republicans fumbled and bungled this nation into the Great Depression. ("Fumbled and bungled" is not mine but one of their favorite oratorical epithets for everything the

Democrats have done for twenty years.) You remember the bitter winters of 1930 and 1931. Farmers in Arkansas—conservative, law-abiding farmers—organized to march on towns and loot the stores. Children left home to spare their parents another mouth to feed; so many of them left that the railroads put on special open boxcars to keep the kids from breaking into the closed ones. Millions of American men and women waited in the breadlines. An army of ragged veterans actually marched on our national capital.

It is little wonder that across the land men and women—and especially the young—began to drift toward the terrible conclusion that free government had reached the end of its rope. Reaching out for a solution—any solution—the communist agents found ready converts among the unemployed, the farmers, the workers. It was then that some persons like Alger Hiss and Elizabeth Bentley, witnessing the devastation of capitalism and the menacing rise of Hitler, became entangled in the communist conspiracy.

In the election of 1932, almost one million Americans voted against the capitalist system. If the paralysis had continued in Washington, the one million votes cast against capitalism in 1932 might have swelled to ten million in 1936.

But in 1933 the Democratic Party brought to this nation a great leader—Franklin Roosevelt.

From that day onward, the swelling menace of discontent and communism in this country began to wane. President Roosevelt brought to us a new spirit, a new hope. The Government acted swiftly and decisively to give the farmer a market, to give the worker a job, to give the unemployed a means of saving their self-respect, to give youth opportunity and hope. America's faith in itself was restored. Under his leadership the American people unlocked from within themselves the strength to drive out communism.

This country was saved from depression and despair. Communism in the United States was turned back and as long as we hold fast to the progressive spirit of human welfare that inspired that leadership we need never fear a communist revolution in this country—and every honest man knows that is true.

And where were the Republican leaders during this fight? They cannot conceal the record. They tried to block, to trim, to obstruct, to prevent, the collective-bargaining laws that mean security to the worker, the price-support laws that mean security to the farmer, the social-insurance laws that mean security to the aged and the infirm.

The plain truth is that the Democratic administrations saved this country from depression and from communism or fascism over the opposition of the Republican leadership, because these near-sighted gentlemen never have understood that the way to make this country secure is to work for the security of all of the people in it. These men still control the Republican Party. That is why thoughtful people of this country are apprehensive that a Republican victory this November would be an Old Guard victory and the forerunner of another great depression. We must prevent another economic disaster, for that would open up the greatest opportunity the Kremlin could hope for to take over the free world, not by arms but by invitation.

We licked the communist hope for a revolution in the thirties. But the years of misery, Republican years, had left a heritage of fanatics and agents in our midst. Communism was finished as a political threat; it survived as an instrument of subversion and espionage. Soviet secret agents and their dupes burrowed like moles in the ground, trying to undermine the foundations of this and every other government in the world.

They penetrated the Nazi Government in Germany.

They penetrated the Government of Imperial Japan—so successfully that they learned in advance about the Japanese plot against Pearl Harbor.

They penetrated the anti-communist Government of Chiang Kai-shek in China—despite the long experience of his secret police in dealing with them.

They penetrated the Governments of a dozen European countries—no matter how anti-communist their policies or pretensions.

No government in the world has been immune from their penetration. Nor has ours. Nor will any government be safe from espionage and the secret communist attack so long as the Soviet Union pursues its goal of world dominion.

We must never forget the dedication, tenacity and fanaticism of this inscrutable, ruthless, restless conspiracy. As General Bedell Smith, the director of the Central Intelligence Agency, warned us last week, we cannot let our guard drop even for a moment. The only safe assumption is that no place is safe.

We must, to protect our Government from infiltration, combine vigilance with vigor. This is a long and continuous struggle—no single action can win the campaign.

And the Democratic administration has been conducting this fight for a long time. In 1939 the Roosevelt Administration made it unlawful for communists to work for the Federal Government.

In 1940 there was passed the Smith Act, under which the Department of Justice in President Truman's administration subsequently convicted the thirty-one leaders of the American Communist Party.

During the war, the Civil Service Commission and the F.B.I. conducted a continuous screening of Federal employes. Nearly 1500 men and women were denied Federal employment because of doubtful loyalty.

In 1947 President Truman set up a new and tighter Federal loyalty-control program. Many people have thought it was too tight, fearing an invasion of our ancient principle that a man is innocent until proved guilty. In the same year the Attorney General established a list of subversive organizations. In 1948 and 1949 the Department of Justice indicted and convicted the communist leaders.

The list of subversives uncovered in these years has been long. By hard, patient, silent work these men were exposed, be it noted, in the years before 1950—before the junior Senator from Wisconsin suddenly appeared on the scene and began his wild and reckless campaign against the integrity of our Government itself. Some people have been impressed by his loud talk. But the record is clear on this, too. For all his bragging and fear-mongering the junior Senator from Wisconsin has yet to produce evidence leading to the conviction of one single communist agent, either in or out of government.

The reason for this is clear. Catching real communist agents, like killing poisonous snakes or tigers, is not a job for amateurs or children, especially noisy ones. It is a job for professionals who know their business and their adversaries.

The professionals of the Federal Bureau of Investigation make up a magnificent instrument for the protection of our Government. For years, the F.B.I. has been quietly and remorselessly uncovering the communist plot against America. It has exposed one conspirator after another. It provided the evidence that sent the thirty-one leaders to prison.

I have often wondered what the Republicans think they would

do to improve the situation if they were elected. The General has joined loudly in the clamor about the communist menace in Washington. First he said the communists in government were the result of incompetent, loose security policies. More recently, I'm sorry to say, he implies that the Federal Government is deliberately concealing communists. But he has offered only thundering silence about a cure. What would he do? Would he fire J. Edgar Hoover? Would he fire General Bedell Smith, head of the Central Intelligence Agency and his own former Chief of Staff? Would he discharge General Smith's deputy, Allen Dulles, the brother of his own chief adviser on foreign affairs? Would he discharge the experienced men who now protect our nation's security?

I think we are entitled to ask, is the Republican candidate seriously interested in trying to root communists out of the Government, or is he only interested in scaring the American people to get the Old Guard into the Government?

For my own part, I will tell you straight out, I believe the F.B.I. has been doing a superb job. I think J. Edgar Hoover and General Bedell Smith are excellent, experienced, devoted and trustworthy men in these posts of great responsibility. I would back them to the hilt.

And let me say one more thing, so there will be no shadow of a doubt. If I find in Washington any disloyal government servant, I will throw him out ruthlessly, regardless of place, position or party. I expect to review thoroughly the present loyalty system and if it can be strengthened or improved in any way, it will be done.

As far as I'm concerned this fight will be continued until the communist conspiracy in our land is smashed beyond repair. And I think my record is the best evidence that this fight will be conducted with full respect for our system of justice, and for the Bill of Rights of the United States.

Let us never forget that tension breeds fear, fear, repression, and repression, injustice and tyranny. Our police work is aimed at a conspiracy, and not at ideas or opinion. Our country was built on unpopular ideas, on unorthodox opinions. My definition of a free society is a society where it is safe to be unpopular.

I want to keep our America that way.

I agree with the Roman Catholic Bishops in their pronouncement last November. "Dishonesty, slander, detraction and defamation of character," the Catholic Bishops said, "are as truly transgressions of God's Commandments when resorted to by men in political life as they are for all other men."

We of the Democratic Party have fought communism in America for twenty years—in the Government, in the union halls, in the farm grange halls, in the schools and in our homes. We have met and destroyed this disease as it has not been met or destroyed in any other country in the world. And we have done it without false accusation, without the assassination of honest characters, without destroying the principles of freedom upon which this society is based. Carelessness about our security is dangerous; carelessness about our freedom is also dangerous.

And let me say another thing that needs saying. I have not said and I do not think for a moment that a single responsible Republican leader in those days of boom and bust in the twenties and early thirties when communism sank its roots in this country was deliberately plotting the downfall of capitalism or covertly encouraging communism. And we will make a lot more progress in solving this problem when we stop capitalizing communism for political advantage and think more of the welfare of the Republic than of how we can spread fear and smear and mistrust.

But if the Republican leaders insist on talking incessantly about softness toward communism, I must point out that the record shows that even today the Republican Party opposes those cost-of-living controls which the Democratic Party supports in order to prevent another boom and bust—another period when the beckoning finger of communism's false light would grow stronger in America.

The record shows the Republican Party has steadily tried to block and hobble our worldwide fight against communism time and time again; the Republican majority in Congress has voted to slash economic and military aid to our allies.

But there is no cheap answer to communism, to world peace, to anything worth having.

The Democratic Party rejects this policy of loud words and soft deeds. We stand for a foreign policy of strength, for that is the only policy that can lead to peace.

We will protect ourselves from communism, and, at the same time, we will protect our liberties, too—those liberties which, above all, distinguish the United States from the police state.

The Area of Freedom

Field House, University of Wisconsin

MADISON, WISCONSIN

October 8, 1952

After what Wisconsin did to Illinois last Saturday I suppose you are here not out of curiosity about a candidate for President, but as a mark of charity to the grieving Governor of Illinois. I think your manners are very good, and therefore I will be charitable and not detain you long enough to tell you the whole Democratic story!

I rarely miss the opportunity of visiting a university. Perhaps I discovered, at long last, the reason for this mysterious attraction a few days ago when I overheard some of my staff talking about "egg-heads." They were quoting some newspaper columnist who said that only "egg-heads" could understand my speeches.

For a few minutes I took this egg-head talk personally in injured silence. But I couldn't stand it and summoned up the courage to ask them what an egg-head was. The answer, I discovered, is that an egg-head is anyone who has gone to college! So at least today I have a lot of company.

It makes me shudder a little to think that I graduated from college thirty years ago last June and how doddering and venerable the thirtieth reunion class looked to me then. If I look to you the way they looked to me, I wouldn't vote for me! Having uttered that sentence, I quickly comfort myself by reminding you that you haven't any younger alternatives!

Nothing so dates a man as to decry the younger generation. Yet this has been a favorite attitude of old fogies throughout recorded time. They were at it 4,000 years ago in Memphis and Philadelphia, Egypt, just as some of their contemporaries are at it today in Memphis, Tennessee, and Philadelphia, Pennsylvania.

Perhaps the solution to this aberration is to be found in the flashing epigram of La Rochefoucauld that "The old begin to complain of the conduct of the young when they themselves can no longer set a bad example."

Sometimes, however, such being the infirmities of these my sere and ivy years, I find myself repeating this maxim to myself so that I may conduct myself with seeming parental grace in the presence of my own young sons. Occasionally the tendency to decry the younger generation—a form of mental arthritis for which there is as yet no cure—takes on large proportions. Before we entered the last war a number of misguided writers busied themselves with telling the country that if we should go to war, all would be lost. The reason, they said, was that the young men of this generation were weak and soft, debilitated by ice-cream cones and Cadillacs for the rigors of armed conflict.

This, of course, was nonsense; a confection of which we are presently having an overproduction. The men of our armed forces in the last war were as courageous and enduring as they ever were in the history of this nation, and indeed they prevailed against conditions more terrible than those known to Andrew Jackson's men. They fought without hate, they griped with fervor, and they laughed at themselves with characteristic and saving American humor. And serving with them, in uniform and out of uniform, were millions of American women.

I have never believed that whiskers and wisdom are necessarily synonymous; sometimes indeed whiskers merely adorn blank spaces on blank faces. Going upon this assumption I have been able to persuade many young men to throw in their fortunes with me in a common fight for good government, and if I should be given a lease on the White House I shall hope to induce many young men to join me in a high adventure as I have done in Illinois.

Most of you students were born, I suppose, in the early thirties and do not remember the state of the world at that time. Looking back, it must be hard for most of you to realize that such a world ever existed. Your world has troubles of its own—perhaps greater troubles than those of twenty years ago. But one worry you are spared is the worry of finding a job. When you finish college and military service, you will enter a world which wants and needs you.

This seems a natural thing—when you have it. It is a terrible thing when you don't. As we look around our booming country, it is almost incredible to think that mass unemployment was ever a problem. Yet a short twenty years ago millions of people were engaged in a desperate search for work.

If you are incredulous, let me say that my generation went into the depression with much the same incredulity. I finished college in 1922. That was the era of flappers, bathtub gin, Freud—the threshold of the gay and carefree period of the twenties—the era of wonderful nonsense, about which a fellow Princetonian of mine, F. Scott Fitzgerald, wrote some enduring prose.

This decade marked a curious pause in American life and growth —a last interlude of national self-indulgence between the testing of the First World War and the testing of depression. It was our last time of daydreams before crisis made us face the dark ordeal of the twentieth century.

The men who ran our country in that decade assured us that they had found the secret of permanent prosperity. Most of us believed them, and bought stocks. Then, in 1929, came the crash— and, as prosperity crumbled away before our eyes, we discovered that its copyright owners had no program against depression— nothing but wails and exhortation and whistling in the night. Our masters in Washington and Wall Street threw up their hands. Some jumped out of windows. In the face of economic disaster we were leaderless.

Of course modesty forbids me to tell you which party was in control of the country and had been for many years at that time!

It was a sullen and hostile world—a world which had little for youth of opportunity, of hope, of a future. The system was running down, like a broken clock. The wonder is, not that so many young men and women turned to socialism or to communism, but that there were so few.

The election of 1932 was, in a way, a last chance for a free America. Nearly a million votes were cast against capitalism that year. That million might well have swelled to ten million by 1936 if the economic paralysis had continued.

But, as you all know, the election of 1932 brought Franklin Roosevelt and the Democratic Party, and also the vitality and guts to tackle our economic problems within the framework of the democratic system. The growth of extreme radicalism was arrested by bringing an end to human distress and economic chaos. In 1936, not ten million but a bare 250,000 people voted for socialism and communism. I firmly believe, therefore, that the man who was more responsible than any other for checking the spread of communism in America was Franklin D. Roosevelt.

We came very near a revolution in 1932—and no place was more revolutionary in those days than our old, sober, sedate farm belt. Hunger and want were turning law-abiding American farmers into rebels. When a season's produce could no longer earn the cost of production or meet the interest on mortgages, it seemed time for action. In Wisconsin, in Iowa, in Nebraska, in Kansas, farmers banded together to resist foreclosures, to prevent the sale of farms for taxes, to keep surplus milk off the market by dumping it on the roads—violence and irresponsibility which we do not condone, but which were symptomatic of a dying faith in our system.

I remember those bitter days well, because my first government job was with the Agricultural Adjustment Administration—the old triple-A. Although a city lawyer in Chicago at the time, I came from the corn belt of Illinois and like many other young lawyers and businessmen and college professors, I jumped at the chance to work for a government which was doing something for the farmer who had not even flourished in the roaring twenties.

In those years, too, we began the process of the reform and reconstruction of our economic system—the process which has made our economy so much more foolproof today than the vehicle in which we careened to disaster in the twenties and which was manned by Republican chauffeurs and mechanics.

I go into this because it is something more than ancient history. I would have hoped that all Americans could accept the gains we have made in the last generation, and that on this basis we could move forward together. But I fear the struggle is not over. The minority which fought this effort at every step along the way is still fighting. Senator Bricker spoke for them when he cried at the Republican convention this year that the "last vestige of the New Deal" must be "destroyed."

I hope this was just partisan elocution, but the record is not reassuring that the constructive work which has been done is secure. And it is well for you who can't remember where we have been to know where we are. This freedom and this security are part of the landscape of your world. But they have only been part of that landscape for a short time.

The remaking of our country in this last generation has made America a beacon of progress on an otherwise stormy and darkening earth. I cannot say that you young men and women will go out today into a safer world than that of 1932. But I do say that you will go out into a stronger America—an America which welcomes you, which has a place for you, and in which you may live and work and serve with dignity and faith.

It seemed to me appropriate to discuss these great changes here at the University of Wisconsin, because the democratic impulse of the thirties owed a great deal to the Wisconsin tradition in our national politics.

There were a number of elements in that Wisconsin tradition. The basic element, of course, was a deep and abiding faith in the American people and the American soil. No matter how much our nation becomes overgrown with the tall towers of great cities, we can never forget that our democracy had its roots in the land. It was a Wisconsin historian—Frederick Jackson Turner—who first made the nation understand that the American democracy came out of the wilderness. In our century, few have symbolized better the ancient Jeffersonian faith than the great leader of Wisconsin progressivism, Robert La Follette.

But the Wisconsin tradition meant more than a simple belief in the people. It also meant a faith in the application of intelligence and reason to the problems of society. It meant a deep conviction that the role of government was not to stumble along like a drunkard in the dark, but to light its way by the best torches of knowledge and understanding it could find. The La Follettes were never ashamed to call on the experts.

Above all, the Wisconsin tradition meant a belief in the value of the free intellectual community—the belief which has found such splendid embodiment here in this city. If we value the pursuit of knowledge, we must be free to follow wherever that search may lead us. The free mind is no barking dog, to be tethered on a ten-foot chain. It must be unrestricted in the play of its inquiry. If we insist on conclusions before the search is over, we are committed to playing the game of the mind with marked cards.

The Wisconsin idea—the faith in the free mind and in the application of reason to government—was one of the hopeful ideas of our century. Today we find that idea everywhere under attack. Throughout the world, the whole conception of the free intellectual community is menaced by those who fear freedom more than they love it. As darkness falls upon this earth, the area of freedom shrinks. New philosophies arise—new theories of the state—which recoil from freedom, detest it, exterminate it, and seek to found new societies upon its extermination.

In the Soviet Union we see the totalitarian state in its gloomy reality. The first casualty of the communist regime is the free mind; and, once the free mind disappears, all else must follow. Thus in Soviet Russia today the last trace of freedom has been extinguished. Not only history and economics and politics, but science and art and music are enslaved by the regime. The unorthodox experiment, the unacceptable melody, the extreme painting, become evidences of disloyalty. Unorthodoxy is treason to the state.

This process reaches its grim climax, of course, in the Soviet courts. Here injustice, wearing the gowns of justice, stages the last act of the cruel joke. Men are accused at random of infamous and fantastic charges; they are transformed into enemy agents, spies, traitors; documents are misrepresented and falsified; past associations are uncovered and distorted, past remarks torn from context; guilt comes in the end, not just by association, but by accusation. And triumphant above all rises the figure of the great accuser whose word can brand men's lives, make falsehood true, create evidence where none existed before, and spread through all society the reign of suspicion and terror.

Because we believe in the free mind, we are opposing communism with all our will. We are opposing it abroad, where its relentless pressure seeks further to narrow the area of freedom. We are opposing it at home, where its agents and its dupes seek to undermine our society and strangle our freedom in its own paradoxes.

As President, I would use all the power of the Federal Government to expose and identify communist activity, to remove communists and their tools from places of position and prestige in our society, and to protect our free institutions from communist espionage, sabotage and subversion.

But, because we believe in the free mind, we are also fighting those who, in the name of anti-communism, would assail the community of freedom itself. The liberties of expression and conscience are the basic liberties of American society. They are sustained by our whole structure of law and justice. That structure has sufficed for us in the great crises of our past. I see nothing in the future which requires us to throw it overboard now.

I would call to your mind the words of a great Republican patriot, Theodore Roosevelt. "No greater harm can be done to the body politic," he said, "than by those men who, through reckless and indiscriminate accusation of good men and bad men, honest men and dishonest men alike, finally so hopelessly puzzle the public that they do not believe that any man in public life is entirely straight; while, on the other hand, they lose all indignation against the man who really is crooked."

And in case you have not been reading all the philosophers, I remind you that Aristotle said: "History shows that almost all tyrants have been demagogues who gained favor with the people by their accusations of the notables." Way back there!

Disturbing things have taken place in our own land. The pillorying of the innocent has caused the wise to stammer and the timid to retreat. I would shudder for this country if I thought that we too must surrender to the sinister figure of the Inquisition, of the great accuser. I hope that the time will never come in America when charges are taken as the equivalent of facts, when suspicions are confused with certainties, and when the voice of the accuser stills every other voice in the land.

So long as America is populated by Americans, this can never be the case. We shall defend the free mind and the free spirit, as we always have in the past. We love and cherish the light of freedom. We will not be stampeded into the dark night of tyranny. With faith in our great heritage of individual freedom, we can— and will—keep America the land of the free.

This challenge to freedom has its compensations. It has forced us to redefine our own values. It has made us restate the ideal of freedom for the complex industrial society of the twentieth century. And the process of redefinition and restatement—for most of us, anyway—has only strengthened our faith in the durability of free society.

We are hearing a lot today about American division, weakness, hesitation, fear. Some, perhaps, find it politically profitable to cultivate the vineyards of anxiety. I would warn them lest they reap the grapes of wrath.

I have said elsewhere in the campaign that this election is a struggle between accusation and fear, and confidence and faith. I say to you today that we need not dwell in fear. We have shown in these twenty years the mighty things we are capable of—if we but maintain faith in ourselves, in our heritage of liberty and in the invincibility of free men.

Fear begets fear, as faith begets faith. My party knows where it has been and where it is going. The opposition doesn't like the road we have traversed and is sharply divided about the road ahead. The future stretches ahead, untrodden and uncharted—but ours to take and to master. That future is mostly yours; the roads yours to choose.

The Proper Role of Government

Kiel Auditorium

ST. LOUIS, MISSOURI

October 9, 1952

A year from now St. Louis will celebrate the one hundred and fiftieth anniversary of Thomas Jefferson's Louisiana Purchase.

That act of statesmanship more than doubled the area of the United States. The price was fifteen million dollars. The value cannot be calculated. Yet the Purchase was opposed by the men of a conservative political party far gone in decay, split into quarrelsome factions, able to unite only in fear of the future and in noisy condemnation of Thomas Jefferson for daring to look ahead.

They remind me of some men today who know the *price* of everything and the *value* of nothing. They are the Old Guard Republicans who are making a desperate bid to direct the future of this country.

What we will really commemorate in 1954 is the triumph of Jefferson's belief in the American future. Because he believed deeply, he dared greatly and so he bequeathed greatness to his country.

St. Louis stands at the keystone of our continental arch. Here the rivers and roads and railroads from the east joined the great north-south highway, the Mississippi. Here, too, people came from all over the United States to begin the great adventure of going west. Beyond St. Louis was an empty land and a great future.

Today great cities lie along the route Lewis and Clark traveled on Jefferson's orders. Along the trails the wayfaring Americans found immense treasures in gold and silver, copper and oil, and other resources. But they found no treasure a hundredth part as valuable as the land itself. The history of a century and a half is the story of how the empty land filled up.

Population, wealth, power, productivity have all steadily increased in the United States. That fact is at the core of American life. An expanding economy has meant a steady rise in the standard of living for all of us.

For every generation the United States has been what the New World was to the first colonists who came here—a land of new and continuing opportunity today and a fairer promise for tomorrow.

Twenty-five years from now there will be thirty-five million more of us than there are now. At every dinner table set for four people today there is an invisible fifth plate. In 1975 the land which has always answered our increasing needs will have to fill that plate as well as the other four. It will have to provide joists and rafters, flooring and roofing, for the now invisible fifth house. This is the measure of the task cut out for us—and of the opportunity the future holds for men of vision and daring.

I would speak to you tonight about our opportunities. I would speak to you of America's new frontier.

Before exploring this frontier, however, before suggesting what lies ahead in the next twenty-five years, let us for a moment glance backward twenty-five years. America in 1927 lived in a fool's paradise. It ended rudely. We came to a stop in 1930. The whole mighty engine flew apart. Numerous thoughtful men actually questioned whether the system of American capitalism could survive.

Well, it is one of history's odd ironies that today the Republicans are accusing us Democrats of being enemies of free capitalistic enterprise—when the plain truth is that it was Democrats that saved the American capitalistic system under the leadership of Franklin Roosevelt.

Today America is more prosperous than any other nation in history. Of course, the Old Guard orators are going around the country these days broadcasting gloomy warnings that our prosperity is a fake, that it is based on war, that a depression will come with peace. This is nonsense. The truth is that our tremendous defense effort is holding us back, gobbling up the goods our people need at home, and when we have at last won through to safer waters, we shall be able to work at a hundred and one tasks that need doing.

But tonight I do not propose to talk to you about the past, nor about the Old Guard of the Republican Party, in whose ranks my opponent has enlisted or been shanghaied; it doesn't matter which. I would speak with you about more important matters.

Today not everyone in this country is sharing fairly in our national prosperity. Schoolteachers, pensioners, old people living on savings, widows living on the proceeds of life insurance—these people often cannot make ends meet today because prices have outrun their incomes. We must stop the price rise—and we know how to do it if only the Republican Old Guard will give us a chance.

Others among us are in a still more serious plight. How can we talk about prosperity to the sick who cannot afford proper medical care, to the mentally ill for whom there is no room in our over-crowded institutions? How can we talk about prosperity to the hundreds of thousands who can find no decent place to live at prices they can afford? And how can we talk prosperity to a share-cropper living on worn-out land, or to city dwellers packed six to a room in an unlit tenement with a garbage-strewn alley for their children's playground?

To these people, national prosperity is a mockery—to the eleven million families in this nation with incomes of less than $2,000 a year.

Do these facts shock you? They shock me. What can we do to improve this situation? There will always be the foolish and improvident. But we are concerned here with much more than that. And what is the proper role of government?

This is one of the great questions on which our two political parties divide.

It seems to me that the answer is this: Government has three duties.

First, government is an umpire, denying special privilege, ensuring equal rights, restraining monopoly and greed and bigotry, making sure that the game is played according to the rules. On this point, the Republicans agree—so long as they write the rules.

Second, government has the duty of creating an economic climate in which creative men can take risks and reap rewards, so that our economic life will have a continuous flow of fresh ideas and fresh leadership; and, of course, it means the building of solid defenses against the greatest threat to that flow—depression.

This, perhaps above all others, has been the great contribution of the Democratic Party in the last twenty years. In taking the nation out of the worst depression in its history, we reformed the economy so effectively that, under continuing wise leadership, there never need be another disastrous depression such as we have known in the past.

The way you stay out of depressions is by stability and maintaining the buying power of the people. In the last twenty years—through price supports for the farmers, minimum-wage and collective-bargaining laws for the workers, social-security measures for the unemployed and the elderly—we have built foundations under the national economy.

The Republicans are against depression just as much as we Democrats are—and especially during September and October of election years! But the rest of the time they are busy opposing and denouncing most of these defenses against depression as "socialistic."

Third, government has the duty of helping the people develop their country.

The Federal Government made the Louisiana Purchase, and on that land a nation grew to greatness. No private corporation would have built Grand Coulee Dam, yet in the Grand Coulee country people are building their homes and establishing their private businesses, and farmers are converting desert into garden.

And this is only one of the frontiers that government has helped the people open in recent years. The Republicans disagree on this. They say that such activity is interference with private enterprise. But the fact is that it is this very activity of government which enables private enterprise to flourish.

Have any great frontiers in human history ever been opened without the help of government? Christopher Columbus discovered the New World, but it was the Queen of Spain who provided his ships. The American Government not only bought the Louisiana Territory but subsidized the railroads that spanned it, opened government lands to homesteaders, built TVA so the Middle South could lift itself out of the quagmire of want. Government achieved the miracle of atomic power which is the new dimension for both good and evil in the world of tomorrow.

It is this partnership of government with free and daring men that we need today.

No doubt the Republican Old Guard would say that that was all very well in the old days—but today the frontier is closed.

I say to you that the American frontier has never beckoned more invitingly to men and women of initiative and adventure.

Even our life span has increased. In less than a generation, a young man at twenty will look forward to a working life five years longer than he could have anticipated in 1930.

Right now there are sixty-two million Americans at work. During the next ten years, there will be ten million more Americans ready and able to work. With their help, we can lift our production from 336 billion dollars a year to 475 billion dollars a year.

These are astronomical figures. What do they mean to you and me? They mean just this: The amount that each of us can spend can be lifted by some $600 per year by 1962. This amounts to $2,400 for a family of four. In other words, we can make the familiar ugly, grinding poverty in this country of ours a thing of the past.

We can make America the land for all of us what we want it to be for each of us. We need more hospitals, more schools, more housing, more electric power, more soil conservation.

And we can achieve these things—if we but have faith in ourselves, in our heritage of freedom and in our limitless future.

In the first six weeks of the campaign I set forth—as clearly as I could—the policies which I think are best calculated to keep our frontiers ever widening and which will enable all the people to share fairly in the new age of abundance.

Let me remind you of these Democratic policies:

One. To repeal and replace the Taft-Hartley law with a new law which promotes the private settlement of disputes, and to work in other ways for an orderly and fair balancing of the interests between labor and management. Production postponed is production lost, and in our industrial society production losses are coffin nails for workers and owners and consumers alike.

Two. Price supports for agriculture; continuing search for practicable methods of supporting the prices of perishables; continuation and improvement of such other programs as rural electrification and soil conservation.

Three. To widen the coverage and expand the benefits available under our social-security system and to honor our obligations to the veteran.

Four. To continue our efforts through private, local, state and Federal action to eradicate discrimination based on race, religion, or national origin.

Five. To move ahead on our well-established housing programs.

Six. To meet our most pressing educational needs.

Seven. To combat relentlessly the inflation which strikes so heavily at family budgets.

Eight. To review our tax policy with an eye to the effect of taxes on incentives to produce and invest, on the ability to consume the full output of the economy, and on the need for a balanced budget.

Nine. To encourage small business and enforce our anti-monopoly laws.

Ten. To continue the progressive development and sound conservation of the nation's land and water resources.

I want to add one word about the matter of a balanced budget. It will be easy to balance the budget in a strong and advancing economy. It will be hopeless to try to balance it in a depression.

Let no one misjudge me on this point. No matter how peaceful and prosperous we are, a balanced budget requires us always to distinguish between the pleasing and the necessary. A government spending beyond its income in prosperous peacetime, or spending carelessly at any time, does not have a proper view of its job and is dangerously vulnerable to adversity. Let us not be too enterprising in discovering additional things for government to do, and more enterprising in defining the essential things that government must do in order to provide an atmosphere in which industry, agriculture and labor can work and prosper and progress together.

That is our program. We take our stand upon the fundamental principle that the role of government is, to sum up, just this: To remove the roadblocks put in the way of the people by nature and by greedy men; to release the energies of the people, so that free men may work the miracles of the future as they have worked the miracles of the past.

No man could travel across our country, as I have done, without being deeply stirred. No man then—his heart touched and his mind moved—could but reflect upon his country's destiny, his love for it the greater as perils encompass it. As we walk through a troubled time, let us remember that the United States was born to greatness.

Greatness was breathed into us at birth by the founders of the Republic, and if we be true to them and their teachings we cannot be false to ourselves.

Let us remember that when men had few rights anywhere, the Declaration of Independence proclaimed the earth-shaking doctrine of the Rights of Man everywhere. As its words went winging around the world, those whose eyes were cast down and those whose backs were bent cupped their ears to listen. They raised their eyes and by ever so little straightened their backs bit by bit. And as, two centuries ago, we were the hope of the world's oppressed, we remain their hope today.

Let us remember that our bigness springs from our fields, forests, mines, and factories; but our greatness springs from the charters of our freedoms, and from countless men and women who believed, and believing, wrought.

If some catastrophe destroyed the things that we have built, we could rebuild them. But if through some catastrophe we lost faith in the principles by which we came to birth and by which we live, we could never return to greatness.

And so I say that when we speak of our abundant future, let us never forget to offer thanks for the riches which are ours today.

A new day is dawning. I do not say all problems are solved. Far from it. But we have dared to try to solve them. We have courage to dare the new, the compassion to help the wretched and the vision to see what men can really be in the society of our dreams.

Tidelands Oil—Foreign Trade

Beauregard Square

NEW ORLEANS, LOUISIANA

October 10, 1952

When I was a little boy I spent several winters here in New Orleans out near Audubon Park and I used to ride up and down Canal Street on the streetcars. No one ever paid any attention to me, and now I come back forty years later and thousands come out to greet me on Canal Street. Something has happened and you've touched my heart. But the fact of the matter is that I love New Orleans—either way!

For here in New Orleans you have made an admirable civilization. It is a jambalaya containing all that makes for the body's pleasure, the mind's delight, the spirit's repose. Here each man seasons the dish to his own taste, for in this amiable society each man is master of his own seasoning.

I wish I could linger over this delectable dish. But such a luxury is not permitted the campaigner. If, then, you will forgive me my bad manners, I shall talk at once about things of mutual concern.

As you know, I stand on the Democratic Party platform with respect to minority rights. I have only one observation to make on this subject, one that must sadden you as it saddens me. It is that, after two thousand years of Christianity, we need discuss it at all.

Let me speak for a moment on a subject of special interest to Louisiana. That is the question of the tidelands or, more accurately, the submerged lands which lie between the low-water mark and Louisiana's historical boundary three miles to seaward.

These are the lands in controversy—and no other. The Federal Government lays no claim to the true tidelands (those between the low- and high-water marks) nor to lands underlying inland waters; and, indeed, it could not because the United States Supreme Court has long since expressly recognized that ownership of all these lands clearly resides in the states. I have no designs upon the oysters of Maryland or the clams of Massachusetts!

Now I have been Governor of a state and I know, better than most, something of the problems of the states. I know that Louisiana, like other states, has important functions to perform for its people. It takes money to do those things and each state needs every resource it can muster for this purpose.

I am not surprised, therefore, that Louisiana has been greatly disappointed in the decision of the Supreme Court holding that the right to the oil beneath the coastal submerged lands is vested in all the people of the United States and not just those of Louisiana. The people and the Governor of Illinois would be equally disappointed had they lost a similar lawsuit.

But I am not running for Governor. And if I am elected on November 4th, I will be representing all of the people and not just some. What will be the position I will then find myself in with respect to this controversy? And how, therefore, should I state my view on it now, if I am to be a responsible President and fair with everyone?

Well, I have stated my position on this—and only *one* position —and I want to make clear that I lack the versatility of my opponent, who has had at least three separate positions on the tidelands question. I tried to make my views as clear as I could at the time Governor Shivers of Texas paid his widely advertised visit to me in Illinois. But what I said then has apparently not been circulated widely or set forth fully in this part of the country, and so I am going to say it again now.

The man who becomes the next President of the United States must, in my judgment, take up the submerged-lands controversy at the point where the Supreme Court left off. He cannot and should not begin to go behind Supreme Court decisions, saying that this one is right and that one is wrong and acting accordingly. I think he takes them as they come, whether they involve submerged lands or the seizure of the steel industry.

There was one great Louisianian who, I am sure, would have agreed with me on this. He was a distinguished Confederate officer who fought long and honorably for this state in the Great War. And as a lawyer on earlier trips to New Orleans I have stopped to look at the statue of Edward Douglas White, Chief Justice of the United States Supreme Court.

If the submerged lands, by virtue of the ruling of the United States Supreme Court, are a national, and not a state, asset, the question presented is one of wise policy in the disposition of that asset. I do not think it is wise policy for the Congress to institute a practice of giving away such national assets to individual states. I believe this in the case of the submerged lands as much as I would believe it in the case of the national forests, the national parks, the national grazing lands, and all of the other public lands which, though located within the boundaries of individual states, belong to the people of all of the states. I believe it is the duty of the President to conserve the national assets, the national domain, be it dollars in the treasury or forests in Oregon.

But to say this is not to solve the problem of the submerged lands. That problem is how to use the submerged lands for the benefit of the people of the country, including the people of Louisiana. The solution lies ultimately with the Congress which makes our laws. At the moment we are on dead center.

I don't believe in keeping matters in an unsettled state so that they may be exploited for political purposes. I believe that what is most needed in the case of the submerged lands is to get rid of the politics, to face the problem with sense and reason and good temper, and to get on with the business so that development can proceed.

I said to Governor Shivers, and I say to you of Louisiana, that my hope and desire is to see the early enactment of legislation which will provide for a fair and equitable arrangement for the administration of these lands and the division of their proceeds. We did this in the case of other public lands years ago—allocating in some cases 37½ per cent of the royalties to the state where the land is located.

I do not know whether the same formula should be followed in the case of the submerged lands. And I do not think that matters of this importance can be settled wisely in the frenzy of a national campaign or as a means of getting votes. I am equally sure that a settlement fair to all, including the people of Louisiana, can be worked out in a realistic, rational spirit. A President who was careless with the people's assets could hardly be a careful steward of your trust.

But there is something else I want to talk about here tonight. The windows of the port of New Orleans open upon seas and continents. They open also upon the incomparable empire of the Mississippi Valley. The great river, the sea, and your energies, have made you—in the romantic old phrase—a company of merchant adventurers.

You are deeply concerned both with foreign trade and domestic trade. But the two are now one. Our economic power in the world is so great that a slight downtrend here produces earthquake shocks elsewhere. These shocks immediately register upon the sensitive indicators of your commerce. So, too, Republican barriers to trade, such as quotas and high tariffs, are quickly reflected upon your docks, in your stores and in your homes as men lose their jobs.

This is a powerful industrial city. Last year, more than $200,-000,000 worth of industry moved into the area. So far this year, more than $100,000,000 of new industries have arrived.

In 1952, this port may handle close to $2,000,000,000 worth of cargo. This is twice the volume of only five years ago.

In brief, a new giant has arisen on the shores of the Mississippi. But giants need more elbow room and more of everything than smaller figures.

Yours has been a long, steady, slow growth. During the past twenty years, however, the progress here has been spectacular. When depressions came in the old days, you could comfort yourselves that you would be less harmfully affected than cities whose growth had been faster than yours. But this is no longer true.

You are geared to a bigger and faster moving wheel than ever before. Louisiana must, therefore, seek the right answer to this question:

Is the Democratic Party or the Republican Party the more likely to promote foreign and domestic prosperity?

Perhaps a few questions may throw light on this subject.

Has not the Republican Party always been the party of quotas and high tariffs?

Did not the last Republican administration raise tariffs to the highest point in history? Didn't that cripple your foreign trade, injure your home market and set in motion events that exploded in the world's most destructive depression?

When these tariffs were rivets on your necks, did not the Republican leadership treat your complaints with contemptuous silence?

What of unfair and discriminatory freight rates that long ran against the South? Did the Republican leadership help right this wrong? Or was it content to see the South pay through the nose?

The Democratic Party has always been for world trade and liberalized tariffs. These are things for which the South has always stood. It is, therefore, no accident that President Roosevelt chose Cordell Hull as his Secretary of State almost twenty years ago. Chief among his great achievements was his program for Reciprocal Trade Agreements to encourage and increase our foreign trade, and incidentally the prosperity of New Orleans.

And what of the Republican record on Reciprocal Trade Agreements? Its leadership has always opposed them. If this leadership prevails, what will happen then to your great port and the thousands of people who earn their living through it? If you have any doubts on this subject, remember the Republican record. Then read the Republican platform and please tell me what it means, if you can.

How do you reconcile the Republican position with your International House or your International Trade Mart; your Dock Board and Foreign Trade Zone? New Orleans has done a magnificent job building cordial personal and business relations with Latin America. How long do you think these relations will last if our Latin-American friends have trouble earning a living by trading with the United States? What will it do to our Good Neighbor Policy—and I say to you that the further strengthening of our Good Neighbor Policy will be a major objective of my administration.

It is not possible for this nation to be at once politically internationalist and economically isolationist. This is just as insane as asking one Siamese twin to high dive while the other plays the piano. And that is exactly what the Republican leadership has long been doing. And that, I believe, is what it would do if it should again come into power.

Even if the Old Guard thinks of foreign trade as a one-way street, that trade is, and must be, a two-way street. We cannot sell without buying and we cannot go on exporting dollars forever.

On October 7th, Senator Taft told an audience at Elgin, Illinois, that he had voted time after time against Reciprocal Trade Agreements.

I cannot exaggerate the deadly importance of this statement. It foreshadows more than the blight that would descend upon New Orleans if his views should prevail. And it foreshadows even more sinister results at the hands of Soviet Russia.

I am not a man given to exaggeration. Nor do I want to frighten you into voting for me. I shall continue to try to appeal to your minds rather than to your solar plexus. Yet I now beg you to listen carefully.

The Soviet Party Congress recently convened in Moscow. Its meeting was described by *Pravda*, the chief Soviet Government newspaper, as "the greatest event in the ideological life of the Communist Party and the Soviet people."

Stalin wrote a book for the occasion. The book is an instrument of Soviet foreign policy. It lays down the line that the Soviets may be expected to follow for perhaps the next decade.

This, briefly, is what he tells communists everywhere: That the world struggle will revolve around Western Germany and Japan; that basic Soviet policy is to emphasize that it will be difficult for Western Germany and Japan to earn a living within the non-communist world. Therefore Soviet Russia will play up the economic opportunities that will be offered these countries to trade with the communist world. And Stalin concludes that conflicts between the free world and Western Germany and Japan will grow as these countries get on their feet and compete more sharply with the free world; that is, with such great trading nations as the United States, Britain and France.

In short what Stalin is saying is this: that he is not so foolish as to engage us in a great shooting war; that he will simply wait it out because we are so blind and so stupid that we will not permit Western Germany and Japan to trade with the free world. They must, then, eventually trade with the Soviet world. So doing they will fall within Soviet domination.

Here I bid you pause and think before it is too late. The mentality of the Republican Party in foreign trade has been well assessed by Stalin. He has seized upon one of the keys that may open the door to our downfall, if we permit him to use it. I say to you with the utmost conviction, that if we follow the suicidal foreign-trade fanaticism of the Republican Party, we may condemn this nation to isolation and destruction.

Stalin, then, proposes to conquer us, not by arms, but by taking advantage of what he believes to be our stupidity. This is not a battle that can be won by cannon or bombs. And it cannot be won by a few minutes' briefing of Army officers on the immensely complicated area of foreign trade and foreign finance—particularly by Republican politicians to whom reciprocal trade is distasteful.

But, to come back to the South after this brief excursion abroad. Friendliness for the South is nothing new in my family. Let me tell you what I mean.

In the 1870's, New Orleans men fought carpetbaggers on Canal Street. Standing with them, there was, I am proud to say, my grandfather Adlai Stevenson. A Congressman from Illinois, he fought a Republican project to compel the use of troops at Southern elections. This project was known as the Force Bill. He expressed his distaste for a measure that would have compelled the South to go Republican at bayonet point.

Time passed. In the 1890's the Republican leadership was still unable to convert Democrats to Republicanism through reason. But it was still determined to do it through force. By then, my grandfather was Democratic Vice-Presidential candidate on a ticket headed by Grover Cleveland, a ticket that was elected. In 1892, just sixty years ago, he again opposed the Force Bill. He said that its passage might mean the election of Congressmen by bayonets, and that the South was faced with the counterpart of the horrors of the Reconstruction Period.

I hope, therefore, that with no violation of grace, I may claim spiritual kinship with you in your struggle for freedom and equity. Today it is the struggle of the ordinary man to get his rightful share of the goods produced by him and his community against those who would grab the greater share for themselves. The struggle never takes quite the same form, but its objective is always the same. Only the weapons change. Yesterday they were bayonets. Today they are a Republican campaign of fear and intimidation.

For decades these forces were pitilessly arrayed against you. The strong exacted of you what they could, and you granted what you must. The sufferings of those times are painful recollections of thousands of Louisiana families. Your physical hardships were great. But—more important—your self-respect was wounded. The wounds of the body are superficial. But the wounds of the spirit are grievous.

These mournful recollections, however, have been fading in the sunshine of happier times. Woodrow Wilson's New Freedom, forty years ago, began your liberation. Twenty years ago, Franklin Roosevelt, leading a strong Democratic Party in the name of a long-suffering people, began to bring you what had so long been denied you. Ever since that time, you have been moving toward a better life.

If I now, for a moment, speak of the past, it is not because of an urgent interest in history. It is because the past and present illustrate two different views of the Republican and Democratic Parties toward man and his place in society.

Let us then look homeward here in Louisiana. It was—and still is—one of our potentially richest states. Petroleum, gas, sulphur, salt exist here in prodigal abundance. Your fisheries are rich. You have a great sugar bowl and a valuable fur catch. Your forest resources are enormous. Your cotton and rice fields are wide.

You long had everything that makes for prosperity. But, for decades, the great majority of the people of Louisiana ate the dry crusts of poverty. Many of them dragged out their lives in the shadowy world of undernourishment. They were too weak to live fully and too strong to die.

Malaria, pellagra and other diseases sapped the strength of thousands. Your health services were pitifully inadequate. How many people died because they couldn't get medical treatment, no one knows except God and their families. Your roads were poor, especially your farm-to-market roads. There were too few schools and teachers for your children. In rural areas, school terms were often too short for genuine education. There was not enough money for longer terms and many men couldn't live at all unless their children worked and added something to wretchedly low family incomes.

Farmers sold their produce for what they could get. Working people sold the sweat of their faces and the toil of their hands for a pittance. And so there rested upon this lovely state, this potentially rich state, the bone-chilling breath of poverty.

By 1933 the people of the United States had lived for almost forty years—except for one eight-year interval—under Republican rule. Most of you had little to show for it except perhaps a corner of the earth where you vainly sought shelter against the arrows of misfortune. By 1933 your condition was little better than that of the natives of India. Your average yearly income per person was then $222.00, or 65 cents a day.

The thin pretense was maintained that you were sovereign citizens of sovereign States. Actually, Louisiana and the South had long been converted through Republican leadership, with its control of money and banking, into an American India. That leadership had succeeded in making the whole South colonies of the rich industrial Northeast. They were your absentee landlords. They used every method possible to keep yours a primitive, agricultural economy through their control of the money and banking systems of the nation. It is only during the past twenty years that you were liberated from colonialism and began to come into your rightful estate as free citizens of a free country, fully participating in all of its privileges.

This process of liberation has been described by the Republican leaders—with their usual skill in calling things by their opposites —as "socialism." I don't need to tell you that our Democratic program is the strongest bulwark against socialism that a free society could have. I have repeatedly said that I do not favor socialization—socialization of medicine, socialization of law, socialization of industry or anything else. Those who say that we cannot meet the people's needs without destroying free enterprise are the worst enemies of free society.

But enough of old, unhappy, far-off things. For some years you have been living in a world bright and fresh. Prosperity walks upon your farms and in the streets of your towns. More people of this state now own—or are on their way to owning—more houses and farms than ever before. Their savings are greater than ever before. Your children can now find opportunities at home instead of having to go elsewhere for them. And we no longer have eroded people living on eroded lands.

In determining our course for the future, I think that there is a simple method. We know what we have. We know how far we have gone. We must now decide how to get from what we have in the present to what we want in the future.

The relationship of the Democratic Party and the people during the twenty years past has been a relationship of good will. The Democratic Party has been responsive to the needs of the people and the people have responded by keeping it in power. I have no doubt at all that this harmonious relationship will be continued at the ballot box next month.

I want to conclude by saying a few words about something that means a good deal to Louisiana—and to me. Some hard words have been said this year by the General—in unmalicious haste, so I hope and suppose—about that great nation which has been the actual motherland for so many of you and a spiritual motherland of us all.

Je voudrais maintenant dire quelques mots à la population de langue française. Je vous adresse mon salut car je suis un grand admirateur de la France et de la civilisation française.

Quiconque dit que la France est en train de dépérir ou de dégénerer oublie les belles qualités françaises qui furent apportées ici, en Louisiane, par les ancêtres de la population de langue française, qualités qui fleurissent toujours dans la patrie d'origine de cette population.

Vous êtes de bons citoyens Americains mais vous avez conservé beaucoup de ces belles qualités du peuple français que vos ancêtres ont apportées dans ce pays, et je vous en félicite.

On Liberty of Conscience

Mormon Tabernacle

SALT LAKE CITY, UTAH

October 14, 1952

I cannot speak tonight in this tabernacle without an awareness of the links between its history and that of the State from which I come.

Many of us who reside in Illinois have tasted the wholesome tonic of humility in contemplation of the mistakes to which our history bears witness at Nauvoo—the Beautiful Place—in Illinois where your forefathers stopped on their long journey and built another temple.

It was 106 years ago now that there were those "burnings," the persecution, the mob violence and the murders which finally drove the men and women of the Mormon faith on westward.

When the caravans of those who today seek public office in this nation stop here with you, to meet with you in this, your tabernacle, they stop their clamor and haranguing. They seek the response of your hearts and your minds rather than of your hands or your voices.

I wish that all of our political campaigning could be conducted in the spirit which this meeting place inspires. It is a spirit of faith, a faith that triumphs over any obstacle.

And tonight I want to talk in this Temple to the great confident majority of Americans—the generous and the unfrightened, those who are proud of our strength and sure of our goodness and who want to work with each other in trust, to advance the honor of our country.

Needless to say this includes many millions of Republicans. If all virtue were in one party the nation would be in a sad way. But this confident majority, I am sorry to say, does not include the Republican speechmakers of this campaign. How do they picture our magnificent America?

Sometimes they whine about our troubles—describing us as half-defeated, half-bankrupt and wholly self-pitying.

Sometimes they boast about our self-sufficiency—describing us as choosing to live alone, friendless, on a remote island, indifferent to the fate of man, a huge hermit-crab without a soul.

Sometimes they call large sections of us dupes and fellow-travelers—a people without a purpose and without a mind.

But at all times they picture us unworthily—scared, stupid and heartless. They thus betray the conquering, hopeful, practical yet deeply moral America which you and I know.

We all know it is nonsense, and that in fact the reverse is true. To the dismay of the enemies of America, we proved after 1945 that we have learned in the last twenty years not only to produce mightily, but to distribute among all our people an increasingly fair share of that production. We have evolved a stronger and a better form of economy, which makes nonsense of the Russian textbooks.

The friends of freedom everywhere have rejoiced. They have noted our rising and widespread wealth and well being. They have noted that we had no depression and no unemployment at the end of the war—in spite of headlong demobilization and disarmament. And remember that all this happened before the Marshall Plan, before the revival of our armed might, before Korea. Every liberty-loving European gave thanks that we had showed ourselves not only strong but stable.

Must this inspiring record now be ridiculed for campaign purposes? Must our credit for using our capitalist system wisely and humanely be undermined in Europe—and by General Eisenhower of all men? Must our proud all-American achievement be pictured as a Democratic Party plot?

During the war, you remember, when we all knew America was in danger, we only wanted the best, the most unselfish. We had no time for building political mantraps or for inventing derogatory tales. It was a heartlifting moment.

But a cold war leads the timid and the discontented into frustration. And out of frustration comes pettiness—the niggling, pitiful picture of a confused, divided country which these office-seekers are now painting. And this, of course, was the very purpose for which the Russians invented cold war and imposed it upon us.

They hoped we would feel frustrated, shackled by circumstance.

They hoped we would fall to quarreling among ourselves and thus betray our mission.

But the American giant will not be shackled!

We shall not be tempted by the cold war to be half-regretful, half-ashamed of our strength—or frightened of it, which is worse. Regretful (God help us!) in the face of the stirring truth that Lincoln's vision has come true, that now we are indeed the "last, best hope of earth"—so recognized by all the free world, which implores us to be great, to lead with magnanimity and, above all, with patience. The very powerful, if they are good, must always be patient.

And still some of us regret it! Some of us say: "Why can't life leave us alone? We don't want to lead. We want to be undisturbed."

What would our Fathers have said to such talk? From the dawn of our Revolution they saw America as the saviour—not merely in terms of power, but in terms of goodness.

They knew that Providence had given us this empty, unexploited Continent for a purpose. And they knew that it must be a purpose which includes all men—for the same God made us all.

In 1787 George Washington said: "The preservation of the sacred fire of liberty, and the destiny of the republican form of government, are justly considered as deeply, perhaps as finally staked, on the experiment entrusted to the hands of the American people."

At that time we had less than four million inhabitants. But there was no doubt, no fear, in Washington's mind regarding our destiny.

In 1858 Abraham Lincoln said: "Our reliance is in the love of liberty which God has planted in us. Our defense is in the spirit which prized liberty as the heritage of all men, in all lands everywhere."

At that time there were about thirty million Americans. And we were threatened with civil war. But there was no doubt, no fear, in Lincoln's mind. He saw the war and the dissolution of the Union as a threat to the new, revolutionary idea of the free man and to democratic aspirations everywhere.

In 1915 Woodrow Wilson said: "The interesting and inspiring thought about America is that she asks nothing for herself except what she has a right to ask for humanity itself."

By that time we were a world power, about to enter into a world war. But there was no doubt, no fear, in Woodrow Wilson's mind. He knew, as in truth we have always known, that we were destined to be an example and to assume the burden of greatness.

So we are marked men, we Americans at the mid-century point. We have been tapped by fate—for which we should forever give thanks, not laments. What a day to live in! What a flowering of the work and the faith of our fathers! Who in heaven's name would want America less strong, less responsible for the future?

And precisely because we are tapped by fate, we must be wise and patient as well as strong. This means that we must live, intensely live, the faith which has made us free and thereby invincible. "Despotism may govern without faith, but liberty cannot."

American power is not just coal and iron and oil; cotton and wheat and corn. It is not just our forests and our mountain-ranges, and the huge meandering rivers of our central plains, and the high dry cattle country, and this lucky land of yours between the mountains and the sea. It is not even all these things plus a hundred and sixty million people. It is these things, plus the people, plus the idea!

So a second temptation of the cold frustrating war—which we also proudly reject—is to become so distracted by our troubles that we take this faith too much for granted, that we salute it (as some of us salute our religion), and then go our own way unchanged. If we do not make it part of us—keep it forever before us, intense and demanding and clear—the faith might die and we should then die with it.

What is this "American idea" which we so justly venerate? I suggest that the heart of it is the simple but challenging statement that no government may interfere with our conscience, may tell us what to think. All our freedoms, all our dynamic unleashed energies, stem from this.

We Americans just naturally talk like this: "No government can tell me what to think. No government can tell me what to do, unless it can prove that the common good is served by such interference." This is the American way of living.

Yet the same Republicans (the dinosaur-wing of that party) who object to service from our Government—who call everything "creeping socialism," who talk darkly of "dictatorship"—these same men begin to hint that we are "subversive," or at best the tools of our country's enemies, when we boast of the great strides toward social justice and security we have already made, and of the still greater strides we plan. They laugh at us, superciliously, when we say we are the political party with a heart.

To honor and uphold our faith, therefore, we must never let them confuse us about the difference between what government should do if possible and what it must never do if America is to survive.

It should strengthen us in our freedom by fostering widespread ownership and as much economic independence as possible. In the towns and counties, in the state capitals and in Washington, that great work goes forward today.

But never must government step across the line which separates the promotion of justice and prosperity from the interference with thought, with conscience, with the sacred private life of the mind.

If you like, this is the distinction between the things that are God's and the things that are Caesar's. The mind is the expression of the soul, which belongs to God and must be let alone by government. But farm prices, minimum wages, old-age pensions, the regulation of monopoly, the physical safety of society—these things are Caesar's province, wherein the Government should do all that is humanly possible.

But those among us who would bar us from attempting our economic and social duty are quick with accusations, with defamatory hints and whispering campaigns, when they see a chance to scare or silence those with whom they disagree. Rudely, carelessly they invade the field of conscience, of thought—the field which belongs to God and not to Senators—and not to protect the Republic, but to discredit the individual.

Let us remember also that the first of the Seven Deadly Sins is spiritual pride: the sin which assures me that I know and you don't, so that I give myself permission to use any dubious or dishonest means to discredit your opinion.

Because we have always thought of government as friendly, not as brutal, character assassins and slanderers in the Congress of the United States have a free hand in the methods they use. We never foresaw that the cult of thought-control and of the Big Lie would come to America. So if their conscience permits, they can say almost anything. And if my opponent's conscience permits, he can try to help all of them get re-elected. But will he have strengthened or weakened the American idea?

This is no small thing, this remorseless attack upon freedom of conscience, freedom of thought. A few peddlers of hate and fear would be of little consequence if they had not been welcomed as satellites by Senator Taft and included in the leadership of this strange crusade. And none of them would be significant if the General—who was implored to come home by Republican leaders so that they might be quit of Senator Taft—had not yielded to the demands of his beaten foe. But because of that surrender, because of those strange allies in his queer crusade, our role in world-history, our faithfulness to the men who made the United States, is challenged in this election.

Finally, then, let us recall that our basic faith in liberty of conscience has an ancient ancestry. We can trace it back through Christian Europe, and through pagan Rome, back to the Old Testament prophets. It is by no means exclusive with us. It is in fact our bond of unity with all free men. But we are its ordained guardians today.

Let us lift up our hearts, therefore—glad of our strength, proud of the task it imposes. So far from being half-defeated, half-divided, half-bankrupt—while we are true to ourselves, we can never be defeated; while we accept the honorable burden of leadership, we can never be divided. And in the name of that burden we shall find the means and the determination to spend in money and in labor and in hard thought whatever is needed to save ourselves and our world.

Second Fireside Speech

Radio and Television Studio

LOS ANGELES, CALIFORNIA

October 16, 1952

A letter to me from a lady in the East the other day said, "I am easily swayed by emotion, except when I think, which I occasionally do."

Well, tonight, my friends, at this fireside, which is really a studio in Los Angeles, I want to talk to you about the question which lies closest to all of our hearts and heaviest on all of our minds.

It has become our custom to sum this up in one word—Korea—a name and a place that many Americans knew little about until two years ago. But we know a lot about Korea now, and perhaps the most important thing we know is that it is a much, much broader problem than that one word, Korea, implies.

In June of 1950, the hopes of the world were lifted by the United Nations' decision to meet force with force in Korea, to fight to halt ruthless, cynical communist aggression.

President Truman's prompt decision to meet the test and his courageous leadership were saluted by all Americans, whatever their party and whatever their station in life, and by free men everywhere.

General Douglas MacArthur said from his post in Japan that the President's action had "lighted into a flame a lamp of hope throughout Asia that was burning dimly toward extinction." "It marked," he said, "for the Far East the focal and turning point in this area of struggling for freedom."

We knew in 1950 that the communist attack on Korea was not an isolated event. We knew that it was part and parcel of a vast drive for world dominion that began long before that Sunday morning when the North Koreans crossed the 38th Parallel. It was intended that the Soviet-directed drive would carry right on through Korea in a few weeks—and far, far beyond, as the West sat indecisive and impotent. Why not? Wasn't that the history of the Japanese invasion of China; of Mussolini's invasion of Ethiopia; of Hitler's conquest in Europe? Wasn't the League of Nations helpless in the face of force?

There is no other problem on which we Americans need to think so clearly as the problem created by this Soviet drive for world dominion. A misstep, an unwise action, a failure of reason and will could touch off world tragedy. But it is equally true where cool heads and straight thinking and unwavering determination are the guides, the only guides which can lead us safely to world peace. It is up to us in America to supply this guidance, accepting the responsibilities of leadership which, whether we like it or not, have sought us out and from which we cannot avert our faces.

We did not choose this struggle in Korea and in the world. We don't want it. But we can't avoid it, and our future depends on its outcome. We face the questions of how we are to wage this struggle and how we are to win it. I want to explore these questions with you tonight soberly and objectively. Like every parent who has sons in the service, I do not want to see the shadows of politics fall across the part your boys and mine must play in the unfolding drama of war and peace.

Politics must end at the water's edge. For it is not as Democrats or Republicans that we live in the world and meet the tests of history; it is as Americans and as free men and women.

And this is why a bi-partisan foreign policy is not only desirable —it is indispensable for the maximum strength and influence of the United States throughout the world because we can be no stronger abroad than we are at home, and no amount of election-year oratory can obscure the truth that our foreign policy has drawn on the wisdom of like-minded men in both parties, that it has been developed with their co-operation, that it has been carried out with their help.

This campaign might have served to unify and strengthen the American people for the tasks that lie ahead. It might have been used to unify and strengthen the free world. It might have given notice to the Kremlin that America is alert, determined and united.

It still can, but not if there is to be a constant effort to create disunity instead of unity, to implant doubt instead of confidence, to claim a foresight that never existed, and to discredit not only the competence but even the motives and the integrity of the men who have borne the burden and the pain of the fateful decisions of these years.

Three weeks ago the Denver *Post*—a newspaper which is supporting my opponent—published an editorial which I wish you could all read. The first four paragraphs of this editorial recite the damaging Republican record on Korea. Then the editorial goes on to say this: "We bring up these unfortunate records only because we are sick and tired of hearing the responsibility for the start of the war pinned on any one or two persons or agencies. Both Democrats and Republicans should remember that and the less said about who did or did not do what, the better. Instead of crying over spilt milk, let's hear the candidates say plainly how they intend to wipe it out."

Now, I believe this expresses the view of most Americans. Everyone wants to end the war and to bring the boys home. The question is not that—the question is how?

What are the alternatives that are open to us?

Some Republicans suggest that we should withdraw our forces from Korea and quit what they call this useless war. This is the policy of scuttle and run. What effect do you think such a policy would have on reckless men? What effect on the free peoples living in the long, dark shadow of the Kremlin?

Well, I will tell you what I think. I think that Korea is not the last ambition of the Soviet rulers. Far from it. I think that weakness will never persuade the Soviet rulers to keep the peace. Once they had us on the run they would undertake new acts of aggression somewhere else, and if we pulled out of Korea, all of South Asia would be uncovered and inviting, like Indo-China, where the French have fought so long, so valiantly and so expensively.

No better plan for certain disaster could be drawn up than a plan to withdraw from Korea. I do not know where the next blow will fall nor do you, but that it would is certain. And if we had just turned tail and run in Korea, would we, do you suppose, resist the next blow?

No, I think we would wait, while one by one our friends and allies fell, until at last, alone and apprehensive, our defense perimeter threatened, we would wait for the blow to fall on us. We might have saved some tax money in the process, in between, but, used this way, saving has a very hollow sound.

Withdrawing then, it seems to me, is not a real alternative.

Some Republicans, including my opponent, say that we should let the Koreans do the fighting.

Well, let us analyze this proposal. It has been common knowledge, I thought, for a long time that the United States has been training and equipping Korean forces and that these forces are taking on more and more of the burden. I pointed this out some weeks ago and it has been frequently reported in the press over the past three years.

We know, too, on the authority and in the words of General Van Fleet that Korean soldiers "will never be able completely to replace American troops in Korea as long as there is an active front."

It takes sixteen weeks to give a Korean infantryman basic training. It takes much longer to train a platoon or a company leader and it takes a long time indeed to develop good regimental and divisional commanders and to give them the experience that they must have if they are to be successful leaders of their troops. General Van Fleet is doing this job as fast as is humanly possible. Already the Korean divisions outnumber ours.

And then there is my distinguished opponent's position that only Asians should fight Asians.

To me this completely misses the significance of the Korean War for America. That war takes place in Korea, but surely no one—least of all the General—thinks that the only object of the attack was the small territory of Korea and the twenty million citizens of the Republic of Korea.

The attack was aimed at America and the whole free world—and that is why many nations have responded.

We fought World War Two in the Pacific and in Europe, far from our shores, but did that mean that America was not under attack? Of course not. Today we are defending America in Korea. The Korean War is not a war that concerns just Koreans. It is our war, too, because—and there should be no mistake about this—world domination is the ultimate target of the communist rulers, and world dominion includes us.

The man who becomes President of the United States is going to have difficult decisions to make, and he is going to need the thoughtful and the understanding support of the American people. And whatever confuses and misleads and deludes the people is destructive of this support—this support without which no President can hope to do his job.

Now there is one other possible alternative to our present course. Some Republicans favor extending the war to China. This course was advocated by General MacArthur. And, following his return from the Far East, exhaustive Congressional hearings were held to assess the wisdom of General MacArthur's advice.

The Great Debate, as it was called, reached an unmistakably clear decision. The Congress and the American people overwhelmingly rejected this advice to extend the war.

As to apparent contradictions in the views of the opposition on this score as the political campaign progresses, I shall make no comments and risk no further charges and countercharges in such a serious matter. But, I do say, regretfully, that the fancied advantage of votes from exploiting our natural emotional reactions to the Korean War have been unfortunate here at home, where the people want enlightenment, and abroad, where the people want confidence that the United States knows what it is doing and why. People's minds should not be clouded about a situation which demands clear thinking.

Now my own views regarding our course of action in Korea offer no miracles. We shouldn't, I think, extend the war to new areas. It would be a serious mistake to tie up our strength in a futile war on the mainland of China, because it would take all our strength and leave the Red Army free to move against the industrial might of Europe. It is not our purpose to bring the world a single step nearer the tragedy and the bloodshed of world war.

Our purpose is peace. We must continue to press in every conceivable way the negotiations in Korea. I am keenly aware of the fact that most people in this country feel that there just must be some way that these negotiations can be pressed to a conclusion. We must keep the United Nations military forces in Korea at that strength which, with Koreans, will be necessary to withstand the communist forces. Otherwise we will lose the negotiations and we will also lose the chance of settlement in Korea which we have now almost won.

We must continue to train and to equip South Korean forces as rapidly as we can so that they can assume as much of the burden as possible.

They are a brave people. You know what they have been doing

only lately in these past weeks at White Horse Mountain. They themselves want to do as much of the job as they possibly can, and I know that our Chiefs of Staff are pressing this training and this equipment program in a way that ought to remove it from the debates of politicians.

We must continue to rotate our soldiers so that the burden will be shared as fairly as possible. So far only a very few men have had to spend more than one winter in Korea. We want to keep it that way, and, if possible, to improve that situation.

We will, by this policy—by perseverance—win the military decision in Korea. With settlement by negotiation and the victory of arms that was substantially won when we drove the invaders back across the 38th Parallel, we will have stopped, or stalled at least, what would otherwise have been the extension of communism all over South Asia, and a long stride in the movement of this menace toward our own shores.

But this does not answer the full question in your hearts. Nor does it even suggest the measure of hope and expectation in mine. What comes after Korea? Are there to be only more Koreas on other soil, but with American boys being called upon again and again to die so that civilization may live?

I have, throughout this campaign, tried to recognize steadfastly the stern demands that the role of leadership in a troubled world makes upon this nation of ours. I have not painted, nor shall I, any false picture of an easy tomorrow. Yet, you must know that in my heart—yes—and clearly in my mind, is only the one expectation that is, I know, in yours—the expectation of peace—of lasting peace —of peace not for future generations but for ours, of peace without another Korea and without another war.

I would not, I could not, say this to you unless my expectation had firm foundations in fact and in reason. First, there is the fact that our strength here at home now approaches that point where Russia can never afford to test it. This strength lies not alone in the nearly four million well-equipped, well-trained men in our armed forces—men whose invincibility of spirit the communists now know at first hand. Behind that front line there is operating now an even more productive supply line than our fabulous industrial genius developed during the last war—the highly skilled and free labor force, a management force of unparalleled inventiveness and resourcefulness, an agricultural force which will supply every demand.

It is an equally important fact that our allies are also growing daily in strength—the strength of restored moral purpose—the strength of the confidence that we have helped to give them—the strength of arms—and, perhaps most of all, the strength of a growing unity that may well emerge in history as the most important development of these times.

Men are at work today drafting a Constitution for the United States of Europe. Age-old rivalries are being replaced by co-operation within Europe and between Europe and Great Britain and the United States. Strong, new ties, based on common interests, are binding closer together the United States and the free nations of the Pacific. Around the world free men are learning how to co-operate in the struggle against poverty and illiteracy and disease; against the ugly conditions which have in the past bred so many wars.

There is also the fact that the United Nations is moving now toward its maturity. All of us feel discouraged sometimes about the difficulties which arise around the United Nations tables. And I know, because I sat there myself for many long, weary, frustrating months. Yet, we know that for every veto there, for every setback which makes headline news, there are new steps ahead. It cannot be expected that nations which have spent thousands of years living aggressively apart will learn now in a moment the art of living harmoniously together. We know that the United Nations will succeed, for all of the peoples of all of the nations know that it must succeed.

It is in our developing strength here at home, in these victories over poverty, in these steps toward unification of the free world, as well as in Korea, that the battle for peace is being won.

I see three stern, menacing realities in this situation. One is the harsh, ugly fact that the communist masters of Russia seek the mastery of the world and that fact will not end with a settlement in Korea.

The second stern reality is the fact that Korea is still a battlefield, and that our boys—our sons—are dying there. No confidence in our growing strength at home can give us any real satisfaction until that day when they come home. We can't take one ounce of real satisfaction from anything else—from any other gain—until the daily human tragedies which are Korea are stopped.

The third stern reality is that the building of our military might at home and the strengthening of the whole free world are placing terrific demands upon our resources. It is costing us awfully in money to build these defenses so that we can be sure that the malevolent lords of communism will not plunge us into a war in which the atom would destroy us all. We dare not stop because of the price tag when what we are buying is the preservation of civilization. But we must take every precaution against weakening ourselves in the process of building our strength. We must practice the most extreme of housewifely economies in our spending. We must, too, be sure that those nations which are our friends and allies realize that there are limits to our strength and that if we overstrain or overtax ourselves they will, with us, suffer the consequences.

We are going to do everything we can to save the free world, and we will save it, but only if they help us to help themselves.

So, there are the stern realities. But there is, too, the light of our hopes and expectations, shining as clear through the clouds as that beautiful evening star that I saw last night from our plane as we came into San Francisco.

We must reckon with realities and find lessons in our failures. But we are entitled, too, to count our gains—and we will err if we take counsel only of our fears. A mad force is loose in this world. Yet scores of other nations have learned now in seven short years to recognize that in co-operation there is salvation. There is war in Korea. Yet, in a dozen other nations we have dug out the roots of war and of communism, for those awful strangling weeds grow from poverty and ignorance and fear of men about their neighbors.

I do not say to you that tomorrow there will be peace. I say to you, though, that we are today moving faster toward peace than mankind has ever moved before. And I say, too, that I find fair and sufficient reason for the belief that we will reach that peace without another war. That must be done, else life itself and the design of its Maker would be a bitter mockery.

And now I'd like to take just the few minutes we have left to chat with you a little more informally. I guess you know my feeling that even the serious business of a Presidential campaign can be improved if we relax a minute now and then while we talk.

I have been on the go a lot lately. It isn't an easy job—this traveling across our country from coast to coast, urging people to support the Democratic Party, our principles and myself. But it is a grandly rewarding experience that has afforded me an opportunity to see so much of our country. And, as it unfolds rapidly, like a motion picture, you get some impression of the variety, the might, the majesty of the United States of America. It is a humbling experience. To confront the possibility of being responsible for at least the execution of its policies and the suggestion of its programs—to do that and do it well—to do it in the interest of all of the people, with so many conflicting views and such a variety of interests, is a job that staggers the imagination, the human mind, the human heart.

This, however, is, under our Constitutional system, an assignment that you give to one man. Anybody who would be so bold as to presume that he had all the answers, or was confident enough of his own intelligence to be sure that he could find the right answer and find it every time, would be a dangerous man. I don't know all the answers myself and I doubt if anyone does.

I do think, though, that our hope of finding those answers lies in this party of ours. I believe the record establishes it and that the projection of our future on the basis of these policies of the past makes it manifest. But, whatever man is assigned this responsibility, he can only succeed—he and your Congressmen and your Senators—with the support, the confidence, the good will—and I must add, the patience, of the people—people like you—and, most of all, with your prayers.

The Idea of Human Freedom

Alamo Plaza

SAN ANTONIO, TEXAS

October 18, 1952

Like many who have made this pilgrimage before me, I stand before these battle-scarred walls with a profound sense of reverence and awe. For this is a hallowed place. It has been hallowed, to the extent that mere human beings can sanctify any place, by the unfaltering sacrifice of life itself in a noble and unselfish cause.

The men who died here accepted that fate by a deliberate and clear-eyed decision. They were under no compulsion of military discipline. Each man had to make the choice for himself, supported only by God and his own conscience. When William Barrett Travis drew a line with the point of his sword on the dirt floor, and invited all who wished to die with him to step across it, every hero in that immortal company knew exactly what he was doing—and why. They knew that the road to escape stretched clear before them; and they refused to take it. Even Jim Bowie, crippled and ill, asked his comrades to lift his cot across that Line of Death.

This story will never be forgotten as long as any American gathers his children about him to read them our immortal literature and tell them of the spirit which has made this country great. In the truest sense, the men of the Alamo will never die. They will live forever in the memory of free men, for they forgot themselves into immortality with a courage of no ordinary sort.

This kind of martyrdom—this sacrifice by deliberate choice—is possible only when men are caught up by a truly magnificent ideal. Men do not die that way for selfish interest. The Texans who stood together inside these walls were not fighting for mere property, or self-advancement, or personal glory. Their cause was not simply a struggle between two nations, as many people wrongly believe. On the contrary, many men of Spanish blood—such as Enrique Esparza, Juan Seguin and Lorenzo de Zavala—stood shoulder to shoulder with Travis, Houston and Austin in the crusade which found its climax on this spot.

They understood that they were fighting for something more precious than the fertile lands of Texas, even more precious than nationhood. They were fighting for an idea—the idea of human freedom.

This struggle is never entirely won, and it can never be entirely lost so long as the spirit of Travis and Bowie survives anywhere in the world. It is the same battle we have fought over and over again. It is the same cause we are defending today on the shell-torn hills of Korea.

I think our young men who hold the line of freedom in Korea—and none among them are more gallant than your Texans—understand this just as clearly as the men of the Alamo understood it 116 years ago. They know that the new autocracy of the Kremlin is an evil and a dangerous thing. They know that tyranny must be halted, at whatever cost, whenever it marches or creeps or crawls against the liberties of free men. They know that if the battalions of militant communism had not been stopped in Korea, we soon would have met them in another place, and another, and, at the end, perhaps on our own soil. And here I cannot overlook the ever-eager response of Texans to our country's call. In the last war, I am told that one of your colleges, Texas A. and M., furnished twice as many officers as West Point.

This understanding, this willingness to defend the simple idea of liberty which is so dramatically symbolized by the Alamo, is the mightiest weapon America can ever possess. If we ever lose it, all our planes and tanks and atom bombs can avail us nothing. In the end, the only true defense we have is the willingness of free men—knowing full well what their choice may mean—to step across a little line, drawn by a sword-point on hallowed ground.

For this reason I have nothing but contempt for those whining politicians who try to tell us that the American people don't know what they are fighting for and what they have been fighting for for more than 150 years. When they tell us the struggle in Korea is unnecessary and meaningless, then they ask us to deny the very meaning of America itself. Such craven words mock the men of the Alamo and our sons in Korea who are defending the same ancient ideal.

It would be easy, and perhaps it would be politically smart, for me to hint obscurely that there is some quick and simple way to end this struggle. It would be pleasant if I could tell you that we can safely withdraw and leave all the fighting to the Asians or the Europeans. But I will leave such deceptive suggestions to someone else. I did not come here to Texas to fight for votes with spears of straw and swords of ice.

That is why I tell you bluntly that there is no easy escape from all our troubles, there is no cheap and painless shortcut to peace. We are engaged in a conflict with forces of darkness which have engulfed seven hundred million human souls. We confront an enemy who is crafty, implacable and far stronger than any foe America has ever known.

Like Santa Anna, he is an enemy who offers no quarter. He cannot be appeased; he can never be bought off by the surrender of territory or by the betrayal of some trusting ally, even if we were capable of such treachery. For his aim is total conquest—not merely of the earth, but of the human mind. He seeks to destroy the very idea of freedom, the concept of God Himself.

Such an enemy cannot be defeated by name calling, by character assassination, by the sowing of distrust among our own people. He cannot be shooed away by the Republican brand of political DDT, guaranteed to contain no taxes, no anxiety and no effort.

If any man promises you a soft path to the future—if he invites you to vote for him and then relax in a tax-free paradise—then beware. In times of crisis our leaders have not promised beguiling comforts. Like William Travis, they have led you, invited you, across that line which is the mark of greatness—and you have always emerged victorious.

This invitation does not come to every generation. And it is our rare privilege to be born in an age of testing and decision.

We are living in one of the great watershed periods of history, which may well fix the pattern of civilization for many generations to come. God has set for us an awesome mission: nothing less than the leadership of the free world.

Because He asks nothing of His servants beyond their strength, He has given to us vast power and vast opportunity. And like that servant of Biblical times who received the talents, we shall be held to strict account for what we do with them.

Let us, then, set out on our mission with rejoicing—not doubting our beliefs and believing our doubts, but free of fears, free of doubt and self-pity. Let us say as Ralph Waldo Emerson did:

> "If there is any period one would desire to be born in—is it not the age of revolution when the old and the new stand side by side and admit of being compared; when the energies of all men are searched by fear and hope; when the historic glories of the old can be compensated by the rich possibilities of the new era? This time like all times is a very good one if one but knows what to do with it."

And of course, need I add, that we Democrats are not afraid. In close communion with the people, we will know what to do with our times because we believe in the wisdom of people, we believe that everyone is wiser than anyone.

I've had a heartwarming experience in Texas—here in storied San Antonio today and among so many Texans in Fort Worth and Dallas who don't seem to have forgotten the great mission of the Democratic Party and what it has done, sometimes with the help of our Republican friends, more often without, to advance the well-being, the dignity and the happiness of all the people— and most of all to pursue relentlessly and to persevere in the quest for peace on earth.

Leadership for Peace

New York Herald Tribune Forum

NEW YORK CITY

October 21, 1952

Thanks to the co-axial cable and, I suppose, other devices about which I know even less, I am able to be with the New York *Herald Tribune* Forum this evening—at least in one dimension. But I am still three dimensional here in Chicago, in spite of seven weeks of campaigning!

The subject, I understand, is "Building Leadership for Peace."

Leadership is a word that we often use these days about America and America's role in world affairs. We mean several things by it, I think. We mean that the United States has become the strongest of the free nations. As the strongest, the task of leadership has fallen to us. And it has to be borne by us—or nobody.

We mean, too, by leadership, that the United States has been the prime mover in many international projects. I could mention the United Nations, the Marshall Plan, the Point-Four program, the collective resistance to the cynical assault in Korea, and our regional security arrangements, such as the North Atlantic Treaty Organization and the Pacific Pacts. Our leadership in these projects grows out of our own self-interest in our security. But it grows, too, out of wider and deeper concern for the safety of the values of Western civilization—the ideas of freedom and equality and justice on which our nation was founded and which are rooted in friendly ground the world over.

Above all, I think we mean by leadership that the United States has shown—and must show—responsibility in the use of its power and influence.

Power means much more than military force. It means the sum total of a nation's ability to influence the course of history. Military force is only one element of a nation's power. It is a necessary element in the world we live in. We must have and we do have, together with our allies, formidable military force.

We hoped that we could follow a different course after the war than we have had to follow. We dealt generously, helpfully and sincerely with our Russian ally in the war. And then we explored honestly and patiently the avenues of friendship and good faith. We were rebuffed.

The Soviet rulers chose a different course. They have tried to achieve a position of preponderant influence and power, not for protection, but to control the course of history. They have certain real advantages, as a tyranny always does. They can organize and concentrate the whole economy of the vast Soviet empire on war and related preparation. They can build as large armed forces as their manageable economy can support. Bound by no moral standards of purpose or behavior, they can try to stir up disorder, and hate, and strife in other countries, knowing that communism breeds best among the ignorant and the needy to whom elocution about democracy and freedom is meaningless. And I got no comfort out of Stalin's speech last week exhorting the communist parties in the free countries, or what he called "the countries under the domination of capital."

The Soviet decision to seek preponderant power as the means to its ends at last left the free nations no alternative but to redress the balance of power. And when we speak of America's role of leadership today, therefore, we mean our leadership in developing a coalition of free nations strong enough to remain the masters of their destiny.

This course has already proven successful. With our help, the Greeks brought superior force against the communist rebels and have succeeded in restoring order to their country. In Berlin, the Western allies refused to budge and over long months demonstrated their will and determination by mounting a giant air-lift. And in Korea, too, the aggressor has been turned back. In each case, the combination of power and patience has been the key.

The two all-important questions for the future are: who is going to adjust to what, and how are the adjustments going to be made? As to the first question, there can be no doubt at all. Imperialism and conquest adjust to independence and freedom. As to the second question, there can be no doubt either. The adjustments must, if possible, be peaceful. In all likelihood that means they must be gradual, for there is only one way to bring about rapid, drastic adjustments—namely, by force. And we all know that the free nations must use force only in self-defense, for war —especially in the atomic age—would destroy what we seek to preserve—the spiritual and material foundations of free society. Moreover, freedom, unlike tyranny, cannot be imposed by force.

This role of leadership is new to us. By and large the United States lived alone—and liked it—so long as this was possible, and somewhat longer than it was desirable. Until the last few years our entrances onto the world's political stage had been largely limited to moments of great crisis—like the First and Second World Wars. On these occasions, the addition of our power to that of our allies tipped the balance against the common enemy.

With the defeat of Germany and Japan, the weakening of Britain and France as world powers and the rise of the Soviet Union, it has become impossible for us to be merely an occasional participant in world affairs. Without our full-time participation, no coalition of free nations could be built which would be strong enough to deal with the Soviet threat.

Now I note a strange and disquieting aspect of this change to many people. Our past experience gave us Americans a somewhat exaggerated notion of the effectiveness of our power. We felt that victory was assured once we made up our minds—and indeed military victory in the immediate battle was assured. But many of us drew the conclusion that any cause that had our support was automatically assured of quick success. And this was not necessarily or even probably so, if the real cause, the real purpose, was not military victory but peace.

For peace cannot be won as a war is won. Peace in the world, like good government at home, is a goal we approach but never finally or perfectly attain. Peace, like religion and the good life, is the task of each new day; it must be worked at in little things and in big things so long as breath we draw.

Our power is now the steadying factor in the world. It would be a tragic error on our part to think that our power is less effective in this role than in the days when we used it to seal the doom of Hitler. Its effectiveness now is to be measured not in the dramatic conquests of war, but in the gradual progress toward a world which will not be afflicted by war and in which the area of genuine freedom and independence gradually widens.

America has thus embarked on a role of leadership which is unique and which places a unique responsibility upon us. The United States is the first great power in history which has dedicated itself to use its strength wholly for peace rather than expansion. We have chosen the patient but fruitful triumphs of peace by which alone mankind can move toward freedom and justice.

So we have these tasks.

We must set a good example. The image we reflect to the world can only be our own image. We want that image to be an image of sanity, serenity and moral as well as economic and military strength, of freedom and justice and confidence. We want other peoples to aspire to the kind of society we have created here and maintain here.

We must meet force when we are challenged by force. For freedom is worth defending, and not for a day or a year or for a limited time, but for as long as it is necessary. We must, therefore, be militarily strong. As Cardinal Spellman put it—it is better to have strength and not need it, than to need it and not have it. We must, of course, keep our efforts in balance. There would be no point in setting a pace so fast that we or our allies would exhaust ourselves. But there can be no genuine relaxation of our efforts until means have been found to achieve honest and safe disarmament.

We must, meanwhile, use our economic strength wisely and carefully to help other nations grow in well-being and thus to strengthen their free institutions. We must work politically to strengthen the unity of the free.

And when we look backward to the weakness and despair and disunity in the free world only a few years ago, we realize how far we have come. Who would have thought only a few years ago that French and German and Italian and Low-Lander would cooperate in a European army? Who would have thought, only seven years ago, that colonialism would now be almost eradicated from Asia without far more violence and bloodshed? Who would have thought that Western Europe would be actually discussing a constitution for a United States of Europe?

Who knows now what economic co-operation and technical assistance can accomplish in Asia and Africa and Latin America?

Who is so fearful as to predict that freedom has now reached its zenith and that once free peoples are enslaved forever?

The future is full of promise if we are willing to take leadership, to use our power responsibly, patiently, persistently.

In the words of our Lord: "For unto whomsoever much is given of him shall much be required."

The Hiss Case

Cleveland Arena

CLEVELAND, OHIO

October 23, 1952

The hour is growing late in this autumn of our political decision.
But I find it necessary to talk here tonight of things which are
more fundamental than the immediate political questions before
us.

For three months now I have done my best to talk sensibly.

I believed with many of you that General Eisenhower's hard-won
victory in the Chicago Convention was a victory of the constructive and progressive men in the Republican Party over its bitter
and reactionary elements.

I believed that an educational and elevating national discussion
would result. But, instead, in the past two months the General
has, one by one, embraced the men who were so savagely against
him at Chicago. He has lost the support of men like Senator
Wayne Morse of Oregon and has won the support of men like
Colonel McCormick of the Chicago *Tribune*.

Meanwhile, his Vice Presidential candidate and other principal
speakers on his behalf have given the Republican campaign its
distinct shape and pattern.

It is not a campaign by debate. It has become a systematic
program of innuendo and accusation aimed at sowing the seeds
of doubt and mistrust.

The Republican candidate for Vice President has himself set
the pace. This week and next—in these last days before the election—the Republican high command is counting heavily on this
kind of campaign.

Next Monday, I'm informed, the junior Senator from Wisconsin is going to make a highly advertised speech—the man who said
last week that, if he were put aboard my campaign train with a
club, he might be able to make a good American out of me.

Now plainly I have no concern about what the junior Senator from Wisconsin has to say about me. As an isolated voice he would be unimportant. But he has become more than the voice of a single individual who thinks the way to teach his brand of Americanism is with a club. This man will appear on nationwide radio and television as the planned climax of the Republican campaign—as the voice of the wing of the Republican Party that lost the nomination but won the nominee. You will hear from the Senator from Wisconsin, with the permission and the approval of General Eisenhower.

Only last week, stung by charges that he had surrendered to the Old Guard, the General said that the decisions in this campaign "have been and will be mine alone." He added: "This crusade which I have taken to the American people represents what I, myself, believe." Crusade indeed!

In 1950 a group of Republican Senators, headed by Senator Smith of Maine, issued a Declaration of Conscience denouncing the tactics of smear and slander. The General might have endorsed that Declaration of Conscience. He might have made it the testament of a real Crusade. Instead, by ignorance or choice, he has turned not to the Republican signers of that declaration, but to the Republican Senator who called Senator Smith a thief and defender of communists.

I had not expected that the General would ever countenance such a campaign by his "crusaders." But this was before the General gave his hand to Senator Jenner of Indiana who had called General George C. Marshall a "living lie" and "a front man for traitors"—Marshall, the architect of victory and General Eisenhower's greatest benefactor. It was before General Eisenhower struck from the speech that he was to give in Wisconsin words of praise for General Marshall at the request of the junior Senator from Wisconsin who had termed Marshall "so steeped in falsehood" that he "has recourse to the lie whenever it suits his convenience." And it was before General Eisenhower last week quietly reinserted the words of praise for General Marshall in New Jersey once he was safely out of McCarthy and Jenner territory.

If the General would publicly embrace those who slandered George Marshall, there is certainly no reason to expect that he would restrain those who would slander me.

The Republican Vice Presidential candidate—who asks you to

place him a heartbeat from the Presidency—has attacked me for saying in a court deposition that the reputation of Alger Hiss was good. And let us always be clear where the responsibility lies. As the Republican Vice Presidential candidate put it last Monday, General Eisenhower "is the captain of the team." Senator Nixon added significantly: "With due regard for his team members and their abilities, he is calling the plays."

Now what are the facts? In the words of Al Smith, "Let's look at the record." I had known Hiss briefly in 1933 when I worked about five months for the Agricultural Adjustment Administration in Washington, where he was also employed. I did not encounter him again until twelve years later, in March of 1945 in the State Department. I saw him intermittently from March of 1945 to March of 1946 in the course of our official duties. Half that time I was in London for the Government. He never entered my house and I never entered his. I saw him twice in the Fall of 1947 at the U. N. General Assembly in New York. I have not seen him since.

In the spring of 1949 I was requested by the lawyers for Alger Hiss to appear at his first trial and testify as to his reputation. I refused to do so because of the burden of my official duties as Governor of Illinois. I was then requested to answer questions submitted under order of the court with regard to his reputation, as I had learned about it from others.

I said his reputation was "good"—and it was. I didn't say it was "very good"; I didn't say he was a "great patriot"; I didn't say any of the things the Wisconsin Senator, whose best weapon is carelessness with facts, says I said. I said his reputation was "good" so far as I had heard from others, and that was the simple, exact, whole truth, and all I could say on the basis of what I knew.

This was his reputation as the General, himself, has good reason to know.

These same spokesmen have challenged my sworn statement that I didn't believe that I had seen Hiss between March, 1946, and the fall of 1947. They say I introduced him at a speech in Chicago on November 12, 1946. All of the records make clear that my recollection was accurate. For on November 12, 1946, I was in official attendance as a U.S. delegate to the United Nations in New York, and was not in Chicago.

I am a lawyer. I think that one of the fundamental responsibilities not only of every citizen but particularly of lawyers is to give testimony in a court of law and to give it honestly and willingly. It will be a sorry day for American justice when a man, particularly one in public life, is too timid to state what he knows or what he has heard about a defendant in a criminal trial, for fear that the defendant might be later convicted.

And I might add that here in your own state of Ohio a Republican Congressman was recently convicted for unlawful acts. Before his conviction, your own Senator Taft appeared and testified that this man's reputation was "excellent without question." Senator Bricker and Congressman Joseph W. Martin, Jr., Republican minority leader, gave the same testimony.

My testimony in the Hiss case no more shows softness toward communism than the testimony of these Republican leaders shows softness toward corruption.

At no time did I testify on the issue of the guilt or innocence of Alger Hiss as a perjurer or a traitor. As I have repeatedly said, I have never doubted the verdict of the jury which convicted him.

I testified only as to his reputation at the time I knew him. His reputation was good. If I had said it was bad, I would have been a liar. If I had refused to testify at all, I would have been a coward.

But while the brash and patronizing young man who aspires to the Vice Presidency does not charge me with being a communist, he does say that I exercised bad judgment in stating honestly what I had heard from others about Hiss' reputation. "Thou shalt not bear false witness," is one of the Ten Commandments, in case Senator Nixon has not read them lately. And if *he* would not tell and tell honestly what he knew of a defendant's reputation, he would be a coward and unfit for any office.

The responsibility of lawyers to co-operate with courts is greatest of all because they are officers of the court. And Senator Nixon is a lawyer.

He has criticized my judgment. I hope and pray that his standards of "judgment" never prevail in our courts, or our public life at any level, let alone in exalted positions of respect and responsibility.

These are the plain and simple facts. I would suggest to the Republican "crusaders" that if they were to apply the same methods to their own candidate, General Eisenhower, and to his foreign affairs adviser, Mr. Dulles, they would find that both these men were of the same opinion about Alger Hiss, and more so. And more important, I would suggest that these methods are dangerous, not just to the Republican candidate, but to the very processes of our democracy.

In December, 1946, Hiss was chosen to be president of the Carnegie Endowment by the Board of Trustees, of which John Foster Dulles was Chairman and several leading Republican businessmen were members. After Hiss was elected, but before he took office, a Detroit lawyer offered to provide Mr. Dulles with evidence that Hiss had a provable communist record. No such report or warning ever came to me. Under date of December 26, Mr. Dulles responded. Listen to what he said:

"I have heard the report which you refer to, but I have confidence that there is no reason to doubt Mr. Hiss' complete loyalty to our American institutions. I have been thrown into intimate contact with him at San Francisco, London and Washington . . . Under these circumstances I feel a little skeptical about information which seems inconsistent with all that I personally know and what is the judgment of reliable friends and associates in Washington."

That, my friends, is what John Foster Dulles, the General's adviser on foreign policy, thought.

In May, 1948, General Eisenhower was elected to the Board of Trustees of the Carnegie Endowment at the same meeting at which Hiss was re-elected president and Dulles Chairman of the Board. This was months after I had seen Hiss for the last time. I am sure the General would never have joined the Board of Trustees if he had any doubt about Hiss' loyalty.

After he had been indicted by the grand jury, Hiss tendered his resignation as president and trustee of the Carnegie Endowment. The Board of Trustees, of which General Eisenhower was a member, declined to accept his resignation and granted him three months' leave of absence with full pay so that he might defend himself. The General was not present at the meeting, but I do not find that he ever voiced disapproval of this concrete expression of trust and confidence. In May of 1949, the month in which I gave my deposition, and again in December, 1949, after the first trial of Alger Hiss, the Board of Trustees, of which General Eisenhower was still a member, again voted to reject Hiss' resignation.

Alger Hiss, General Eisenhower and Dulles continued as fellow members of the Board of Trustees until after the conviction of Hiss.

I bring these facts to the American people not to suggest that either General Eisenhower or John Foster Dulles is soft toward communists or even guilty of the bad judgment with which the General's running mate charges me. I bring them out only to make the point that the mistrust, the innuendoes, the accusations which this "crusade" is employing, threatens not merely themselves, but the integrity of our institutions and our respect for fair play.

I would remind General Eisenhower of the wisdom of yet another General. One day, after inspecting his troops, the Duke of Wellington said: "They may not frighten the enemy, but gad sir, they frighten me."

I might observe to the General that although his troops do not frighten us they ought to frighten him.

I do not suppose that the Hiss case exhausts the arsenal of accusation with which the General's high command hopes to obtain victory. But these things I can tell you about myself and they are on the record. In 1943, during the war, after leading an economic mission to Italy, I warned against the spread of Soviet influence in the Mediterranean. In 1945 and 1946, just after the war, I engaged in constant and heated debate with Soviet representatives in the United Nations in support of the interests of the United States. I repeatedly pointed out that appeasement doesn't work. In March, 1946, I said to an audience in Chicago that: "Russia and communism are on the march . . . We must forsake any hope that she is going to lie still and lick her awful wounds."

This was not long after General Eisenhower had told a House Committee: "Nothing guides Russian policy so much as a desire for friendship with the United States." As late as June of this year he said, "There is no more reason to fear the 190 million backward people living on the Eurasian continent than there is to fear pollywogs swimming down a muddy creek."

I would never have believed that a Presidential contest with General Eisenhower would have made this speech necessary.

It may well be that the General has been misled by his lack of experience in civil life. This is not a war; it is a political contest in a free democracy; and the rules are different. We who believe in our system have always considered it to be the responsibility of candidates to promote wider understanding of the true issues— and not to stir up fear and to spread suspicion.

I resent—and I resent bitterly—the sly and ugly campaign that is being waged in behalf of the General, and I am deeply shocked that he would lead a so-called "crusade" which accepts calumny and the big doubt as its instruments.

Because I believe in freedom I am opposed to communism. And I think I know more about it and more about the Soviet Union than most of these self-appointed Republican custodians of patriotism. I even went to Russia more than twenty-five years ago to see for myself, before, I dare say, some of these crusaders even knew what was going on in the world, and I have negotiated face to face with the Russians and their satellites in San Francisco, London and New York.

We are opposing communism abroad, where its relentless pressure seeks further to narrow the area of freedom. We are opposing it at home where its agents and converts seek to undermine our society and corrupt our government. As I have repeatedly said, the Federal Government must use all its resources to expose and identify communistic activity, to keep communists out of places of responsibility in our society, and to protect our institutions from communist espionage, sabotage and subversion.

But I know and you know that we do not strengthen freedom by diminishing it. We do not weaken communism abroad or at home by false or misleading charges carefully timed by unscrupulous men for election purposes. For I believe with all my heart that those who would beguile the voters by lies or half-truths, or corrupt them by fear and falsehood, are committing spiritual treason against our institutions. They are doing the work of our enemies.

In the end such tactics serve directly the interests of the communists and of all other foes of freedom.

Even worse, they undermine our basic spiritual values.

For in the final accounting, "What shall it profit a man if he shall gain the whole world, and lose his own soul?"

The United Nations: Our Hope and Our Commitment

United Nations Day Radio Broadcast

SPRINGFIELD, ILLINOIS

October 24, 1952

We do more today than to observe the anniversary of an institution. What we do today is to hold communion with an idea.

I speak of the idea of peace on earth.

The pursuit of this idea is at once old and new. It is as old as man's discovery that he could conquer and enslave other men. In the same sense it is as old as the will to resist, as old as the power of a righteous cause. But it is also a young idea, this pursuit of peace, for it is only in our century that human wisdom and energy have sought to bring all the nations of the earth under a rule of law through world organization.

If the pursuit of peace is both old and new, it is also both complicated and simple. It is complicated, for it has to do with people, and nothing in this universe baffles man as much as man himself. Much of nature's mystery has come under man's mastery. Heat, cold, wind and rain have lost their terrors, but the environment man has created for himself has yet to be brought under control. Nature's jungle has been conquered, but man still lives in the larger jungle of his fears.

Yes, it is complicated, this pursuit of peace, but there is also an inspiring simplicity to it. We can win the war against war because we must. Progress is what happens when impossibility yields to necessity. And it is an article of the democratic faith that progress is a basic law of life.

If I thought that the human race was no longer capable of

human progress, I would not be trespassing now upon the time and attention of the American people. Instead, I might be off on a remote hilltop silently contemplating the closing scene of the final act of the human comedy.

But I do not believe it is man's destiny to compress this once boundless earth into a small neighborhood, the better to destroy it. Nor do I believe it is in the nature of man to strike eternally at the image of himself, and therefore of God. I profoundly believe that there is on this horizon, as yet only dimly perceived, a new dawn of conscience. In that purer light, people will come to see themselves in each other, which is to say they will make themselves known to one another by their similarities rather than by their differences. Man's knowledge of things will begin to be matched by man's knowledge of self. The significance of a smaller world will be measured not in terms of military advantage, but in terms of advantage for the human community. It will be the triumph of the heartbeat over the drumbeat.

These are my beliefs and I hold them deeply, but they would be without any inner meaning for me unless I felt that they were also the deep beliefs of human beings everywhere. And the proof of this, to my mind, is the very existence of the United Nations. However great the assaults on the peace may have been since the United Nations was founded, the easiest way to demonstrate the idea behind it is by the fact that no nation in the world today would dare to remove itself from membership and separate his country from the human hopes that are woven into the very texture of the organization.

The early years of the United Nations have been difficult ones, but what did we expect? That peace would drift down from the skies like soft snow? That there would be no ordeal, no anguish, no testing, in this greatest of all human undertakings?

Any great institution or idea must suffer its pains of birth and growth. We will not lose faith in the United Nations. We see it as a living thing and we will work and pray for its full growth and development. We want it to become what it was intended to be—a world society of nations under law, not merely law backed by force, but law backed by justice and popular consent. We believe the answer to world war can only be world law. This is our hope and our commitment, and that is why I join all Americans on this anniversary in saying: "More power to the United Nations."

Franklin Delano Roosevelt

Balcony of the Nelson House

POUGHKEEPSIE, NEW YORK

October 25, 1952

I am sorry I kept you waiting. I have just been up at Hyde Park and the Roosevelt Library and then I went over to Val Kill cottage for breakfast with Mrs. Roosevelt and Franklin Roosevelt, Jr. It was hard to tear myself away from a scene so thronged with memories for any Presidential candidate or, indeed, for any Democrat— or for any American.

As I came across upstate New York yesterday, I reflected a little on the meaning of Franklin Roosevelt for our time and for our nation.

As a man, he remains a vivid and unforgettable figure in all our minds. His courage, his gallantry, his world vision and his passion for democracy will stay always alive in the national memory. Of course, I know he had—and has—his enemies too. Like all great historical figures, he aroused contention and controversy. But, when I look at those enemies, I can only remember the statement made about another great New York Democrat: We honor him for the enemies he has made.

He made enemies because he led the party of progress—and those who benefit by the vested privileges or injustices of an existing order always resent and resist change.

Franklin Roosevelt became President at one of the turning points in our history. The old order had reached the end of its tether. Our nation either had to revolutionize itself from within—or risk revolution from without. It had to recognize the existence of the twentieth century.

At home, the disorder and collapse of the security markets and then of the economy, the misery and despair of the people, threatened revolt and violent social change.

278

Abroad, the old order had built one wall after another, insulating America from the world, until it had succeeded totally in neutralizing our power and withdrawing us from the world balance of forces. War threatened.

Fortunately we had in President Roosevelt a man with the historical insight to understand the problems and with the will and leadership to do something about them.

At home, he knew that the economy of a great nation could not be weak, anarchic, undermined by speculation and influenced by selfish and unscrupulous concentrations of wealth and power. He stood for a strong economy—and he knew that the people's government had an essential role to play in releasing the energies of the people.

Under his leadership, the American people drew up programs by which they could gain the assurance of economic and social security. His New Deal put solid foundations under our free economic system—foundations designed to maintain the buying power of the people and thus to prevent another collapse into the dark pit of depression and despair. Sense and sanity and responsibility were restored to our economic life.

The result was that our nation, so weak and battered and despairing in 1932 in the greatest economic misfortune of our history, was able ten years later to serve as the arsenal of democracy in the greatest war of our history—and today is riding the crest of the greatest prosperity of our history.

As Mr. Roosevelt believed in strength at home, so he believed in strength abroad—because he knew that, without strength, America would be without influence, and without influence America could not make her proper contribution to the maintenance of peace. From the beginning of his administration, he led the way in building up American military and naval power.

Some of you will remember that his early requests for naval appropriations horrified certain of his liberal friends. They tried to explain it away by saying that it was a kind of hobby for him, like sailing his favorite sailboat! Well, if it was a hobby, it was a fortunate one for the American people. Those aircraft carriers and destroyers built with PWA money turned out to be mighty useful just a few years later.

But Roosevelt did not believe in strength for the sake of strength. He believed in strength for the sake of co-operation with other free nations in the service of peace. Unfortunately, by the time he could persuade the rest of us of the vital importance of an affirmative foreign policy, the Second World War was upon us. Once war had begun he understood that we could best defend America by helping our friends in the world defend themselves. And in the fire and fury of war, he never lost sight of the ultimate objective—the building of a structure of world security which would reduce the chances of another such global holocaust.

The concept of the United Nations was his final legacy to the American people. It is one of the proudest incidents in my own life that I was able to play a role in its birth and its formative years. The United Nations and its specialized agencies are today the world's best hope for peace.

At home and abroad, President Roosevelt understood the moral and historical imperatives of our age. Under his leadership America came to terms with the needs of our own industrial society and with the needs of the emerging world community. We shall continue his struggle for sanity and responsibility at home and for the collective strength of freedom abroad. We shall never go back to the pre-Roosevelt period—to the reign of the Republican Old Guard—no matter how much the old enemies of Roosevelt inveigh against us, nor how successful these men are in recapturing the Republican Party.

Some of them have spoken loudly and defiantly of their determination to destroy the last vestiges of the works he wrought. But I don't think they will do any better this time than they have in any election since 1932—even with a General to lead their legions.

I have said that this nation would never retreat from affirmative, forward-looking policies at home and abroad. Nor shall we stand still. We shall move ahead—and I hope we may do so with some of the same creativeness and enterprise and the same faith in free Americans which Franklin Roosevelt has written large across our history.

New conditions create new problems. We will not be bound by the past, any more than Roosevelt felt himself bound by Woodrow Wilson's era. Nor would he have it so, for his deepest belief was that the obligation of government was to keep pace with the changes wrought by science and experience in our society—and by ideas in the minds of men.

We cannot rely on past solutions in 1952, any more than he

could in 1932. But, as we move ahead, we shall always be faithful to the spirit of Franklin Roosevelt. We shall always be fired and inspired by his courageous example. We shall attempt to achieve at last that America—free and friendly and strong and responsible —of which he always dreamed.

On Religion and Politics

Volunteers for Stevenson Breakfast

BOSTON, MASSACHUSETTS

October 26, 1952

I think perhaps the most gratifying exhibit I have seen in my political adventures in the last few months is right over here. It is a small baby. How can I lose?

I was amused the other day when I had one of those announcements of the birth of a baby through the mail from people I didn't know—"Mr. and Mrs. So and So announce the birth on October 18th of their son James." And on the reverse side of this little card was printed, "I was only born yesterday, but I am for Stevenson. Jimmy." It excited all sorts of ideas about "time for a change"!

This is Sunday, and this is a day of rest for candidates. And, therefore, I am not even going to worry about Senator Nixon's conscience. What I did want to talk about, and I should like to if you could bear with me for just a few minutes, is something I have become much more conscious of as my experience developed, and I think is important: That is, the connection and the union, if you please, between our religious beliefs and political aims in a democracy. Some of us worship in churches, some in synagogues, some on golf courses. (I don't know whether there are any Mohammedan Volunteers who worship in mosques.) Yet, we are all children of the same Judaic-Christian civilization, with very much the same religious background basically.

In the heat of a campaign—and I must say the disciplines of the tongue get looser and looser as these ordeals proceed—some of us forget about the religious sources of democracy. In times like this the brush of politics is dipped pretty deep into vats of paint, black and white, and seldom any other shades. And everything that is put on display is painted in these rather sharp tones. We are told that this man is a man of unsurpassed virtues, and that man is an out-

282

and-out crook, or he is a communist, or he is subversive, or he is a traitor, or, he is possibly just a soft-headed imbecile who didn't want the nomination and won't accept any mortgages to get the election either.

I remember a remark that comes down to us from earlier American politics when some candidate said, "If my opponent were twice as good as he is, he would still be the most degraded human being in the history of civilization."

Some day, perhaps, we may show a bit more charity in the conduct of our public discussions or, rather, I should say that we can never show enough charity. For, I am reminded that even in heaven, where there is no need for faith, because it is confirmed, and no need for hope, because it is realized, charity still flows in measurable abundance. I emphasize charity because I feel most strongly that the great body of people who give their loyalties to our two main political parties are really not divided between the forces of light and darkness. (You may doubt that from listening to some of them!) Both alike consciously seek the good, and consciously try to avoid the evil.

In the political forum, as in private life, we can and do differ on what is good and what is not so good, and what is simply terrible. We have developed political parties to help to define these differences in public questions. If one political party wins a majority for its point of view and the point happens to be wrongly decided, then all of our society suffers, but there is nothing you can do about it. It pays heavily for it. Yet, it seems to me that even here our great and important differences are not over the ends of social effort, but over the means by which they can be approached.

I am not unaware that there are men in our midst who love evil just for the sake of evil. And other men believe that the end can justify and purify, somehow, the means. And still others raise a cloud of smoke over truth and then cry that where there is smoke there is fire. This is the most common and garden variety of political technique in our country. Yet, among the great body of our people, if our divisions were of a different sort, if they were over ends instead of means, we could never have a peaceful transfer of power between the vanquished and the victor. And this would be a dreadful thing. If either party had a valid reason to feel that victory or defeat would usher in a planned and radical transformation of our social order, neither one would consent voluntarily to the decision reached by the electorate. Hence you have revolution. We have counterparts of that to the south of us, even in our times. Our politics would swiftly degenerate into endless vendettas, conspiracies, plots and resorts to force.

The Declaration of Independence—and do not spell it "ents" —and the Constitution assert in unmistakable terms that justice, and not oppressive force shall be the essence of our politics. They assert that there must be absolute limits to the lawful powers of those who govern. They assert that there is reserved to each man an area of spirit where no secular arm can encroach. And, they assert that any decision affecting the community shall be reached through reflection and choice by all who are affected by that decision, and not by the accidental whims of those who wield the instruments of force in a society.

All of these concepts are now locked in a mortal struggle, of course, challenged basically by communism and this new imperialism. There is no doubt in my mind that we will win this struggle, that our people will triumph, because of the fact that they express eternal truths and because of the fact that the communists embrace eternal wrongs in their meanings. It would be improper for me to detail, of course, the measures of a foreign policy that might quicken the victory of our beliefs over those of the wretched men who have been trapped by this new disease. Any such description would of necessity invite a note of partisan controversy, I am afraid, which I have tried to avoid on Sundays. Yet, I believe it would be proper to apply to the international scene that concept of fraternity of which I have been speaking.

First, we must recognize that not alone for Americans, but for men everywhere, body and spirit are co-principals of the same being. Each needs a special sort of ministry. Let us remember that, while Christ preached the doctrine of eternal salvation, he also did the work that needed to be done in the kingdom of man. He healed the sick, fed the poor, sustained the weak, and sheltered all those who were in want. So must we, I think, as Americans continue prudently to extend to the needy of this earth that material help which we almost alone can give. And we ought to do this not grudgingly, but with a clear recognition that it is far better to give than to receive. In a word, the first answer to communism is not a lesser, but a fuller application of Judaic-Christian ethics to the neighborhood of nations around us.

This isn't a give-away program. This can be—but here I am making a speech!

Second, I feel that we, the first great Federal democracy, can find a major defense against communism by stimulating the growth of Federal organisms like ours all over the world. Some of them are visible already, as they have never been before, in modern history at least, in the form of the Atlantic Community that is emerging, in the Schuman Plan and the European army, and even in present discussions about a conference for the United States of Europe that are going on abroad. Others are just beginning to shoot their first slender stalks through the earth in the emergence of a Pacific community. All these must be strengthened and encouraged. They will be born in the greatest travail, even as everything is born in travail, but they are much more basic and much more fundamental, some of these developments.

But what we are to talk about in political campaigns and what I should have talked about here is my great sense of indebtedness and gratitude to the Volunteers for Stevenson all over the country for what they have been doing. I am deeply touched and flattered by the presence of so many of you here on such a lovely autumn Sunday morning when I am sure you have more useful things to do than to come and listen to me, and I suppose that the most useful thing you had to do was to come and listen to my old and beloved friend, Archie MacLeish.

The New Force in America

Madison Square Garden

NEW YORK CITY

October 28, 1952

We are reaching the final hours of the long campaign voyage. A week from today you and millions of your countrymen will retire to the solitude of the voting booth for a moment of communion with your conscience. The blare of the loud-speakers will be silenced; the Republican air raid will be over; the all-clear will have sounded; the candidates, the politicians, the experts, the pollsters will all have slipped into the shadows, and the people will take the stage.

As I speak here I am aware that the world will quickly forget what I say tonight, but it will long—(*voices say "no."*)—oh, yes, it will, but it will long remember what you do on next Tuesday. And I will long remember your welcome to me, a son of Illinois, here in New York tonight.

To stand here in Madison Square Garden on this traditional occasion is to be enveloped with the memories of two great men of this State and of the Democratic Party—Alfred Smith and Franklin Roosevelt. It was these men who led the Democratic Party to its great revival. Picking up after a long period of Republican rule and ruin, they gave to New York State and then to this nation a whole, complete program of liberal social reform. They took up once more the spirit of the idea of an immortal American—that government must be of the people, for the people, and by the people. It is the principle immortalized at Gettysburg which animates and guides our party today—the principle of government with a heart—government not content with merely governing, but dedicated to reflecting and expressing the interests of people—their needs, their dreams, their highest hopes and aspirations.

To travel this country as I have these past two months is to

realize that there is a new force alive in America. People are looking for something more in the conduct of their public affairs. I
sense at this mid-point of this great century of revolution a kind
of driving desire in people to find a more exalted meaning in democracy. They are willing to do for their party more than they
have done before, and they are demanding of those who would be
their leaders, some new, not wholly defined, imperfectly perceived
element of uplift in the execution of democracy's purpose. The
record of this election will be the record of the response of our two
great parties to this new challenge of the people.

The Republican Party rose last spring from a generation of
lethargy and caught for a moment the spark of this new desire and
exaltation. They cradled the fire in the slogan of change. And then,
as the nation cheered, the Republican Party cast out its old and
weary rigid leadership and turned instead to a man whose name
has become a national symbol of high purpose.

However, that the spark which had been kindled in the higher
desires of thousands of our Republican friends was then snuffed
out in a sordid triumph of expediency over principle. These hopes
and aspirations were shaken to their roots when the Republican
crusader said "I do" to the lifelong cheer-leader for a dear, departed, quiet past that is also dead. These hopes were wholly
destroyed in the chain reaction of compromise which followed the
first surrender of principle to expediency. Today there is the dreary
dullness of disillusion; the stark realization that the venerable
Republican Party has within it forces of reaction once more unconquerable. It is in all ways proper that Democrats extend a warm,
affectionate welcome to these thousands of courageous souls—
these refugees from all walks of life who were thrilled by the General's victory at Chicago, and are now disheartened by this negotiated peace with the enemy. It has been part of the price of that
surrender that much of the purpose of this campaign and of this
election has been lost—for us as well as them.

America faces today great questions of its destiny. This should
have been a time, in this campaign, for the two great parties to
lay before America their precise programs for America's future. I
have tried to do this—for you, for the Democratic Party, for the
independents who wear no label—to the fullest of my ability. I
have enjoyed it. There have been great satisfactions in honoring
as best I could my commitment to talk sense to the American

people. But there has been no opportunity for actual debate, for evidently part of the price of the embrace on Morningside Heights has been to lay no affirmative program before this nation for its approval.

The general headquarters of the great crusade are agreed upon what they are against, which is, in a word, Democrats. But, they are not agreed on what they are for. And the record is clear that most of what they are for is what most of the people of America are against—and have been for twenty years. So, speech after speech has come forth from Republican rostrums, always in the same pattern. Volumes of sound about all that the Democrats have done wrong, followed by an angels' choir—the angels in costume, of course.

The biggest single fact before the American people in this election is that there is no Republican program for the future. It is not enough that they tell us they are against high prices. It is not enough that they cry out in alarm about false prosperity. They offer no facts to support their prophecies of doom and no evidence that they have departed from their 1930 patented formula of "let boom and let bust."

It is not enough to be told that every decent Republican hates communism. So does every loyal American. What we wanted to know was how the Republican leadership would meet this problem. And, of that we know nothing, except that the General gives us his assurance that we can do it justly and fairly and in full observance of the American system of justice. We do not know even whether the Republican program would include fighting communism by helping our allies, as the General professed before he was a candidate; or, whether he changed his mind when he took up Senator Taft's demand for tax reductions that could only be accomplished by halting virtually all aid to Europe.

There is no point in going on. The pattern is clear on issue after issue. To recognize the problem, to engage in self-righteous denunciation, and then to present two offerings: one, unspoken but plain from the record, is the persistent answers of a group of Old Guardians who are once again in the places of decision. We have said in five straight elections that we don't like those answers— and will say it again. The other answer which has come so often these past two months is the assurance that a great General will somehow continue to deal with these problems fairly and justly.

It is in no disrespect that we say this is not only too little—it is dangerously too much. A democracy cannot afford to make its elective process simply a determination to rely on the unrevealed wisdom of one man. History offers too many warnings against that course.

On July 12th, in Chicago, speaking to a group of old-line Republican leaders, the man who was then seeking the Republican nomination sought to reassure his listeners against their doubts about his political qualifications. Would he do, they were asking in effect, what they considered necessary to win the election? He gave them full and sufficient assurance, and these were his words: "In the military, when strategical principles conflict with the tactical, the tactical always goes. Which means that long-term programs are not nearly so important as winning the next battle."

Now, it isn't perhaps for me to argue before the bar of the American people whether a background of military or civilian experience is a better qualification for the Presidency. Anything I might say would be misinterpreted as a denial of my unqualified respect for those who have served our country with courage and with devotion. Yet the Republican candidate, drawing upon his own military experience to explain his campaign tactics, gives those tactics he has subsequently employed a fuller meaning which the voters of America are entitled to have made clear.

High prices, labor relations, farm programs, social security, communism—are these in the General's view matters right now only of campaign tactics? Are America's long-term programs for meeting these problems of lesser importance than winning this election? Is this only a battle that we have before us? Do the tactics of winning it justify false fears and false promises? Is it all right to count the American people too ignorant to understand? Are no long-term answers necessary? Is it just bread and circuses, and if there has to be an answer, is it to offer fairness, justice and the services of a man whose familiarity invites respect?

In this record is the complete rejection by the Republican Party of what I have called earlier the new force alive in America today, the desire of people to find a new, a more exalted kind of meaning in the public life of this democracy.

Are we ready, we of the Democratic Party, to meet this challenge? I say that we are. An awareness of it has been the guiding star of this campaign. I have spent—and my colleagues with me—

two long, yes, hard months, spelling out a complete program of policy for the people to consider and to vote on next Tuesday. In any campaign there may be some words uttered that one wishes later had remained unspoken. I am not above reproach. I have not been able in the exigencies of time and circumstances to spell out every problem, every question in minute detail. But my conscience —that thing that usually feels so bad when everything else feels so good—my conscience does not trouble me.

I have spoken my piece with candor, and often. I have been subjected to the solemn charge that I am being too funny, and at other times I have been accused of being too intellectual and somber. I shall have to let you judge whether I am too prone to invite people to laugh or weep. Both, in my judgment, are good for the spirit, and I hope the Republicans don't contemplate any legal prohibitions against them!

I can approach this day of the people's judgment with the confidence that I have never attempted to be different things to different men. There is only one candidate for the Presidency on the Democratic ticket. It will never, I hope, be said that the Governor of Illinois has ever whispered anything to the Governor of South Carolina that he would not say aloud to the Governor of New York. I have said the same thing about the great cause of equal rights for all men in Virginia and in Harlem. I have not been an isolationist in Chicago and an internationalist in New York. I have not praised my friend in one breath and then moved on quickly to grasp hands with those who slander him.

We have talked to—not down or up—we have talked to the American people. This is the beginning of our answer to men and women who are saying, "We want no smallness of vision in those who seek our trust—no compromising with what some mistakenly think are our weaknesses."

It was a great poet who said, "Not failure, but low aim, is crime." Those who aspire to the leadership of America, if they offer Americans something unworthy of their own beliefs and interests, will fail.

I do not say to you that I, or any member of our party, has a vision of America large enough that its people will not outstrip that vision in a score of years. I say to you only that it is our purpose, our intent to work up toward the level of high purpose for America which you hold unspoken in your hearts. We offer you what we think is an awareness of your aspirations for our country as it turns into the second half of this troubled century. You want your public affairs to be in the hands of a government which is clean so that it may be strong. You want the tremendous affairs of America administered so that you can live in a world of plenty and of peace. You accept the obligations of leadership of the world of free nations, asking only that these obligations entail no more of sacrifice than is wholly essential and required.

We have learned that to act with enthusiasm and faith is the condition of acting greatly.

We have learned that to plan boldly is to make dreams come true.

We offer for America, for leadership, no fear, no counsels of little cautiousness—nothing small and petty. Facing America, we offer an awareness of its call for something better, and nothing less than the finest which is in us.

And finally, my friends, you have been very patient, and I have some good news for you. On Sunday last, the Chicago *Tribune* came out for the General, and Colonel McCormick is in the forefront in the great crusade, without any loss of rank. But the Milwaukee *Journal* came out for Stevenson—and guess who lives in Wisconsin?

Business and Government

Railroad Station

READING, PENNSYLVANIA

October 30, 1952

There have been many things I don't understand about this campaign, and one is why so many people value my signature. I wish I could give you all autographs. If I give one of you an autograph, I have to sign a lot of pieces of paper, and one of them might be on a check, and it might bounce. A politician can't be too careful!

I am very happy to be here with you, and we are very grateful to you for coming out at this inconvenient hour to afford us an opportunity to talk to you. I know Berks County is the home of good farmers and of good pretzels, and is also the home of good Democrats. I don't think the United States can ever have too many of any of those things—and especially at this season of the year, of good Democrats!

I have selected Reading for a solemn speech, and I hope you will forgive me. I wanted to talk this morning about one group of forward-looking people who seldom get mentioned in political campaigns. I mean businessmen, the people who make up the industrial and the commercial leadership of this country. I think that that neglect is a serious mistake, not from a vote-getting viewpoint, because the business vote is not very massive, but because there are principles of justice and of equity involved to which politicians—and I call myself one—ought to pay more attention.

If my destiny takes me to Washington I propose to do the best I can to end this noisy and largely unnecessary war between some segments of government and some segments of business. It doesn't get us forward with the all-important business of making America stronger and more united and secure in this terribly dangerous world.

I think we should get two things straight: The name for all

government is not bureaucracy—and the name for all business is not reactionary. I ought to know. I have spent time on both sides of the desk—both in business and in government. And, so far as I know, I am the only candidate in this campaign who has. As a lawyer practicing in the Middle West for many years before I entered what we call public life—and, believe me, it is public!—I did work for many businessmen and for many corporations, large and small. I think I learned what some of those problems were. I never had much trouble understanding them, and I never had to wrestle with my conscience in representing their reasonable points of view.

If any of you think that this is strange talk coming from a Democratic candidate, let me say that I can see no legitimate reason for hostility between business and the Democratic Party. We are for private, and profitable, business. Indeed, we don't see how America could survive with any other kind. We are for the productive and the dynamic system of enterprise which the great partnership of public and private initiative has forged in this country. The Democratic Party is against socialism in our life in any form—creeping, crawling or even the imaginary kind which shows up so often in the Republican oratory.

I am opposed to socialized medicine, socialized farming, socialized banking, or socialized industry—and I think all of you are too.

Now, I am emphasizing these points with all the force at my command because there has been an intensive propaganda campaign to misrepresent the Democratic Party as anti-business. Unfortunately, a certain number of businessmen—intelligent men who ought to know better—have been misled by this propaganda. I have been somewhat puzzled to understand why. Certainly it is not because the Democratic Party has actually harmed American business. On the contrary, I would say that it has done more for business during the last twenty years than in any other interval in our history. It rescued industry from nearly total collapse in 1932, restored confidence in our banking system and created a purchasing power which was felt in every cash register in the nation.

Nor can this misunderstanding be laid to a lack of profits, for today American business has bigger profits than ever before in history—not just before taxes, but after taxes as well. More new businesses are being created today than even in the fabled '20's—

and the one thing that a businessman does not do when he is really alarmed is to start a new enterprise.

So, I conclude that it is a—(*Someone in audience raises an "I like Ike" sign*) you know, I don't mind the Ike signs. I even like Ike myself. You would be amused at an incident that happened to us out in the West the other day when we were driving through the streets of a big city out there, and a little boy ran out in front of the crowd and shouted at the top of his voice, "Hooray for Stevenhower." I am going to give that kid a job in the State Department.

So, to resume, I conclude it is no simple matter of dollars and cents which makes some businessmen look on the Democratic Party with something less than blinding love. And, in an honest concern to understand the reason for this attitude, I have come to believe that it rests less on fact than on emotion.

You know, I had a letter from a woman not long ago commending me on some speech I made. She went on to say, "You know, Governor, I am very easily swayed by emotion until I think, which I occasionally do." Well, I think some more of those businessmen ought to do some thinking.

It seems to me, therefore, that the businessman has been unhappy not for lack of profits, but for lack of understanding, a feeling that there is no knowledge of his problems and less sympathy for them.

At the very beginning of this century, we had a business setup quite different from anything that exists today. Much of our industry was organized into old-fashioned trusts, with water in their stock and monopoly in their eye.

Today the business picture has changed beyond recognition. Management began to learn that many buyers at low prices provide a sounder market than a few buyers at high prices. Management developed its own unwritten code of ethics, and it gradually came to recognize its responsibility to the community.

We still have a few snake-oil peddlers in the business world, but they are a small and dwindling crew. Today the vast majority of businessmen are eager to live within the letter and also the spirit of our laws. They can distinguish between legality and morality. Their aim is no longer ruthless monopoly, but, rather, genuine service to the nation—on the very sound theory that he who serves best will profit most in the long run. As a consequence, our industry has achieved an almost incredible volume of production, which is the very cornerstone of American strength and prosperity.

I don't believe that these changes in the nature of business have been adequately recognized by everyone in government. I think we must sweep out of the corridors of government, at all levels, national and state, those lingering suspicions which are a holdover from an earlier and very different time.

This is a problem which concerns me very deeply, for I am convinced that both government and business must learn to live together in harmony, before an era of bad temper turns into something infinitely worse. We must avoid at all costs the bitter struggle of class against class, which results inevitably in a drift either to the extreme left or to the extreme right. And you and I know that either kind of drift would end up at the same dreadful destination: a police state with all of the horrors that we have seen in Hitler's Germany and Stalin's Russia.

And that is why I am determined to go to Washington only as the servant of all the people, without obligation to any class or interest. I have made no deals or any commitments to any individual, any political clique, or any pressure group. And I haven't had to or even been asked to.

I have done my level best to talk sense to the American people, in the very firm belief that you want honest words and an honest President. For this ultimate honesty—an honesty of mind and conscience—my friends, is the only solid foundation on which we can build the unity which is the true strength of a democracy.

So long as the people can have a government they can trust, they will not hesitate to trust each other. So long as they can be sure of even-handed justice in Washington, they will not be led by fear and bitterness to deal unjustly with one another.

We must do nothing that might array class against class, or citizen against citizen, in quarrels which tear apart our blessed American family. I shall do all I can to sustain a feeling of mutual confidence and understanding among all segments of our society. I see the American people rejoicing in their strength and sure of their destiny—and I see them from coast to coast—and for such a brotherhood among our people, I think everything is possible.

I apologize to you for talking too long. I sometimes—

A VOICE: "We don't want to go back to school yet."

Well, there is at least one honest guy in this crowd— He says he wants me to go on talking so he won't have to go back to school.

(Applause and Cheers)

There seems to be some unanimity of opinion about that. Well, you have been in school with me this morning, I am sorry to say, and I apologize for this lecture. I am afraid that sometimes when I go from town to town and talk interminably that I am a little like the girl in school who was asked to spell "banana," and she said, "I can spell banana, but I never know when to stop."

The Fundamental Issues

Academy of Music

BROOKLYN, NEW YORK

October 31, 1952

Brooklyn has meant good fortune for Franklin Roosevelt and good fortune for Harry Truman. In fact, it seems to have meant good fortune for practically everybody, except the Dodgers.

I will never forget the time during the war when I was driving through Brooklyn from the Navy Yard with the Secretary of the Navy behind a motorcycle escort; we slowed down at a crowded corner, and I overheard somebody in the curious crowd say, "It must be dem bums." I was never more flattered in my life.

Now, as usual, my friends, the pre-election thunder comes from the Republicans. They have most of the nation's newspapers and magazines. They have the slickest slogans and the shiniest posters. They win most of the pre-election polls, and sometimes they win them in a "Gallup." It is not a very good pun but it is the best I could do.

Then—then the people will vote on Tuesday. I understand that on Wednesday the newspapers plan to publish a 5-Star Final.

Many thousands of our votes will come from rank-and-file Republicans who will vote with us. No doubt some Democrats will vote for the Republican candidates. We have already, for example, traded a couple of Southern Governors for the Senator from Oregon and the Vice Chairman of the National Young Republicans. And I regard this as a profitable exchange for us. I would be happy to throw in a second baseman—but not Jackie Robinson.

But, let's not speak of the approaching Republican sorrow without compassion. You in Brooklyn, of all places, know how melancholy is the sound of the words, "wait till next year."

The choice next Tuesday is a fateful one. It is a choice of parties, between the party whose affirmative leadership for many years is written in the strength and the prosperity of our nation and in the widening opportunity and security of our lives, and the party whose only consistent record is one of opposition, obstruction and stubborn negation. It is also a choice of leadership. My opponent has been making a great effort—here in the East anyway, and especially in New York—to persuade the people to forget the last three months. His friends are suggesting that what he said in Champaign, Illinois, doesn't count, that those words in Milwaukee really weren't uttered, that none of his Midwestern tour expressed the real Eisenhower. But those words were spoken, those speeches were made; the visits with Senator Jenner and Senator McCarthy were all too real. The General may forget, but those Senators won't, and if they should be returned to the Senate and the General sent to the White House, they won't forget and they won't let the General forget either.

A man who has the confidence of the public has a public trust not to abuse that confidence for any ends, let alone his own.

In the field of foreign policy the obligation is even stronger. The issues are the relations of our country with our allies and our enemies, the issues of peace or war.

Deception cannot be condoned as campaign oratory. I thought for a time that the issues of foreign policy and of our future could be freely and honestly debated between us on a level worthy of the American people. But the Republicans have concentrated not on discussing, but on systematically disparaging the policies which, with all their defects, have brought the United States to a peak of world prestige and power and responsibility never before dreamed of. Confronted with the great achievements and potentialities of the Marshall Plan, the Truman Doctrine, the North Atlantic Pact, Point Four, the Trade Agreements Program, the Good Neighbor Policy, they have fallen back upon the parrotlike repetition of a monotonous charge. The Democratic foreign policy, they say, does not promise quick solutions; the answers are not all to be found in the back of the book.

As a result, they have now got their own candidates into a trap. For, they feel, unless he can come up with the big answer, unless he can promise a quick and easy road to peace and world leadership, the American people will begin to find out how good our foreign policy really has been. The General's advisers seem to have assured him that the American people will buy any merchandise so long as you package it gaudily enough. But the public has rejected the General's merchandise, piece by piece as second-hand and deceptive.

Now, let us, if you will, review this dreary history because it is important in these last hours of this fateful campaign.

The General's experience in Europe and in working with Europeans should have made him unusually sensitive to the importance of guarding and strengthening our European alliances. Yet in his first major policy speech last August, what did he do? He said, speak "with cold finality," to the Soviet Union and prepare to roll back Soviet power and liberate the satellite states. How we were to accomplish this, he did not say; but these words, spoken on the General's eminent authority, raised momentary hopes among those Americans whose friends or relatives were trapped behind the Iron Curtain.

As the idea sank in, however, the effect was greatly different. It became apparent that the General's proposal would lead, not to the liberation of the captive peoples, but to their obliteration—not to release, but to war.

Caught out in this manner, the General explained that he didn't mean what he had said. Yet the damage in Europe had already been done—damage not only to the General himself—which you and I have all regretted—but, far more important, to that funded capital of confidence in American stability and judgment which we have so carefully built up in the postwar years.

And this was only the beginning.

I was surprised that the General should have recklessly gambled with the confidence of our European allies in view of his experience as the head of the North Atlantic Treaty Organization. I was even more surprised when he showed a willingness to undermine that organization itself. In May of 1952, the General had told the Congress that a cut of more than one billion dollars in the foreign-aid program would endanger the proposed military buildup which he said he considered essential in the interests of United States security.

As soon as he took off his uniform, however, he changed his tune.

What this country needed, he said, was a forty-billion-dollar budget cut and a major tax reduction. Pressed by his own astonished colleagues, he qualified this claim. He did not propose, he said, to cut the budget immediately by forty billion, but to work toward a reduction of that amount over a period of five years.

It was at this point that Senator Taft took the General firmly by the hand. The forty-billion figure, he apparently dismissed as a typographical error. In his Morningside Heights Manifesto he pledged the General to a mere ten-billion-dollar cut next year, and a twenty-five-billion cut the following year.

Again false hopes were raised—hopes that we could quickly reduce our taxes and still not reduce our safety. And once again the hopes were doomed to disappointment.

Before the Chicago Convention the General appeared willing to keep Korea out of the campaign. Last June, at Abilene, he denied that there was, and I quote him, "any clear-cut answer" to the Korean problem. He said he did not think it would be possible for our forces to carry through a decisive attack; he ruled out the alternative of retreat; and he ended with this candid conclusion: "We have got to stand firm and take every possible step we can to reduce our losses and stand right there and try to get a decent armistice."

But a few weeks as a political candidate began to alter his opinion. Where once he had sought to unite public sentiment behind our stand in Korea, he now sought out the possibilities of division and of mistrust, echoing the views of his Republican advisers who had even called this first, great, historic case of collective security under arms a "useless war" and "Truman's war."

He first began to speak of what he called the truly terrible blunders that led up to the Korean War, including the very decision to withdraw our troops from Korea, in which he had participated as Chief of Staff of the Army.

Then he reversed his position on the all-important question of bombing the Manchurian bases across the Yalu and expanding the war—a question which the nation had pondered through the weeks of the MacArthur hearings and had decided in the negative. On June 5th, at Abilene, the General declared that he was against bombing bases in Chinese territory on the other side of the Yalu. Yet in September, he could say that he had always stood behind MacArthur on bombing those bases.

And now, as this political campaign has grown in intensity, and as each day sees the increase in Democratic strength, the General is indulging in something far more insidious than self-contradiction. He is seeking one easy solution after another for the Korean War.

Early this month in Illinois, the General propounded the startling theory that the American forces could soon be withdrawn and replaced by South Korean troops. "If there must be a war there," he said, "let it be Asians against Asians."

Now, there are several things wrong with this proposal. In the first place, the General put it forward as though it were a brand-new idea, although he knew that it has been our policy since the start of the Korean conflict to arm and train South Korean forces as fast as possible. In the second place, he suggested that it would be relatively easy to replace our American boys with Koreans; yet our Commander on the spot immediately stated that no matter how much training and equipment we supplied, it would be impossible for the South Koreans to take over the entire front.

Apart from these military questions, however, the General's statement displayed an alarming disdain for the sensibilities of our allies both in Europe and in Asia. The General talked as if we had entered Korea to fight Asians; yet he must know that we entered Korea to resist communist aggression, and that in such a fight there can be no color line. And, as the former head of NATO, how could the General be unaware that such talk would undermine the confidence of all our allies in the sincerity of our world leadership?

"Let Asians fight Asians" is the authentic voice of a resurgent isolationist. In 1939 the Republican Old Guard, faced with the menace of the Nazi world, was content to say, "Let Europeans fight Europeans," ignoring completely the fact that the menace of Nazism was a menace to Americans as much as to Frenchmen and Englishmen. What a curious remark for a man who led the crusade against a Nazi tyranny!

Again the General raised false hopes of a quick solution, and again the false hopes were doomed to disappointment. Confronted with scathing comment for this proposal, even from members of his own party, such as Senator Smith of Maine, the General has now put forth a new proposal—a proposal suggested not by an experienced diplomat, or even by an experienced soldier, but rather by one of the General's new ghost writers, recruited from the staff of a slick magazine.

This new proposal is simplicity itself. "Elect me President," the

General says, "and you can forget about Korea; I will go there personally." I don't think for a moment that the American people are taken in by a promise without a program. It is not enough to say, "I will fix it for you." The principle of blind leadership is alien to our tradition. And, unfortunately, the ghost writer who provided the proposal failed to give it content. The General was to go to Korea, but nobody indicated what he should do when he got there. The American people were quick to realize also that the conduct of a military campaign is the task of a field commander, whereas the making of peace requires negotiation with the central adversary—and in this case the central adversary is in Moscow, not in Korea.

And so, once again having raised the hopes of American families, he has been forced to beat a retreat from his first proposals. In a series of statements in the last two days he has abandoned his promise of making peace. At Kew Gardens he said that he was going out only to—and I quote him—"improve our plans." At Mineola he referred to his duty to go to Korea to see what our problems were and—I quote him—"how we can bring that situation under better control."

In the Bronx, on Wednesday, he referred to his Korean trip as an opportunity, "to see how we stand in organizing the forces of the Republic of Korea in order to prepare the Koreans to defend their own line."

And in New York City on the same day he again talked in terms of increasing the contribution of the Republic of Korea.

Now, these are admirable objectives, and such a trip would be informative. But, the label on the bottle was different, and the contents are misbranded.

If we are to bring about an honorable peace in Korea—which is what the General talked about in his Detroit speech—we must face the facts. There are only four possible courses open to us: Get out, or enlarge the war, or purchase a truce through the abandonment of our moral position, or continue the negotiations with all of the resource and self-discipline at our command.

Last summer the General excluded the alternatives of extending the war or retreating from it. I don't know what his position is now. Retreat can only mean the loss of the whole Far East to communism. And extending the war to China would tie up the bulk of our armed strength in Asia while the Red Army was left free for new adventures in the industrial heart of Europe.

But if he would neither enlarge the war nor abandon it, what would he do? Would he make new concessions in the truce negotiations, or has he forgotten the nature of the problem which has caused the deadlock?

Negotiations with communists are never easy, always exasperating, but not necessarily hopeless.

At the time we instituted the Berlin Airlift many impatient Americans said that we were undertaking a hopeless task; but we regained access to Berlin and our prestige in Europe was greater than ever.

The Korean truce negotiations have dragged on through many months, but they have not been without result. Most of the problems which first confronted us in reaching an agreement have now, one by one, been eliminated. Only one major issue remains, and this is not a military but a moral issue.

It is whether we and the other United Nations fighting in Korea should force thousands of Chinese and North Korean prisoners to return to communist territory and almost certain death.

We sent our troops into Korea two and one-half years ago because we knew that mobsters who get away with one crime are only encouraged to start on another. Korea was a crucial test in the struggle between the free world and communism.

The question of the forcible return of prisoners of war is an essential part of that test. Fifty thousand prisoners have stated that they would rather kill themselves than return to their homeland. Many of those prisoners surrendered in response to our own appeals. They surrendered to escape the communist world. They surrendered because in their eyes the United States stood for freedom from slavery. So far the United States *has* stood for freedom—and this is our greatest asset in our struggle against communism. How many of you suppose that we could retain that asset if we sent these men back to their death at the point of a bayonet?

This is the sole question remaining unresolved in the truce negotiations. Is this the question General Eisenhower intends to settle by going to Korea? I do not ask this idly. Quite recently at Richmond, Senator Capehart, one of the Republican Old Guard whom General Eisenhower has embraced, accused President Truman of prolonging the war by refusing to force these prisoners to return. The Senator's position with respect to these prisoners is identical with that of the communists. It is a position which no government in the world has taken except the Soviet Union and its satellites.

And I think it is worth noting that this was the same Senator Capehart who said on October 12th, "In another two weeks, General Eisenhower will be thinking and talking on foreign policy just like Senator Taft."

Now I think the General should answer one question. In embracing the Republican Old Guard has he embraced their contention that we should give up our moral position? And in asking the General this question, let me state my own views.

I have the profoundest sympathy for every mother and father in the United States who is affected by this tragic war. No one is more determined than I to see that it is brought to a conclusion. But that conclusion must be honorable, for if we do not maintain our moral position we have lost everything—our young men will have died in vain. If we give up on this point, if we send these 50,000 prisoners to their death, we will no longer lead the coalition of the free world. Today we stand in that position of leadership not merely because we are physically strong but because our cause is just. Once we commit a gross injustice, our allies will fall away like the leaves in autumn.

With patience and restraint and with the building up of our strength the communists will be compelled to yield, even as they yielded on the Berlin Airlift.

As of the moment we have a stalemate, and stalemates are abhorrent to Americans. But let us not deceive ourselves. A stalemate is better than surrender—and it is better than atomic war. And let us not forget that a stalemate exists for the enemy as well as for ourselves.

There is no greater cruelty, in my judgment, than the raising of false hopes—no greater arrogance than playing politics with peace and war. Rather than exploit human hopes and fears, rather than provide glib solutions and false assurances, I would gladly lose this Presidential election.

There is strength in freedom—strength far greater than we know. I have no fear that our present ordeal is without end. Working together, united in respect for human beings, and united in respect for ourselves, the free peoples can stop the communist conquest, save the peace, and move together to build a new and spacious and friendly world.

If we have the courage and the fortitude to walk through the valley of the shadow boldly and mercifully and justly, we shall yet emerge in the blazing dawn of a glorious new day.

The Campaign Is Over!

Chicago Stadium

CHICAGO, ILLINOIS

November 1, 1952

Tonight we have come to the end of the campaign, and a long, long journey—and I have come home to old friends and to familiar surroundings. There's no place like home.

There have been times when I have wondered whether you, my friends here in Illinois, couldn't have found some easier way of getting rid of me. In fact, before the Convention I wrote a song about it, only the Democratic Party took the song and changed the words. My song was called "Don't Let Them Take Me Away."

It has been a great campaign. I have enjoyed every minute of it. It has been the most exhilarating and most heartwarming and most uplifting experience a man could have.

The story of this campaign is written in the record of the changing meaning of the Republican talk about change. It was, in its July form, the one thing they had to offer the nation. And what a different meaning it has in November can, it seems to me, be illustrated by one fact. Never once in this whole campaign, so far as I have been able to determine, has the General ever mentioned the name of Wendell Willkie, who was really the founder of the modern tradition of progressive Republicanism. I can understand that it is difficult to mention him, for Wendell Willkie placed the principles of the new Republicanism above compromises and expediency. And there are evidently a lot of Republicans who haven't forgiven him yet.

This stadium reminds me most vividly of Wendell Willkie, for it was here, in March of 1941, and at my invitation—which I personally went to Rushville, Indiana, to extend to him—that he spoke eloquently to a great mass meeting on the life-and-death issue of aid to our friends abroad who were then sorely pressed by the Nazi tyranny.

It was this kind of selflessness following so closely on the disappointment of political defeat that has kept, and will always keep, Wendell Willkie's memory alive for all Americans, and especially for those of his party who wanted to perpetuate his tradition.

My friends of Chicago, it has not only been a great campaign for me—it's also a winner. There has been an electric feeling of victory in the air all the way home.

Well, that's the way it always goes with Democratic campaigns. In July the Republicans pull each other's hair and kick each other's shins, and practice up for the rest of their campaign by calling each other the names they are going to call the Democrats later on. This is known as creating unity in the Republican Party.

Then, in August, the newspapers compete with each other in predicting Republican landslides. They tell us we might just as well save the expense of campaigning because we don't have a chance. The polls show that the Republicans will carry every State except Rhode Island and Georgia, and they're doubtful. This is the month, my friends, when the Republicans place their big orders for confetti and balloons.

In September the newspapers tell us that the Democrats are gaining a bit, but that no one needs to worry, for reason has prevailed and the Republicans are really truly united. In September the polls begin to worry them a little, so they accuse us of talking over people's heads. They even accuse us of having a sense of humor.

Then, by the first of October, the newspapers sense that something is wrong and they begin to get nervous. They accuse their own candidate of running like a dry creek.

By mid-October the pollsters begin to concede that the election will be fairly close. This is the time of year when the Republicans start to complain that the campaign is going on too long—it is too hard on the candidates, and, besides, the Democrats are socialists, communists, crooks, or a little of each.

By the first of November the newspapers say that it's impossible to predict the outcome of the election; and now they say that the Republic is in danger and that they have documentary proof that all Democrats are dreadful and depraved, and that to find out how dreadful we are everyone should tune in on Monday night to hear the real low-down—although, of course, they disapprove heartily of such techniques.

And then, of course, on Election Day, the Democrats win. And so it goes, my friends, election after election.

I think you know and I know that they have never really been ahead at any time. They just throw so much confetti at each other, read so many of each other's editorials, and cheer each other's speeches so loudly, that they begin to think that everyone agrees with them. Well, they don't. And I think you can rely on the American people every time to tell who is really talking sense and who isn't.

And it's even more than a question of sense. It is, above all, a question of which party has faith in the future of America—which party has a program—which party has earned the people's trust. The answer to this question is now, as it has been for these many years, the Democratic Party.

Then this time, perhaps because the Republicans wanted discipline in their ranks, they chose a General to lead them. He and they have taken a bewildering variety of positions. And in the Republican choir the General has shown an admirable capacity to sing bass and baritone and tenor all at once. When he was here in the Middle West he identified himself with the most reactionary and isolationist wing of the Republican Party. But he recognized that the songs he sang in what he mistakenly considered isolationist territory would not be music to the ears of Eastern Republicans. So, when he went East he summoned a new ghost from the Republican haunted house and asked for a new script.

Which General do you read? And which do you believe? Is it the one who is in agreement on all basic issues with Senator Taft in Taftland? The one who signs up Senators Jenner and McCarthy on his team? Or, is it the General who proclaims in New York and California his devotion to all the social gains achieved by the Democratic administrations in the past twenty years?

We have been offered a strange picture of an anguished, reluctant, respected figure reciting distasteful words, shaking hands that make him shudder, walking in strange, dark alleys, caught in a clamor of conflicting voices. And that picture, I fear, appeals not just to soft hearts, but to soft heads.

I do not ask you to withhold your compassion for my opponent in the ordeal he has endured. But I say, does he, therefore, deserve your confidence and trust?

It occurred to me last night, on Hallowe'en, that the General

who started out with a new broom has ended up on an old broom-
stick, and he is surrounded by a vintage collection of ghosts, of
spooks and bogeymen.

Some still cling to the fact that he doesn't really mean it; that
immediately after the election he will wave a wand and there will
be a flash of fire and he will be transformed into what they call the
"Old Eisenhower." And that will be the neatest Hallowe'en trick
of them all.

They say that then he will turn in righteous wrath upon those
who have held his hands throughout this melancholy autumn.

Well, I don't believe it, and neither do they. This suggestion
that he will double-cross his new-found friends as soon as he gets
into office does credit neither to the General's integrity nor to
Senator Taft's vigilance.

Can independents really believe that victory would strengthen
progressive Republicans? Will Senator Taft, having laid down the
General's program, be humbled and routed by the General's success? Will the big gun—the not-so-secret weapon of these last
weeks of the Republican campaign—the Junior Senator from Wisconsin—will he be enlightened and chastened by the heady wine
of triumph?—the Wisconsin Senator who told the country the
truth for once the other day when he said that his power in Washington depends upon the General's election? Let's not deceive
ourselves, because it is quite clear who will run the country in the
event of a Republican triumph.

Many progressive Republicans, like Senator Wayne Morse, for
that reason are fighting on our side because they know what the
fate of the progressive Republicans would be under an administration like that. Hence, I have noticed as I have traveled in this
autumn weather that the Ike buttons are falling faster than the
leaves.

This, my friends, is the transformation that has been wrought in
three months. And, as a result, instead of the hopeful, resurgent
Republican Party, the contrast between the two today is exactly
what it has been for twenty years. The Democratic Party remains
the party which has fought for a strong America—a nation strong
at home, strong abroad, dedicated to strengthening the purpose
and the meaning of life for all of our citizens.

The Republican Party, despite the honorable efforts of many
individuals, remains the party not of a strong America, but of a

little America. Its leadership stands for a rudderless and drifting economy, at the mercy of every gust and squall, careening recklessly between the extremes of boom and bust.

That's a change, my friends, we need just as much as we need a good attack of appendicitis.

And, abroad, the Republican Party stands similarly for a little America—fearful to take its place in building the strength and the unity of free peoples.

We entered this campaign with a bipartisan foreign policy, virtually united except for a few stubborn men—united as the leader and the hope of the free. The campaign closes with an alarming chasm reopening between us. Here is change indeed—frightening change—that reflects a guiding purpose no higher than political ambition.

It was irresponsible politics first to hold out hopes of early liberation to those among us with families and close friends behind the Iron Curtain.

It was dangerous politics to promise tax cuts of tens of billions at the risk of endangering our own defenses and those of our allies in Europe and Asia.

It was sorry politics to urge the re-election of the few figures in public life who still preach unreconstructed isolationism.

And it was cheap politics to suggest that one candidate is more deeply concerned than the other about getting our sons home from Korea. And, on this let me add just one thing. Yesterday the New York *Times* published a poll taken among some of our troops in Korea—and the Democratic candidate got twice the votes of the Republican candidate.

I grieve, and so should you, that the Republicans have made an issue of war and peace when there was none four months ago, because this far transcends politics or the political fortunes of any man. The stakes are life and death; the stakes are civilization itself, and not votes in an election campaign.

It's time for a change. It's always time for a change. And we Democrats have accomplished tremendous changes despite stubborn obstruction and resistance, consecutively for twenty years. But, we are far from where we seek to go. So let's talk in these closing moments of this campaign about the future, and not about the past—about our hopes, and not about our fears.

The things we seek for ourselves we seek for all Americans:

good education for our sons and daughters; the dignity of security in advancing age; the equality of opportunity for all, not just some of God's children.

The only guiding stars are those which reflect the needs and the aspirations of people—of living men, women and children.

Let us build our program for change not on fear, but on faith—faith which we know is rooted in the vast resources of this land and the unmeasured capacities of its people.

I wish you could all have made this two-month journey with me. No American could travel the long road I have traveled and not find his faith renewed, his faith in his country and its future.

I have traversed the New England hills, ablaze with autumn color, and felt the touch of the soft air of the Southland.

I have flown over the mighty mountains to the Golden Gate and the blue Pacific.

I have flown over the fir-clad slopes and the rolling wheatlands of the great Northwest, and over the lonely cattle lands of the old Southwest.

I have traveled the route my forebears followed westward to Illinois. I have seen the old stone houses in the Pennsylvania hills, and I have come home to the sweep and the swell of the free soil of our beloved Illinois.

I have seen an America where all of the signs read "Men at Work."

But, we have much to do in this century in this country of ours before its greatness may be fully realized and shared by all Americans.

As we plan for change let us be sure that our vision is high enough and broad enough so that it encompasses every single hope and dream of both the greatest and the humblest among us.

I see an America where no man fears to think as he pleases, or say what he thinks.

I see an America where slums and tenements have vanished and children are raised in decency and self-respect.

I see an America where men and women have leisure from toil —leisure to cultivate the resources of the spirit.

I see an America where no man is another's master—where no man's mind is dark with fear.

I see an America at peace with the world.

I see an America as the horizon of human hopes.

This is our design for the American cathedral, and we shall build it brick by brick and stone by stone, patiently, bravely and prayerfully. And, to those who say that the design defies our abilities to complete it, I answer: "To act with enthusiasm and faith is the condition of acting greatly."

The Good Fight

Radio and Television Broadcast

CHICAGO, ILLINOIS

November 3, 1952

In this city of Chicago, in the early hours of a July morning last summer, I accepted the nomination of the Democratic Party for the Presidency of the United States and Senator John Sparkman was nominated for the Vice Presidency. By the calendar that was just fourteen weeks ago. That is not so long as time is measured, but to one who has spent weeks, as I have, writing, traveling, and speaking incessantly, yes, and listening, to countless thousands of the American people, it has been a long, long time.

The end has now come, the cheers and jeers, the tumult and the shouting are almost over, and these are the last words I shall speak to you before the balloting begins tomorrow morning.

Anyone who runs for office wants to win. I want to win, of course; but, win or lose, if I have kept faith with myself during the campaign, then I can await tomorrow—and the day after—and all the days after that—in good temper and sober contentment.

I did not seek my party's nomination for the Presidency. I said on that July night that the burdens of that office stagger the imagination; that its power for good or evil smothers exultation and converts vanity to prayer. Today, fourteen weeks later, the solemnity and the enormity of the responsibility we ask you to entrust to us grows ever more sobering and humbling.

I said when I accepted that I would fight to win with all my heart and soul. That I have done, sparing nothing of myself, encouraged and assisted along the way by many friends, new and old, who have spent themselves no less.

I've enjoyed the fight because I believe in our cause. I believe the Democratic Party, over the long sweep of its history and our history, has performed a great mission as a mechanism for the expression of political opinion, the development of policy, and the

313

attainment of a truly democratic society in which the people are sovereign. I believe in a people's party—call it what you will—a party that reflects in policy, program and action the interest of all, not some of the people.

I believe the Democratic Party *is* the people's party. It belongs to no one, because it belongs to everyone; and the world, the nation, and everyone in it, are the better, the safer, for it. I believe that with even greater conviction than when I uttered those words fourteen weeks ago.

And I also said when I accepted the nomination—let's talk sense to the American people. I said that it was better to lose the election than mislead the people; that this was a great opportunity to educate and elevate a people whose destiny is leadership, not alone of a rich, prosperous, contented country, but of a world in ferment.

Looking back I am not wholly content that I have said or said well everything that was in my heart. I am not sure that I have kept all of our concerns, national and international, in proper balance and perspective. I am not sure that I have made my views on all of our concerns as clear and precise as I would have liked.

But I have not evaded and I have tried and tried diligently, day and night, to talk sensibly, honestly, candidly about our many problems. I have tried to explain the issues as I see them, and the records of the parties. I have tried to educate. If I have not succeeded altogether, I have certainly educated myself about those questions, and also about those wonderful human beings that are America.

Talking sensibly and honestly is not always easy. It means saying things that sometimes people don't like to hear; it means risking votes, and candidates are not supposed to do that; it means saying the same thing in all parts of the country and at all stages of the campaign.

It means avoiding political expediency and dealing forthrightly with individuals regardless of the party labels they wear or the votes they can deliver. It means trying to find out what really are the major problems, to get under their surface, to say exactly where one stands on them and what one proposes to do about them.

It means trying incessantly to keep the important things foremost, and not be diverted by the sideshows, the assaults and the falsehoods that clutter our campaigns.

As I think of these things here at the end of the long road, a lot of memories of these crowded weeks flood in upon me.

I remember the night at Dallas, when I spoke to Texans of my views about tidelands oil.

I remember the crowd in Detroit on Labor Day when I said I would be the captive of all the American people and no one else.

I remember the evening in the railroad station at New Haven when I identified a powerful Democratic leader as not my kind of Democrat.

I remember the American Legion convention when I said that those who have served this country must always be Americans first and veterans second, and that our free-enterprise system must include free enterprise for the mind.

I remember the audiences down South listening to what I had to say on the subject of civil rights.

In these and many other cases there were those who pointed to their perils and urged another course. That would have been easy —but I would not feel as good as I do sitting here tonight on election eve.

Looking back, I am content. Win or lose, I have told you the truth as I see it. I have said what I meant and meant what I said. I have not done as well as I should like to have done, but I have done my best, frankly and forthrightly; no man can do more, and you are entitled to no less.

I have told you over and over how our economic well-being has been built step by step for all the people, not just the few, and why I am concerned that the economic well-being of America, why your prosperity, cannot be safely entrusted to the party of fear, inaction, boom and bust. I have told you about our vision of an ever-growing abundance in this heaven-blessed land.

And I have told you over and over that we are winning the worldwide struggle with communism; that step by step from Greece and Turkey to Korea the grand alliance of the free has thrown back the enemy; that it is years now since any new peoples or new lands were enveloped by the Kremlin's dark shadow.

The Korean War and the miserable stalemate there must be freshly reviewed by fresh minds. Solution, settlement and an armistice there is the first order of public business. But Korea is only one aspect of the communist conspiracy against the free.

And this is no time to hesitate in doubt and confusion about the dangerous world we live in, for "on the plains of hesitation bleach the bones of countless thousands, who, on the eve of victory, rested, and resting died."

As I said earlier this evening, I have been listening as well as traveling and talking these past three months. And what I've heard all across the land belies the sorry campaign picture of a nation divided, feeble in faith, ruined by debt, threatened with bankruptcy, a nation afraid, a nation cowering before her destiny.

No, I've seen and heard the deep-throated courage and confidence and faith of strong men and women and happy children —people who still believe in one another, in spite of all the timid, doubting men. And I thank them every one for the reception they have given me—for their infinite courtesy and their heartening friendliness.

I have asked you for your support for my candidacy. I ask you now for support of our common faith in this country. The confidence we've inherited is our greatest wealth, the source of our strength.

Whatever the electorate decides, I ask that we close our ears, once and for all, to the cowardly voices of hate and fear and suspicion which would destroy us; that we dedicate ourselves, each one of us alone and all of us together, to that belief in ourselves, that trust in each other, on which the greatness of our country rests. For, believe me, the future of the world depends on it.

Tomorrow you will make your choice. I would urge every eligible American to exercise the greatest privilege bestowed upon us—the right to participate in deciding his own destiny.

If your decision is General Eisenhower and the Republican Party, I shall ask everyone who voted for me to accept the verdict with traditional American sportsmanship. If you select me, I shall ask the same of the Republicans—and I shall also ask Our Lord to make me an instrument of His peace.

To Future Citizens

I would like to ask all of you children to indicate, by holding up your hands, how many of you would like to be Governor of Illinois, the way I am. (*Show of hands.*) Well, that is almost unanimous.

Now I would like to ask all the Governors if they would like to be one of you kids. (*Whereupon Governor Stevenson cheered.*)

I don't know whether you understand what is going on here this morning very well. I am not sure I do myself! But what you see here is something that does not happen everywhere in the world. Here are a lot of your parents and your neighbors going over to the schoolhouse there to cast their vote. That means they are deciding for themselves who is going to lead them—who is going to be their leader. You understand that? They are going to decide over there who will be their officers and who runs their Government, all the way from the county up to the United States.

In other words, what that means is that we decide who governs us. It is not everybody in the world who can do that. These are the things you read about in the history books, that your ancestors have been struggling for for generations—not only to get the right to govern themselves, but to keep it.

Anyway, I think you are going to remember today for one thing only, that you got a half day off from school. I am sure I have enjoyed this as much as you have, and I would like to spend the recess this morning playing with you in the school yard. But I don't know what we would play. What would we play?

(Shouts: "Baseball, football.")

The same old fight between the cattlemen and the sheepmen. Wouldn't anybody like to have a little mock game of politics?

(A *Little Boy*: "*We don't like mud fights.*")

Well, I never saw a kid who didn't like a mud fight!

You are very good to let me talk to you this morning. What I hope, as time goes on and you go further along in school, is that you will study more and more about what you have seen here this morning—this business of voting—why we vote and what we vote for. The more you study about it, the more precious it will become to you. The more you do it, the better and more intelligently you will vote, and the better government you will have. Does everybody understand that? (*Chorus of yeas.*) One of the highest degrees of intelligence in the whole United States is political intelligence.

Good-bye, kids. I hope you will all come over and see me on St. Mary's Road, but I am not over there very often any more. Good-bye. (*Chorus of "Good-bye, Governor."*)

The Verdict—We Pray As One

Leland Hotel

SPRINGFIELD, ILLINOIS

November 5, 1952

I have a statement that I should like to make. If I may, I shall read it to you.

My fellow citizens have made their choice and have selected General Eisenhower and the Republican Party as the instruments of their will for the next four years.

The people have rendered their verdict and I gladly accept it.

General Eisenhower has been a great leader in war. He has been a vigorous and valiant opponent in the campaign. These qualities will now be dedicated to leading us all through the next four years.

It is traditionally American to fight hard before an election. It is equally traditional to close ranks as soon as the people have spoken.

From the depths of my heart I thank all of my party and all of those independents and Republicans who supported Senator Sparkman and me.

That which unites us as American citizens is far greater than that which divides us as political parties.

I urge you all to give General Eisenhower the support he will need to carry out the great tasks that lie before him.

I pledge him mine.

We vote as many, but we pray as one. With a united people, with faith in democracy, with common concern for others less fortunate around the globe, we shall move forward with God's guidance toward the time when His children shall grow in freedom and dignity in a world at peace.

I have sent the following telegram to General Eisenhower at the Commodore Hotel in New York:

"The people have made their choice and I congratulate you. That you may be the servant and guardian of peace and make the vale of trouble a door of hope is my earnest prayer. Best wishes,

Adlai E. Stevenson."

Someone asked me, as I came in, down on the street, how I felt, and I was reminded of a story that a fellow-townsman of ours used to tell—Abraham Lincoln. They asked him how he felt once after an unsuccessful election. He said he felt like a little boy who had stubbed his toe in the dark. He said that he was too old to cry, but it hurt too much to laugh.